LANDMARK LAW CASES

&

AMERICAN SOCIETY

Peter Charles Hoffer
N. E. H. Hull
Series Editors

Titles in the series:

ROBERT J. COTTROL, RAYMOND T. DIAMOND,
AND LELAND B. WARE

Brown v. Board
of Education

Caste, Culture, and the Constitution

UNIVERSITY PRESS OF KANSAS

© 2003 by the University Press of Kansas

All rights reserved

Published by the University Press of Kansas (Lawrence, Kansas 66049), which was organized by the Kansas Board of Regents and is operated and funded by Emporia State University, Fort Hays State University, Kansas State University, Pittsburg State University, the University of Kansas, and Wichita State University

Library of Congress Cataloging-in-Publication Data

Brown v. Board of Education : caste, culture, and the Constitution / Robert J. Cottrol, Raymond T. D amond, and Leland B. Ware.

p. cm. — (Landmark law cases & American society)

Includes bibliographical references and index.

ISBN 0-7006-1288-2 (cloth : alk. paper) — ISBN 0-7006-1289-0 (pbk.: alk. paper)

1. Brown, Oliver, 1918– . Trials, litigation, etc. 2. Topeka (Kan.). Board of Education—Trials, litigation, etc. 3. Segregation in education—Law and legislation—United States. 4. Race discrimination—Law and legislation—United States. 5. African Americans—Civil rights. 6. United States—Race relations. I. Title: Brown versus Board of Education. II. Cottrol, Robert J. III. Diamond, Raymond T. IV. Ware, Leland, 1948– . V. Series.

KF4155.B758 2003

344.73'0798—DC21

2003013217

British Library Cataloguing in Publication Data is available.

Printed in the United States of America

10 9 8 7 6 5 4 3 2 1

The paper used in this publication meets the minimum requirements of the American National Standard for Permanence of Paper for Printed Library Materials z39.48-1984.

CONTENTS

Near the end of the nineteenth century, when Jim Crow was in full flower and violence against Americans of African extraction was common at the polling place, in the streets of the cities, and along the rural lanes of the backcountry, a United States Supreme Court justice declared that law, courts, and judges' decisions could never change folkways. One of those folkways was the separate and unequal treatment of black Americans by their white neighbors. Not every American indulged in this self-serving and racialist philosophy, but intellectuals, politicians, and lawyers all agreed that public policy could not undo what private prejudice had wrought. In fact, the highest court in the land repeatedly displayed its unwillingness to use its moral or legal authority to insure equal protection and due process for the black minority.

In the series of Supreme Court decisions gathered together under the label of *Brown v. Board of Education* the justices proved, however, that courts and law can redress long-standing biases in attitude and behavior. A little over fifty years after the Court in *Plessy v. Ferguson* had announced that supposedly separate but equal treatment of persons under state law satisfied the requirements of the Fourteenth Amendment, another high court found that no state or locality could permit segregation in public schools. Such segregation was inherently unequal, branding the segregated minority with a lifelong stigma of inferiority. Later years would see massive resistance in some parts of the South and covert opposition in some areas of the North to the evolving goal of one nation, equal under law, but for all Americans, of all backgrounds, the world after *Brown* is profoundly different from and infinitely better than it was before that decision. For *Brown* bespoke the conscience of a nation too long divided by race and distracted by racism.

Many legal scholars, historians, political scientists, social psychologists, journalists, and participants have written about the cases covered in this superb addition to the Landmark Law Cases and American Society series, but rarely have the issues been so clearly delineated, the long historical context of the drive for legal equality so strikingly portrayed, and the impact of the cases so wisely assessed. The authors, law professors, historians, and close observers of the events bring to the story a passion for its affective as well as cognitive side. They have worked on this volume for almost a decade, and the results of their broad survey of materials and careful thought will be obvious to every reader.

There are also a great many works on cases that second-guess the Court. From its inception, the opinion for the Court was attacked, even by those who supported the outcome. It should not have cited or used the studies of social scientists, said some critics. Others decried the absence of "neutral principles" in the decision. One legal scholar, almost two generations ago, argued that the issue of desegregation was not a matter for courts but for democratically elected legislatures (ignoring, if that was possible, the way that blacks were prevented from taking part in those "democratic" legislative proceedings). A few years ago, another press published in book form essays by a distinguished group of scholars and lawyers on how *Brown* should have been decided. No one objected to the result, but every one of the scholars would have written a different opinion, using different constitutional logic, from that assayed by Chief Justice Earl Warren in *Brown*. To their credit, the authors of this book make patently plain that the decision and its language was a product of converging historical realities—the need to bring nine justices together to face what was then the greatest social issue in the land.

Finally, the authors provide us with sharply incisive portraits of the key players, the dangers they faced, and the opportunities they grasped. The road to and from *Brown* is one of the most dramatic, wrenching, uplifting, and remarkable stories in our history. In short compass, with great clarity and force, this book travels that road.

ACKNOWLEDGMENTS

We have incurred many debts during the writing of this volume. It has been our privilege to discuss our ideas concerning *Brown* with numerous colleagues, friends, and family members. These conversations have greatly improved our understanding of the case and our ability to discuss it in this volume. We would like to especially single out Davison M. Douglas, Tanya K. Hernandez, and two anonymous referees who read earlier drafts of the entire manuscript and made detailed comments that greatly assisted in our writing of the final version. Other colleagues read portions of the manuscript and made helpful and encouraging comments in bringing their expertise to bear on specific chapters. These include Harriet F. Adams, Miriam Galston, Philip Hamburger, Thomas Kohler, Cynthia Lee, C. Thomas Long, Richard Pierce, Alfreda Robinson, Jeffrey Rosen, Steven Schooner, Judith Schafer, Gregory Squires, and Michael Young. One of the authors, Robert J. Cottrol, would like to thank the George Washington University Law School for a sabbatical, at just the right time, that greatly aided in the completion of this book. All of the authors would like to thank the following students who acted as research assistants: David Eldridge, Wendy Elmendorf, Troy Larkin, José Martin Dávlia, Kamala Miller, and Keela Seales. Finally, we would like to express our gratitude to our editors, Peter Hoffer, the series editor, and Michael Briggs of the University Press of Kansas. Both played a major role in encouraging the project and offering valuable criticism and support during the course of the project.

Introduction

Early in the afternoon on Tuesday, December 8, 1953, Thurgood Marshall stood before the Supreme Court of the United States and asked the central question in American history, "Why, of all the multitudinous groups of people in this country, you have to single out Negroes and give them this separate treatment?" Marshall, who would later be the first American of African descent to serve as solicitor general and later as an associate justice of the Supreme Court, was representing Harry Briggs and other black parents in South Carolina who were suing state officials because state law forced their children to go to segregated all-black schools. On that Tuesday, Marshall was representing Briggs and the other South Carolina parents in oral argument before the nation's highest tribunal. We will discuss Briggs, the other parents, and the case that Marshall was arguing later in this book, but for now it is sufficient to say that the *Briggs* case was a companion case to the case more famously known as *Brown v. Board of Education* (1954), the case that declared legally mandated school segregation unconstitutional.

All cases are important to the parties involved. They must be so, or presumably rational people would not undergo the expense and difficulty that comes with fighting a case, particularly one that takes a long time and goes through several layers of appellate review. A few, a very few, cases are significant because they establish important legal precedents—precedents that shape and perhaps change the law in fundamental ways. *Brown* had a significance that went far beyond the concerns of the parties involved or even the precedent-making decision that was rendered. *Brown* touched on the core contradiction in American life. More than two centuries after its writing, Thomas Jefferson's Declaration of Independence still speaks eloquently of the unalienable rights of the individual. The American Constitution, particularly its Bill of Rights, remains the world's most enduring example of legally enforceable limitations on government power and protection for human liberty. The American nation, at least since its founding, has long celebrated the rights of individuals, equal rights before the law, the democratic ethos, Jacksonian democracy, the common man, the classless nature of American society. These were long a part of the nation's official and unofficial ideology, celebrated in story and folklore, passed on to generations of grammar school pupils in the nation's textbooks.

Still there was an exception, a great exception. The founding generation that boldly declared independence and carefully crafted a Constitution enumerating the rights of citizens lived in a nation in which nearly 20 percent of the inhabitants were enslaved. The same Constitution that protected habeas corpus and the free exercise of religion also contained a fugitive slave clause requiring that those slaves who sought for themselves the kind of liberty for which the Revolution had been fought or the Constitution written would be forcibly returned to their owners.

It would get worse. If there was more than a touch of hypocrisy displayed and ideals betrayed as the founding generation wrestled with the dilemma of maintaining slavery while otherwise proclaiming their fealty to individual liberty, that generation at least found slavery troubling to the conscience. The northern states began the process of legally abolishing slavery after the Revolution. In a number of southern states, the law made manumission—the private freeing of slaves—somewhat easier. Many of the major statesmen of the time, including southern statesmen like George Washington, James Madison, Thomas Jefferson, and George Mason, expressed their discomfort with slavery, their recognition that it betrayed the ideals of the new nation, and their hopes that it might somehow be ended.

That discomfort with slavery would lessen considerably in the nineteenth century. The invention of the cotton gin and the opening of new western lands to cotton cultivation increased slavery's economic importance to the South. That development, the creation of what has come to be called the "cotton kingdom," would help bring about a new, less apologetic defense of "the peculiar institution." Slavery would no longer be defended as an embarrassment that must be prudently endured until it might be made to yield to some new, more equitable arrangement. Instead slavery would be championed as a positive good. That new, more muscular defense of human bondage would bring with it a renewed emphasis on race and alleged racial difference as the prime justification for slavery. In a nation that prided itself on its democratic politics and its egalitarian social ethos, slavery was hard to justify. This task was made easier because American slaves were black, descendants of Africans captured and brought to the Americas in the seventeenth and eighteenth centuries. In a society where whites were not slaves and 90 percent of blacks were, a racial rationale for slavery was always likely. American society would become more democratic and more egalitarian in the nineteenth century. Democracy spread as more and more white men were enfranchised as property qualifications were dropped for prospective voters. By the beginning of the nineteenth century, fewer and fewer white men and women would experience indentured servitude, a form of temporary bondage that was the nearest thing to slavery that whites had experienced in American history.

Custom and law presumed the freedom and autonomy of white individuals and the slave status of blacks. The doctrine of racial inferiority became more than the proffered rationale explaining the anomaly of chattel slavery in a free society. Instead it became a full-fledged ideology that allowed the South and the nation not only to reconcile slavery with the nation's ideals, but also to proclaim that the institution was not merely good for whites but indeed a positive benefit to the inferior and dependent Negro as well. By the early decades of the nineteenth century, it was clear that many whites had a considerable psychological as well as economic investment in the doctrine of black inferiority.

And it was not only in the slaveholding South where many whites had a strong commitment to notions of white supremacy and black inferiority. True, the northern states had abolished slavery after the Revolution. There was even, in the late eighteenth century, a promising start on the road to de jure equality for blacks and whites. At the end of the eighteenth century, most northern states allowed both black men and white men to vote— if they owned sufficient property. In the nineteenth century, that would change. Black men were disenfranchised. They encountered strong prejudices. Vicious riots and constant threats of mob violence menaced free Negro communities throughout the North, many black men and women could only get jobs no white person wanted, steamships were segregated, separate common schools for black and white children were established. As one of antebellum America's keenest observers, French social critic Alexis de Tocqueville noted in 1835:

> Whoever has inhabited the United States must perceive that in those parts of the Union in which the Negroes are no longer slaves they have in no wise drawn nearer to the whites, on the contrary, the prejudice of race appears to be stronger in the states that have abolished slavery than in those where it still exists.... The electoral franchise has been conferred upon the Negroes in almost all the states in which slavery has been abolished but if they come forward to vote their lives are in danger. If oppressed they may bring an action at law, but they will find none but whites among their judges; and although they may legally serve as jurors, prejudice repels them from that office.

These developments—the rise of the positive good view of slavery and the strident bigotries endured by free blacks in antebellum America—are critical to an understanding of the question that Thurgood Marshall posed on that December afternoon in 1953. They are also critical to an understanding of how *Brown* was planned, argued, and decided and ultimately how it changed the American nation. *Brown* was about caste. A caste system, or perhaps more accurately an attempt to impose a caste system, had developed in antebellum America. It existed in the North as well as in the South, with differing degrees of intensity in different regions. It was, we believe, in large part brought about by the attempt to reconcile slavery with the liberal precepts of the American nation. We would argue that this caste system reached its modern form in the antebellum America of the nineteenth century. Race-based slavery had, of course, existed in the English colonies that would become the United States since the seventeenth century. Laws detailing a clearly unequal status for blacks slave and free had existed since colonial times. But we would argue that the Revolution and the liberal ideology that informed the nation's institutions in the Revolution's wake forced a new consideration of the anomaly of slavery in an otherwise free society. That consideration was largely responsible for abolition in the North. It would also help bring about a new, more systematic strain of racism that served as an apologetic for American slavery. These developments gave long-standing patterns of racial differentiation and discrimination a more castelike character in nineteenth-century America.

The principal elements of the caste system were at once simple and yet peculiar. A slave woman might be a cook for a white family, a wet nurse to a white child, a mistress to a white man. A man who was a slave might ride with his owner on a coach or steamship. Yet a free black man in, say, Connecticut could not ride in a coach with whites. His children would be forced to go to the common school for colored children. It was a caste system that could allow quite intimate contact when a black person's inferior status was unquestionable and yet preclude ordinary contact when there might be even a hint that members of different races were meeting as equals.

It was this system, born in antebellum America, that would be challenged in *Brown*. Between antebellum America and *Brown*, many things would happen. The Civil War put an end to slavery. The Thirteenth Amendment would outlaw the institution. The Fifteenth Amendment granted the vote to black men. The Fourteenth Amendment established the principle of equal protection before the law. That principle, included in the Constitution to prevent unequal treatment of the races by the states, would provide the foundation of the legal argument in *Brown*.

{ *Introduction* }

After the Civil War, there was a promising but brief attempt, Reconstruction, to legally attack the system of castelike restrictions that was the legacy of antebellum law and custom. The Civil War amendments to the Constitution and the federal civil rights statutes of the 1860s and 1870s were designed to protect the newly freed Afro-American population from the pervasive discrimination, public and private, then existing in the nation. But Reconstruction proved to be all too brief to do serious damage to the pattern of castelike attitudes and practices that had become part of American law and culture. The withdrawal of federal troops from the South would pave the way for that region's return to a legally enforced system of white supremacy, the demands of the recently amended Constitution notwithstanding.

It should not be forgotten that the Supreme Court played a critical role in dismantling federal protection for blacks and allowing a system of castelike restrictions to be reestablished and strengthened after Reconstruction. Two Supreme Court cases of the era, *United States v. Cruikshank* (1875) and the *Civil Rights Cases* (1883), severely limited Congress's power to protect blacks from hostile action by private parties—even, as was the case in *Cruikshank*, where those private parties were violently seeking to prevent black men from exercising constitutionally protected rights like voting, assembling for political purposes, or carrying arms for protection. This would pave the way for an extralegal reign of terror designed to restore white supremacy with the aid of private violence. The black man who tried to vote, the Negro family deemed too prosperous or too uppity, the sharecropper who demanded the money owed him, the black man or woman who failed to get off the sidewalk when a white man wanted to pass—all faced the threat of physical violence, even murder. If federal authorities were prevented by Court decision from protecting the lives and rights of black people under these circumstances, state authorities often supported, abetted, and indeed led these actions. They were helping to solidify white control of state politics and state law.

But by the eve of the twentieth century, white control would take a somewhat different form than had existed in the era before the Civil War. Slavery had been abolished, the Negro's citizenship proclaimed. These were stubborn constitutional facts that even the Redeemed South's most militant champions could not undo. These constitutional facts probably heightened the search for ways to clearly define an inferior status for African Americans. Before the Civil War, white supremacy was an unquestionable fact of American life. Slavery had made it so. But could white supremacy survive the constitutional changes that followed in the wake of the War of the Rebellion? Could status, could caste lines survive the Constitution's new mandate of equality before the law?

They could. As the nineteenth century was yielding to the twentieth, the South, and indeed places in other regions, would find a new way to remind black and white of their differing statuses, of the respective places of superiors and inferiors. It would be called Jim Crow. It was an American form of apartheid with a somewhat whimsical name that had its origins in an antebellum minstrel show. It was enforced by law and custom, by sheriff and vigilante. At its zenith it prescribed a ritualistic separation of black and white in almost every visible facet of public life. Public water fountains and rest rooms had White or Colored signs over them. Movie theaters forced Negro patrons into segregated balconies. Black and white witnesses had to swear on separate Bibles in court. Afro-Americans rode in the Jim Crow coaches on the railroads and were restricted to the back seats of municipal buses. And, of course, in the South and elsewhere, schools would be rigorously segregated. This was true of the most preliminary instruction in grammar schools. It was also true of the most advanced graduate and professional courses in the state universities.

This new legal regime would also receive the support and sanction of the United States Supreme Court. The 1896 case of *Plessy v. Ferguson* placed the high court's imprimatur on the South's ritualistic reaffirmation of a caste system. The *Plessy* decision held that separate but equal facilities were not repugnant to the Fourteenth Amendment's equal protection clause. This meant that the state, indeed the law itself, could actively and vigorously reinforce inequality. Negroes, as Thurgood Marshall noted, could be singled out for special and stigmatizing treatment. This was the law of the land. It was an option that would be followed by many state governments and indeed the government of the United States for much of the twentieth century. It should also be noted that states that adopted policies requiring segregation usually assigned blacks to facilities that were separate, but rarely to ones that were equal.

Brown was shaped by this background, by the struggle against the caste system that had deep roots in American culture and strong protection in American law. This is in part the story of a group of visionaries who early in the last century retained their faith in the Constitution and its ideals even when the highest legal authorities in the land were willing to compromise them. It is also about the legal strategies those visionaries fashioned and how those strategies helped shape the decision in *Brown*.

If *Brown* had simply been the case that pronounced "separate but unequal" unconstitutional and had lent the Supreme Court's authority to those who had long argued that the law cannot lend sanction to a system of caste distinctions, its significance, indeed its preeminence in American legal history, would have been insured. *Brown* certainly played a pivotal role in the postwar civil rights movement in the United States. It would probably be fair to say that it helped precipitate a more assertive civil rights movement in the 1950s and 1960s, a movement that would ultimately bring about far-reaching change in American race relations.

But ultimately, *Brown* would do more than help change the equation of race and caste in American society. *Brown* would also come to change the way many Americans would view the courts and their proper role in American governance. *Brown* was initially criticized by many as a severe kind of judicial overreaching, the forging of a constitutional mandate not originally intended by the framers of the Fourteenth Amendment. That view still exists in some quarters. But for many, *Brown* has become exhibit A in the case for a more activist judiciary, an argument that courts, because of their relative insulation from political pressures, might in fact be better vehicles to resolve knotty social problems. That, too, is part of the legacy of *Brown* and one that we will discuss.

A few words before we begin. Although we will be discussing the concept of caste throughout the book—indeed it is a key concept in the book—we must confess to not being entirely comfortable with our use of the term. It has always seemed to us that a true caste system requires an acceptance of caste distinctions on the part of members of different castes. If we look, for example, at the classical caste system in India, that system appeared to have the acceptance of members of the different castes. The system was rooted in the Hindu religion, and presumably the logic of separate castes and separate spheres was part of the belief system of those who were born, who lived, and who died in that culture, at least classically. Such was not the case with blacks in America. Indeed a strong case can be made that the history of free African Americans is a history of struggle and resistance against castelike restrictions. This was true of the free Negroes of the antebellum North who began the civil rights movement fighting for the right to vote and fighting against segregated schools. It was also true after general emancipation during Reconstruction, and in the twentieth-century struggle against Jim Crow. In short, Afro-Americans resisted the caste system. It should also be noted that from the beginning, there were always a substantial number of white Americans who saw that the attempts to impose a racial caste system were repugnant to the founding ideals of the nation. This rejection of the caste system by blacks and a not inconsiderable number of whites throughout American history makes the use of the term *caste* problematic. Yet we use the term because it captures the rigid and separate nature of the distinctions that were imposed or attempted, even though the considerable resistance to caste throughout American history should never be forgotten.

We will be discussing race, racism, and racial discrimination throughout the book. Some may find it strange that we will largely confine our discussion to relations between blacks and whites. Our purpose is not to ignore the experiences of American Indians and those Americans with Asian and Latin American ancestries. These groups have had important and often painful histories with racism, discrimination and the attempt to overcome these evils. Indeed the same may also be said for many white ethnic groups at different times and places in American history. But we would argue that although many groups in the nation's history have experienced racism, often severe racism, black people have been uniquely singled out for treatment as a separate caste. This unique treatment was sanctioned by the nation's laws, including its highest law, the Constitution, and the Supreme Court, its most important interpreter. It is for that reason and because *Brown* was a case brought by Negro parents on behalf of Negro children that we largely confine our discussion to relations between blacks and whites.

One final word on terminology. There has been a tendency for the better part of the last generation for historians to explain, often somewhat apologetically, about their use of the term *Negro* in their texts. We will explain, but not apologetically. Negro was the name most African Americans called themselves throughout most of American history. They did so with pride and respect. We will treat the name the same way. The men and women that conceived of, struggled for, and ultimately won the victory in *Brown* took great pride in the term. Thurgood Marshall would use it with pride all of his life, even after it became unfashionable. Different generations of Afro-Americans have preferred different names. That is perhaps natural, but it is not a reason to discard or denigrate names honored by previous generations. That will not be our practice in this volume.

CHAPTER I

"A People Apart"

Sarah, the Printer's Daughter:
The Yankee Preface to Separate but Equal

Boston, Massachusetts, in the year 1848 is undoubtedly a curious place to begin our discussion of law, race, and caste in American society. The black population of Boston in that year was small—less than 2 percent of the city's total of roughly 137,000 people. Even in the colonial era when slavery was legal, the institution had not been particularly important in Massachusetts society. By the 1780s, the Supreme Judicial Court—the Bay State's highest tribunal—had declared slavery repugnant to the new state constitution in the case *Commonwealth v. Jennison* (1783). Black men had also gained the right to vote in the Massachusetts Constitution of 1780. Some local officials in the 1780s and 1790s had tried to prevent black men from voting. Their efforts failed. Protests and petitions by free Negroes and sympathetic whites made black voting rights a reality in Massachusetts before the end of the eighteenth century.

By law, at the beginning of the nineteenth century, the free Afro-American population of Massachusetts enjoyed almost all the rights of their white counterparts. They were citizens. Men voted. A few black men would serve as jurors in antebellum Boston. There would even be a handful of African American lawyers. Boston's free Negro population exercised the rights of other free Americans in the antebellum era. They organized politically both to protect their rights and to provide crucial support to antislavery organizations. They formed and supported churches. They legally owned firearms, and indeed quite a few were armed to resist fugitive slave catchers. Boston's antebellum free people of color would even support a private military company—a fairly common practice in antebellum America, although their petition to have the company recognized as part of the state militia would be rejected by the legislature.

But equal or nearly equal rights under law tells only part of the story of black life in antebellum Boston. The other part of the story is one of virulent, frequently violent antiblack prejudice, as well as legal and extralegal restraints caused by that prejudice and the struggle against those restraints. Part of this story involves the complex history of race relations in Boston and the Northeast more generally in the early nineteenth century—an area that we can only quickly touch on here. We might briefly summarize that history by observing that in the late eighteenth century, after the Revolution, there seemed to be fairly strong antislavery sentiment in the North. That sentiment was particularly strong in New England. This sentiment was translated into law. Some northern states passed legislation mandating the gradual abolition of slavery. In other states, like Massachusetts, judicial decisions would put an end to slavery. What was perhaps even more remarkable in the late eighteenth century was the tendency of the new states to treat the newly freed Negroes as citizens. While discriminatory laws and practices certainly existed at the time, there was nonetheless one significant recognition of equality before the law: free black men were legally eligible to vote on the same basis as white men in every northern state. To be sure, property qualifications for suffrage probably prevented the vast majority of recently freed northern black men from voting, but at least the principle that race would not be a factor limiting a fundamental right of citizenship was recognized by the law—at least initially.

The liberal sentiment that had helped to bring about northern emancipation and a degree of de jure equality in the late eighteenth century would, in the early nineteenth century, change, giving way to a harsher, more strident antiblack sentiment. The attack on the rights of black people in the North would become especially strong after the War of 1812. Black voting rights were curtailed in most states, although they would survive in Massachusetts. Blacks found themselves barred from all but the most undesirable jobs. In Massachusetts, where black legal rights would survive this period of intense Negro phobia, blacks were forced to use separate railroad cars and ride on the outside of stagecoaches, were barred from theaters, and were prevented from practicing most trades and professions. Until 1843, Massachusetts had a law prohibiting interracial marriages.

There was also strong antiblack violence. A number of northern cities in the 1820s and 1830s were witness to vicious antiblack riots. Boston had one such riot in 1826. The riots of this era were evidence of the rising tensions between northern free Negro populations and working-class whites. Historians have offered a variety of plausible explanations for these tensions: competition for jobs, competition for status, rival political mobilizations, among others. Whatever the origins of these tensions, they caused fear of racially motivated violence to be a major concern in Afro-American communities in many cities. That fear caused some black parents in Boston to petition the Massachusetts legislature for separate schools for their children in the 1820s when the state established common schools and mandatory state-supported education.

By the 1840s, Boston's black community was developing a vigorous civil rights movement designed to combat the discrimination that had developed in the previous decades. That movement was not simply a reaction against the daily discrimination Negroes encountered in Boston. It was that, of course. But the movement was also the product of the strong and increasing identification with America and as Americans on the part of Afro-Americans in Boston and indeed elsewhere in the North. In Boston that identification was certainly bolstered by the fact that large numbers of black men from New England had fought in the Revolution. Resentment against being treated as outcasts in a country that their fathers and grandfathers had helped to create was a commonly expressed sentiment on the part of the free Negroes of Boston. That sentiment helped cause blacks in

Boston and elsewhere to reject colonization—expatriation of free African Americans to Africa.

Free Negroes also played a major role in convincing the abolitionist movement to reject colonization and to join the fight for equal rights in America. This would prove to be a significant and far-reaching development. The American Revolution had caused many whites to question slavery for the first time. This new sentiment helped bring about the end of slavery in the North and even caused many southern statesmen to question the institution. Still the Revolution did not produce a sustained national movement to abolish slavery. Free blacks opposed the institution. Members of Boston's black community founded the Massachusetts General Colored Association, an abolitionist organization, in 1826. The organization advocated immediate national emancipation. Its most prominent activity was the publication of *David Walker's Appeal*, a widely read antislavery pamphlet written by Boston resident David Walker, a free black man who had been born in North Carolina.

By the 1830s, Boston's free Negroes would find whites enlisting in and extending the reach of the abolitionist cause. William Lloyd Garrison began to publish the antislavery newspaper *The Liberator* in 1831. Blacks in Boston and free Negroes in other parts of the North were among the earliest and strongest supporters of Garrison's efforts and subscribers to his newspaper. Garrison's black supporters convinced him to not only press the antislavery cause but also reject colonization. The alliance between Garrisonian abolitionists and free Afro-Americans also aided Boston's antebellum civil rights movement.

By the 1840s, advocates of equal rights were becoming increasingly critical of Boston's system of segregated common schools. Boston was the only locality in the state that maintained separate schools for black and white children. Separate facilities, colored schools, were not required by state law; instead they were the results of the policies of the Boston School Committee. Historical evidence indicates that the curriculum in the colored schools was inferior to that offered in the white schools. At one point, the Boston School Committee's policy was to forbid the teaching of English grammar in the colored schools. The schools for blacks were also often in locations that were inconvenient for their students. Throughout the 1840s, Afro-American community leaders urged a boycott of the segregated schools.

Sentiment against the colored schools was not unanimous in the black community. Some members of the community wanted to maintain the separate schools, fearing violence if black children attended schools with white children. Others believed that the colored schools could be a source of community pride and control of the education of the community's children. The colored schools employed Negro teachers, a rare professional accomplishment for blacks in the 1840s. A number believed that black children would be better taught by sympathetic black teachers instead of hostile white ones.

Still, by our best historical account, the majority of Boston's Afro-American community resented the separate schools. They termed them "caste schools." In 1846 a number of black parents and community activists unsuccessfully petitioned Boston's Primary School Committee to integrate the schools.

It would take the efforts of black printer Benjamin Roberts to have his five-year-old daughter, Sarah, attend a school near their home to bring the antebellum school integration struggle into the nation's constitutional history. In February of 1848, Roberts attempted to enroll Sarah in the primary school closest to their home. That school was reserved for white students, and Sarah was ejected by a teacher. Roberts was required to enroll his daughter in the primary school for colored children located on Belknap Street, considerably farther away.

Sarah's rejection caused Benjamin Roberts to bring suit on his daughter's behalf against the city of Boston. His primary attorney was abolitionist Charles Sumner. Sumner would later go on to become a senator from Massachusetts and would play a major role in the drafting of the Fourteenth Amendment. He was assisted in his representation of Sarah Roberts, who was technically the plaintiff, by Robert Morris, one of the nation's first African American attorneys. Sumner framed the principal issue in the case in a way that would have a lasting impact on American jurisprudence.

Sumner centered his argument on the Massachusetts Constitution. Article 1 of that document had declared all men to be free and equal. It was a powerful constitutional expression. It had provided the basis for the judicial outlawing of slavery in *Jennison* in 1783. Sumner believed it might also provide a rationale for the elimination of caste schools in 1848.

Sumner's strategy was to zero in on segregation as an inherent violation of the principle of equality before the law. The gravamen of Sumner's case was not that the two colored primary schools—one located on Belknap Street, the other on Sun Court Street—were necessarily inferior in physical facilities or quality of teachers. Instead, Sumner argued, separate schools helped implant in students a sense of caste distinction unacceptable under Massachusetts' liberal constitutional principles. Sumner argued eloquently that the law could not sanction caste: "He may be poor, weak, humble, or black—he may be of Caucasian, Jewish, Indian or Ethiopian race—he may be French, German, English; or Irish extraction, but before the Constitution of Massachusetts all these distinctions disappear. He is not poor, weak, humble, or black; nor is he Caucasian, Jew, Indian, or Ethiopian; nor is he French, German, English, or Irish; he is a MAN [*sic*], the equal of his fellowmen."

The case was ultimately heard in the Massachusetts Supreme Judicial Court presided over by Chief Justice Lemuel Shaw. Shaw had had a somewhat mixed record with regard to slavery. Although he regarded the institution as unjust, he also rejected the idea of immediate abolition. Despite his relatively conservative views with respect to slavery, Shaw issued opinions based on the Massachusetts Constitution that aided the antislavery cause. In the 1836 case of *Commonwealth v. Aves*, Shaw declared that a six-year-old slave girl who had been brought into Massachusetts by her owner was free. In writing that opinion, Shaw affirmed a long-standing principle in Anglo-American law that slaves brought into free territory became free persons. In *Aves*, Shaw carefully distinguished between that case, where the slave had been voluntarily brought into the state by the owner, and the case of fugitive slaves.

If Shaw was prepared to be conservative with respect to issues of slavery and abolition, he proved to be even more so when confronted with the issue of racial discrimination and the meaning of equality before the law. Shaw's opinion in *Roberts v. City of Boston* (1850) rejected Sumner's argument that separate schools perpetuated caste distinctions. Shaw went further. He made a distinction between law and custom and expressed his view that strong prejudice was a deeply rooted part of the culture of the day that could not be eradicated by legal change. His was an argument that would be repeated many times in the nation's future:

> It is urged, that this maintenance of separate schools tends to deepen and perpetuate the odious distinction of caste, founded in a deep rooted prejudice in public opinion. This prejudice, if it exists, is not created by law; and probably cannot be changed by law. Whether this distinction and prejudice, existing in the opinion and feelings of the community, would not be as effectually fostered by compelling colored and white children to associate together in the same schools, may well be doubted; at all events, it is a fair and proper question for the committee to consider and decide upon, having in view the best interests of both classes of children placed upon their superintendence, and we cannot say, that their decision is not founded on just grounds of reason and experience, and in the result of a discriminating and honest judgement.

Roberts was a remarkable case, far ahead of the time in which it was argued and decided. It involved the issue of equal protection under the law nearly twenty years before the Fourteenth Amendment with its equal protection clause would be added to the nation's Constitution. It dealt with the relationship between legal segregation and stigmatization half a century before the United States Supreme Court would touch these issues in *Plessy* and more than one hundred years before the Court would revisit these concerns in *Brown*. Shaw's view that caste, status, and stigmatization were dependent on popular mores and were not caused or reinforced by government segregation would be repeated by the Supreme Court in *Plessy* and by subsequent defenders of legal segregation. Shaw's decision in *Roberts* would be used by the Court in *Plessy* to show the compatibility of segregation and a mandate of equality before the law.

The case of *Roberts v. City of Boston* would have many post-scripts. Two are important for our purposes. One of these is that the Massachusetts legislature outlawed segregated schools in 1855. Another is that attorney Charles Sumner would become a Republican senator from Massachusetts. In the Senate, he would provide a strong antislavery voice and would play a leading role in the drafting of the Fourteenth Amendment. That amendment would, among other things, bring Massachusetts' constitutional concept of the equality of all before the law into the formal Constitution of the nation.

That New Birth of Freedom

Roberts v. City of Boston affected only a minuscule portion of the black population in mid-nineteenth-century America. For the time, Shaw's opinion was remarkable not for its grudging recognition of Negro citizenship and equality, but because it recognized those concepts at all. Over 90 percent of African Americans were slaves. Over 95 percent lived in the slave states of the South. There the law allowed no recognition, not even a reluctant or theoretical recognition, of black citizenship and equality. Slaves, of course, were property, and the law of the southern states was carefully constructed to safeguard white interests in that region's most valuable commodity—human chattel. Slaves could be bought and sold, leased and traded. They could be inherited by will or intestate succession. Slaves were assets that could be seized to satisfy debts. Children could be sold apart from their parents, wives and husbands separated, depending on the business needs or even personal whims of their owners.

But it was more than their status as an article of commerce that separated the mostly enslaved black population from the free white population. Southern jurists and legislators recognized the paradox embedded in a legal system designed to protect property in people. They also were aware that that paradox was made even sharper because southern law was informed by the liberal postulates of the American constitutional order and indeed the common law—which had not recognized slavery in England—as well. Slaves were not like furniture, or cattle or real estate, although at various points in southern history, slaves were legally classified as various species of property, sometimes chattel, sometimes even real property. Slaves were thinking, aware human beings—thinking, aware human beings who were often quite dissatisfied with their enslavement. Southern lawmakers became adept at developing and administering a body of law that took into account the slave's dual status, property for some purposes, person for others. The slave was, for example, regulated as an article of commerce. Some of this regulation even resembled modern consumer protection laws. Statutes might specify when a contract for sale of a slave could be considered final and binding. Other statutes or court decisions might deal with the issue of whether or not a hidden defect in a slave—an undisclosed tendency to run away, for example—might render a sales contract null and void.

But it was in the law governing slave discipline where the contradiction between the slave's humanity and his status as property became most glaring. On one level, southern law had no difficulty recognizing the slave's humanity. By the nineteenth century it was a criminal homicide to murder a slave, even if the murderer was white, indeed even if the murderer was the slave's owner. That was somewhat different from the prevailing legal rule in many southern colonies before the American Revolution. Then the killing of a slave was often just a civil matter, basically a trespass to the owner's property, a matter to be settled by compensation, not criminal sanction. Antebellum southern law also recognized the slave's humanity by treating the slave as a responsible, moral agent who could be held responsible for crimes. Slaves accused of the more serious crimes, particularly capital crimes, were generally deemed to be entitled to have jury trials and legal counsel.

Still the recognition of the slave's humanity only went so far. It might be an illegal homicide or even murder for a master to kill his slave, but slave owners were given wide latitude in disciplining slaves. Courts repeatedly recognized that a master was entitled to use "moderate correction" to discipline recalcitrant slaves, and if the slave died during the course of such action—which might include flogging or branding or some other horror—that was not murder nor any other kind of unlawful homicide—but was the unfortunate result of "moderate correction." Similarly the murder of a slave by a white person witnessed only by other slaves was highly unlikely to receive the law's punishment. The other slaves could not be witnesses in court. The white killer would go free.

Southern law probably came closest to a realization of the precarious duality of the slave's status in its regulation of slave attempts to gain freedom. The white South was painfully aware that slaves were discontented with their lot and desired freedom. It was a human desire, fed by the example of the free people, black and white, that slaves encountered and by the ideology of freedom that prevailed in antebellum America. The appetite for freedom was even whetted by slaves' imprecise and often distorted knowledge of the successful revolution of Haitian slaves at the start of the nineteenth century. Southern whites knew of and feared these longings for freedom even as they sought to reassure themselves and the outside world with the comforting moonlight- and magnolia-soaked myth of the devoted, contented slave.

As the nineteenth century unfolded, southern law became increasingly concerned with curtailing this desire for freedom. While the law in some southern states had become sympathetic to manumission, the voluntary freeing of slaves by masters, in the liberal atmosphere that immediately followed the Revolution, that changed by the nineteenth century. The growth of the cotton kingdom and the fear of slave rebelliousness brought about a new hostility to the growth of free Negro populations. Statutes and court decisions made private manumissions increasingly difficult. Free Negroes were deemed a threat to the slave order; their very ability to survive on their own challenged the assumptions of black inferiority and dependency that were used to justify slavery. Laws became more stringent, restricting the rights of free Afro-Americans. In some locations they were in danger of being reduced to slave status if they could not produce documents proving their free status. They could not travel without passes. Their ability to get together in political and social groups was severely curtailed. They could not own or carry weapons for their defense. Free Negroes in the South could not testify against whites in court. Nor could they bring actions against white parties. One historian, Ira Berlin, has gone so far as to describe antebellum southern free blacks as "slaves without masters."

And southern law was constantly afraid of the potential for rebellion and running away. Insuring that slaves remain in their place became the business of the entire white community, not merely slave owners. Slave patrols—posses of white men whose sole function was to police the slave population—patrolled roads and fields to capture would-be runaways, to demand passes from slaves who were off their owners' property, and to provide a constant reminder to slaves that swift and severe punishment would be meted out to those who stepped outside their physical and social place.

The subject of slave law and the slave's status could and has filled numerous volumes, and it is not our intention to go deeply into the subject here. One aspect of the topic is important, though, for our purposes. The southern law of slavery could not simply exist and survive in a vacuum—or at least southern lawmakers did not believe that it could. The slave South was in a union with free states in other regions. A few of those states, like Massachusetts, accorded their Afro-American populations almost, at least on paper, the same rights granted their white populations. Others, like Oregon, were so restrictive that black people were legally barred from settling in the states. Most free states were somewhere in between. Free Negroes could live in those states, but with fewer rights than whites. But in all of those states, the presumptions of southern law were reversed. Slavery was illegal. The law presumed that a person, black or white, was free. From the time of the drafting of the Constitution, southern lawmakers recognized that the free states would be a magnet for slaves who sought freedom. They demanded and got a fugitive slave clause in the Constitution. In 1850 Congress enacted a stringent fugitive slave statute that imposed the South's presumption that a black person was a slave nationwide. Under that statute a white person could claim a black person as a fugitive. The person alleged to be a fugitive was to be returned to a slave state and reduced to slave status without benefit of a trial by jury or other safeguards. This would be true whether the individual was in fact a fugitive slave or a free Negro from a northern state. Under this statute the alleged fugitive could not testify on his own behalf.

The 1850 statute was seen by many in the North as an effort to in effect spread the southern law of slavery to the free states. The case of *Dred Scott v. Sanford* (1857), more popularly known as *Dred Scott*, further fueled this fear. *Dred Scott* touched on many issues, but the most important question involved the issue of Negro citizenship. By 1857, when the case was decided, it is clear that the southern states, with some minor exceptions, had rejected the idea that blacks, even free blacks, were citizens of the different states and of the United States. The defense of slavery rested too strongly on presumptions of black inferiority and dependency to seriously entertain notions of black citizenship. In the North the record was more mixed. Clearly some states, most prominently but not exclusively in the New England region, recognized their free Negroes as citizens. Discrimination existed and indeed was often mandated by law. Outside of New England and New York, black men were unable to vote, but nonetheless most northern states extended a range of other rights to free Negroes that were generally denied blacks in the South. *Dred Scott v. Sanford* in part called on the Court to decide between the southern view, which rejected blacks as citizens, and the northern view, which accepted the possibility.

In the majority opinion, Chief Justice Roger Brooke Taney emphatically chose the southern view. His opinion rejected the idea of Negro citizenship and went on to starkly proclaim what had become the antebellum South's legal position with respect to the rights of blacks under the Constitution. As Taney (in)famously stated it: "The negro has no rights which the white man is bound to respect."

Taney's opinion sought to preserve and nationalize the world of southern slavery with its body of laws crafted to preserve property rights in human beings and to reject Negro citizenship. That world would come to an end with the end of the white South's unsuccessful rebellion against the Union. Even during the Civil War, the Lincoln administration moved to nullify one significant part of the Taney decision. In 1862, before Lincoln issued the Emancipation Proclamation, Attorney General Edward Bates issued an opinion expressing the view that free Negroes were citizens of the United States and thus entitled to military commissions and other privileges reserved for citizens. During the war the Lincoln administration acted on the Bates opinion commissioning over one hundred black men in the Union army.

The most important result of the Civil War was, of course, the end of slavery. The end came in stages. Lincoln's Emancipation Proclamation of 1863 freed only slaves in states in rebellion against the United States. Slaves held in loyal border states like Maryland, Kentucky, and Delaware were not freed by the proclamation. However, the Thirteenth Amendment to the Constitution was ratified immediately at the war's end in 1865. It outlawed slavery throughout the United States.

Slavery's end immediately raised the question of exactly what kind of freedom the newly emancipated slaves would enjoy. The defeated South quickly indicated that it intended to permit the freedmen only a very limited kind of freedom. Immediately after the war's end, southern state governments passed a series of statutes known as the Black Codes. While these codes recognized the free status of the former slaves, they also imposed the kinds of legal disabilities on blacks that made it clear blacks were in no way entitled to equal rights or any claim of citizenship. The codes restricted public meetings, imposed curfews on blacks, and prohibited blacks from owning firearms. In an attempt to insure that former slave owners still had a large labor supply, the Black Codes also forced former slaves to sign labor contracts or face the alternative of prison and forced labor for vagrancy.

The Black Codes played a major role in spurring Republicans in the Thirty-ninth Congress to pass and send the Fourteenth

Amendment to the states. Although the Fourteenth Amendment was designed to accomplish a number of different goals, two purposes of the amendment would profoundly affect and alter the American law of race and caste. First, the Fourteenth Amendment would end the dispute concerning Negro citizenship. Its language clearly established that every person born in the United States was a citizen of the nation and of the state in which he or she resided. This provision would ultimately become of extreme importance not only for Afro-Americans but indeed for other groups that experienced severe discrimination, including later generations of Chinese and Japanese Americans, among others.

The second provision that would fundamentally alter the American law of race was the amendment's equal protection clause. That clause generated intense controversy during the debate over the Fourteenth Amendment. Indeed, it probably generated more controversy than any other provision of the amendment. Critics saw that it would profoundly alter the status of black and white before the law. It would do so in the recently rebellious South, but it would also do so in the Unionist states of the North and West as well. Opponents, mostly Democrats, argued vigorously against the measure, some claiming that it would permit interracial marriages, others that it would force associations between black and white. Their arguments failed. The Fourteenth Amendment passed both houses of Congress in 1866. By 1868 enough states had ratified the amendment for it to become part of the Constitution.

The passage of the Fourteenth Amendment was a critical part of the larger process of Reconstruction. The Reconstruction era would see far-reaching federal civil rights legislation, legislation designed to protect the newly freed African American population not only from state discrimination but from harmful private action as well. Important constitutional change would come during Reconstruction. In addition to the Thirteenth and Fourteenth Amendments, the Fifteenth Amendment prohibiting discrimination in the exercise of voting rights was also added to the Constitution.

And most important, during Reconstruction federal authorities acted to enforce the grand pronouncements of the new constitutional provisions and civil rights statutes. The right of black men to vote was enforced, guaranteed by the presence of federal troops and prosecutors from the newly formed Justice Department. Southern politics changed dramatically. Black men were in the state legislatures, the U. S. House of Representatives, and the Senate. South Carolina and Louisiana had black lieutenant governors. One of these, P. B. S. Pinchback of Louisiana, even served as acting governor for a brief period. During Reconstruction the first public schools for either black or white children were established in the South. In New Orleans there was even, in the early 1870s, a brief, highly controversial experiment with integrated public schools.

Initially the Supreme Court seemed inclined to give a reasonably broad reading of the Civil War amendments—at least as far as those amendments were seen as limiting the ability of the states to engage in racial discrimination. Two early cases, *Strauder v. West Virginia* (1879) and *Yick Wo v. Hopkins* (1886), illustrated the willingness of the Court to take the Fourteenth Amendment's equal protection language and use it to closely examine state-sponsored racial discrimination. Briefly put, *Strauder* involved a statute that restricted jury service to white men. The Court pronounced the statute and practice repugnant to the Civil War amendments, looking at the amendments as a whole. This was an important decision. Although the Thirteenth Amendment abolished slavery, the Fourteenth Amendment mandated equal protection of the law, and the Fifteenth Amendment prohibited racial discrimination in voting, none of these amendments specifically prohibited racial discrimination in jury membership. Certainly the Court could have given a narrow technical interpretation of the amendments that denied that they necessarily applied to the selection of jurors. Instead the *Strauder* opinion, authored by Justice William Strong, stressed that the three Civil War amendments should be read broadly and with the idea that they had a common purpose in mind, namely to give the newly emancipated slaves the same rights as the white population.

In some ways the case of *Yick Wo* might have been even more significant than *Strauder*. That case—which, interestingly enough, involved Chinese immigrants, not African Americans—dealt with a more subtle kind of discrimination. Authorities in San Francisco refused to give licenses to Chinese immigrants who wanted to operate laundries. The statute under which the authorities operated said nothing about race. There was no language restricting licenses to white people or prohibiting Chinese or others from obtaining licenses. Nonetheless the discrimination existed. The Court ruled for the Chinese complainants. This case was of paramount importance because it required the Court to look at the actual behavior of state actors instead of merely confining its inquiry to the stated language in a discriminatory statute. This decision potentially made the Fourteenth Amendment's equal protection clause a tremendously powerful tool for those suffering state discrimination. The demands of the clause could not be thwarted by a statute that on its face appeared not to discriminate.

But if the Supreme Court's decisions in *Strauder* and *Yick Wo* suggested that the Civil War amendments might provide a shield against state discrimination, other developments were working to weaken the legal protections that had developed in postbellum America. Reconstruction would come to an end in 1877 with the withdrawal of federal troops from the South. The recently freed Negroes of the region would theoretically retain the civil rights granted by constitutional amendment and federal statute in the previous decade, but increasingly they would be forced to look to state government to vindicate those rights.

The Supreme Court would play a major role in restricting the federal government's ability to protect the civil rights of Afro-Americans. If the Court in the 1870s and 1880s was willing to be far-reaching when it examined state discrimination in light of the equal protection clause, it took a very narrow view of Congress's ability to protect blacks and others from private action. In 1875 Congress had passed a far-reaching civil rights statute outlawing discrimination in inns, theaters, and steamships—what we today would call public accommodations. In 1883 in the *Civil Rights Cases*, the Court declared that Congress lacked the power to do this under the Thirteenth and Fourteenth Amendments. The

Court opinion held that the Thirteenth Amendment simply pro-hibited slavery and that the Fourteenth Amendment only cov-ered state actors, not private actors such as the owners of theaters or steamships. Justice John Marshall Harlan, a former Kentucky slaveholder, issued a telling dissent:

> I do not contend that the Thirteenth Amendment invests Congress with authority, by legislation, to define and regulate the entire body of the civil rights which citizens enjoy. . . . [S]ince slavery . . . was the moving or principal cause of the adoption of that amendment, *and since that institution rested wholly upon the inferiority, as a race, of those held in bondage, their freedom necessarily involved immunity from, and protection against, all discrimination against them, because of their race, in respect of such civil rights as belong to freemen of other races.* (italics added)

The Court's earlier decision in *United States v. Cruikshank* (1875) was of even greater importance. That case involved a Ku Klux Klan attack on a group of black men in Louisiana who were attempting to vote. Klan members were charged with violation of the constitutional rights of the victims. The Klan members were charged under the Enforcement Act of 1870, which made it a crime for private individuals to deprive people of their civil rights. The Court ruled that the Klan members were private cit-izens and that their actions could not be reached by Congress. The Court went on to say that citizens had to look to their state governments, not the federal government, for protection of their rights from other citizens.

If the *Cruikshank* Court saw the fine distinction between state and private infringement of civil rights, the distinction would be-come more academic than real to southern blacks in the 1880s and 1890s. White rule would be reestablished in the South to a great extent by means of private extralegal violence—which fre-quently was done with the approval and not very clandestine as-sistance of state and local officials. The Ku Klux Klan played a key role in this. With bullet and torch, rope and whip, the Klan threatened black voters, killing some, driving many more away from the ballot box. While black voting would not be completely eliminated in this period, it was severely weakened. White rule returned to the South. Fewer and fewer blacks dared exercise the franchise. The number of black officeholders diminished. Historians of the American South have called this retreat from Reconstruction and the return of white rule "the Redemption." By the 1890s southern state governments were firmly in the control of white voters and white politicians. There was still, at the beginning of that decade, a question of what direction state governments might take with respect to race. Law and custom had changed, profoundly so, in the previous decades. Emancipation was irreversible. The Civil War amendments remained even if federal authorities were no longer actively protecting the rights of blacks. There were still a significant number of Negro voters, even if their numbers were diminishing. Blacks too had changed. They had experienced a liberation. Men had voted and for a time had exercised real political power. Black mothers and fathers had sent their children and often themselves to school, first the schools established by the Freedmen's Bureau, later schools run by the states. How would the "Redeemed" southern state governments confront these new realities?

***

Jim Crow, *Plessy*, and the Triumph of Caste

One way southern governments approached this new reality was to develop a rigid system of segregation. At its zenith this system of segregation would turn Negroes into a group of American untouchables, ritually separated from the dominant white population in almost every observable facet of daily existence. It was an etiquette of discrimination. It would not be enough for blacks to be second-class citizens, increasingly denied the franchise and other rights of citizenship. Instead black subordination had to be reinforced by a racialist ritual, a punctilio dictating separate seating on public accommodations, separate water fountains and rest rooms. Separate seats were to be found in courtrooms, along with separate Bibles with which to swear black and white witnesses. The list of separations would become ingenious and endless. The system would have the somewhat whimsical name of Jim Crow, named for an antebellum minstrel act.

Jim Crow as a system did not appear overnight. Indeed, at the close of the nineteenth century, many whites as well as blacks fought vigorously against the idea, arguing that such rigid separations would lead to absurdities. Some of the critics, in fact, cited such ideas as separate park benches or railroad cars or Bibles for witnesses as the kind of absurdities that would cause right-thinking people to reject segregation. Their arguments were to no avail. What critics of Jim Crow cited as far-fetched absurdities would in fact become mandated and mandated by law in many states in the South and in a few other regions as well.

This system of state-mandated segregation would gain the support of the nation's highest court in 1896. That year the Supreme Court handed down its decision in *Plessy v. Ferguson* (1896). *Plessy* was a case that originated in Louisiana. In 1890 the legislature of that state passed a statute requiring separate railroad cars for whites and blacks. The statute specified that the facilities were to be of equal quality. The statute also prescribed fines or imprisonment for passengers who sat in the cars reserved for members of another race. The law did permit one exception to the rule of rigid segregation. Servants attending children could sit in cars reserved for those of another race. This exception was made to accommodate black nannies of white children.

Plessy became part of the Court's and the nation's history when one Adolphus Plessy of New Orleans was arrested on June 7, 1892, for attempting to ride in the first-class coach reserved for white passengers. When told that he must move to the coach reserved for colored passengers, he refused. He was arrested. The case was on.

Before we discuss *Plessy* the case, a few words about Plessy the man are in order. That Plessy was considered black at all can tell us much about caste and race in American culture. Plessy was an octoroon—a term most of us today scarcely remember, except perhaps for those of us who are devotees of a certain kind of melodramatic novel that was popular in the nineteenth and early part of the twentieth century. Plessy had one-eighth African ancestry;

the rest of his ancestry was white. Racial discrimination, especially racial discrimination by law, requires racial classification. American law and custom had long dictated that if a person had virtually any traceable African ancestry, that person was a Negro. This view stands in marked contrast to the view that has been held in other societies. In most of Latin America, for example, blacks and people of mixed race are often considered distinct groups. Also in most of Latin America, many individuals are classified as white who have some acknowledged African ancestry, indeed often relatively recent African ancestry. Not so in the United States, where most jurisdictions have held by law that even highly attenuated African ancestry will make an individual black.

Louisiana was in some ways a hybrid of the American and Latin American views on racial classification. Before the Civil War, there was a distinct class of French-speaking mulattoes, called *gens de colour libre*, who did not regard themselves as black. With American annexation and Louisiana's adoption of American law, particularly American law with respect to slavery and race, the group was legally classified with the free Negro population. Despite this, the lingering Latin culture of Louisiana allowed this group to carve out a separate status different from free Negroes in the rest of the South. Some members of this group voted quite openly, even though it was illegal. Some were large slaveholders. Others participated in the slave patrols. There are even a few cases of members of this group formally marrying white persons, despite the fact that this was technically illegal. Some members of this group even formed military units and offered their services to the Confederacy, although they switched sides and joined the Union ranks with the federal occupation of New Orleans in 1862.

After the Civil War, this group increasingly was treated as simply part of the Afro-American population. Plessy, who was from this group and who by all accounts was not visibly of African descent, was not only protesting his assignment to the colored coach. He was also protesting the railroad's right to define him as black. His was in part a complaint against the system of legally required racial classification—a system of racial classification that was necessary to maintain the emerging world of Jim Crow restrictions. If the law could classify him as black, Plessy reasoned, it could do so at great injury to his reputation. Plessy and his associates used discrimination on the railroad to launch a test case against racial classification and Jim Crow restrictions.

Plessy was argued and decided along many of the same lines as *Roberts* nearly half a century before. Plessy's attorneys, led by Louisiana lawyer Albion Tourgée, focused on the stigmatizing effects of forced segregation, as had Sumner and Morris when they argued for Sarah Roberts in antebellum Massachusetts. This time Plessy's attorneys could argue that the amended national constitution supported their claim. They argued that the Thirteenth and Fourteenth Amendments prohibited this kind of segregation, that it stamped a badge of inferiority on blacks.

The majority opinion authored by Justice Henry Billings Brown also echoed much of the Lemuel Shaw opinion in *Roberts*, which he cited. Brown rejected the claim that the Thirteenth and Fourteenth Amendments prohibited segregation. His opinion saw segregation as reasonable regulation, a valid exercise of the police power. Brown dismissed the argument that mandated segregation stigmatized blacks:

> We consider the underlying fallacy of the plaintiff's argument to consist in the assumption that the enforced separation of the two races stamps the colored race with a badge of inferiority. If this be so, it is not by reason of anything found in the act, but solely because the colored race chooses to put that construction upon it. The argument necessarily assumes that if, as has been more than once the case, and is not unlikely to be so again, the colored race should become the dominant power in the state legislature, and should enact a law in precisely similar terms, it would thereby relegate the white race to an inferior position. We imagine that the white race; at least; would not acquiesce in this assumption. The argument also assumes that social prejudices may be overcome by legislation, and that equal rights cannot be secured to the negro

except by an enforced commingling of the two races. We cannot accept this proposition. If the two races are to meet upon terms of social equality it must be the result of natural affinities, a mutual appreciation of each others' merits and a voluntary consent of individuals.

The lone dissenter in *Plessy* was Justice John Marshall Harlan. One of the ironies of the case is that Brown, the author of the majority opinion, was born in New England, a region of the country traditionally associated with racial liberalism. Harlan, the dissenter, had been a Kentucky slave owner before the Civil War. He argued that the Civil War amendments should be read together as preventing the law from making racial distinctions:

These notable additions to the fundamental law were welcomed by the friends of liberty throughout the world. They removed the race line from our governmental systems. They had, as this court has said, a common purpose namely, to secure "to a race recently emancipated, a race that through many generations have been held in slavery, all the civil rights that the superior race enjoy. They declared, in legal effect, this court has further said that the law in the States shall be the same for the black as for the white; that all persons, whether colored or white shall stand equal before the law of the States, and, in regard to the colored race, for whose protection the amendment was primarily designed, that no discrimination shall be made against them by law because of their color.

Harlan also went on to express his view that the Constitution required the law to be color-blind:

The white race deems itself to be the dominant race in this country. And so it is, in prestige, in achievements, in education, in wealth and in power. So, I doubt not, it will continue to be for all time, if it remains true to its great heritage and holds fast to the principles of constitutional liberty. But in view of the Constitution, in the eye of the law, there is in this country no superior, dominant, ruling class of citizens. There is no caste here. Our Constitution is color blind and neither knows nor tolerates classes among citizens. In respect of civil rights, all citizens are equal before the law. The humblest is the peer of the most powerful. The law regards man as man, and takes no account of his surroundings or of his color when his civil rights as guaranteed by the supreme law of the land are involved. It is, therefore, to be regretted that this high tribunal, the final expositor of the fundamental law of the land, has reached the conclusion that it is competent for a State to regulate the enjoyment by citizens of their civil rights solely on the basis of race.

But the *Plessy* court had reached that conclusion, exactly that conclusion. It said that a state law that separated people simply because they were of different races violated no provision of the Constitution, not even the recently enacted Thirteenth and Fourteenth Amendments. Still the statute the Court upheld did require that facilities for black and white passengers be of equal quality. The Court had allowed states to treat Afro-Americans separately as long as they received equal treatment. In 1896 government separation of the races was certainly growing. Would the courts insure that that separate treatment was equal? Could they?

CHAPTER 2

"Separate and Unequal"

An American Apartheid at the Dawn
of an American Century

Half Speed Backwards

The new century would provide new opportunities to test *Plessy*'s separate but equal doctrine. Segregation was on the rise. What perhaps started in the 1890s as tentative steps to separate the races in a few areas would, by the early part of the twentieth century, become a full-fledged effort to subjugate and stigmatize the South's black population. That effort would be accompanied by the virtual repudiation of the Civil War amendments and the egalitarian sentiment that helped bring about their enactment. Along with increased segregation came increased disenfranchisement. Blacks would largely disappear from the voting rolls in southern states. In those states—home to nearly 90 percent of the nation's black population in 1900—Negroes would become politically irrelevant and disenfranchised, victims of a new brand of politics that effectively reestablished white domination in the region. That white domination was maintained through the often vicious politics of race baiting.

The reestablishment of white domination in southern politics was accomplished with and maintained by an incredibly high level of illegal violence. Mob murder, lynching, was condoned, no celebrated, by some of the most eminent public figures in the turn of the century South. Newspaper editors wrote editorials justifying these murders. Governors and senators delivered speeches praising the handiwork of mobs, proclaiming lynchings a necessary tool for dealing with blacks who got out of line, who forgot their place. Federal officials ignored these crimes. The

Supreme Court's decision in *Cruikshank* in 1875 had effectively ended the federal government's role in protecting black citizens from private terror. Besides, there was a new politics in this new century. Whites totally dominated the politics of the new South. They had an unchecked political power in the region. Few politicians outside the region, even those somewhat sympathetic to the ideal of equal treatment, were inclined to challenge the ruling order in the South.

Historians of the Afro-American experience have rightly termed the beginning of the twentieth century as the "nadir" of American race relations, a time—at least after the Civil War—when race relations and protection of the rights of African Americans hit rock bottom. A number of historians have offered insightful explanations as to why this occurred. Some have explained this retreat from equality as a reaction to the nation's new imperial adventures and new contacts with nonwhite peoples in Hawaii, the Philippines, and Latin America. Others contend that waves of immigration from southern and eastern Europe, not to mention China and Japan, gave influential people outside of the South new skepticism concerning the concept of equality before the law. Many historians have persuasively argued that politicians from the North and West were, by the early twentieth century, inclined to give the South a free hand with its black citizens as a way of fostering national unity—a unity that was particularly important for a nation that was increasingly looking outward.

These explanations can help us to understand why the Fourteenth and Fifteenth Amendments were becoming virtual dead letters in the South, the region for which these two constitutional provisions were especially designed. But something even more fundamental was at work. A good portion of the nation, particularly those who shaped the nation's opinions, the men and to a lesser extent the women of law and letters, those who dominated the intellectual life of the nation, were helping to give the nation a case of buyer's remorse over the Fourteenth and Fifteenth Amendments. The newly emerging historical profession was rendering a very severe judgment on America's recent past. The generation that had supported abolition in the 1850s and had fought the Rebellion in the 1860s and later supported Reconstruction at the end of that decade and in the 1870s were either quite elderly or already dead by the beginning of the twentieth century. Their lives and their works were being judged and judged harshly by a new generation of university trained historians at the beginning of the twentieth century.

The most prominent of these historians, William A. Dunning, taught in the history department at Columbia University in New York City before the First World War. Dunning would provide a vivid picture of Reconstruction that dominated the thinking of most Americans for most of the twentieth century. In Dunning's view, Reconstruction was a "tragic era"—to use the title of a book by one of Dunning's disciples, Claude Bowers—a time when a vengeful North imposed its harsh rule on the South. Part of that imposition was the forcing of Negro equality down the throats of the white people of the region. This, it was argued, was accomplished through unparalleled corruption and military brutality. The return of white rule to the South was an unmitigated blessing, even if it was occasioned by the illegal work of the Ku Klux Klan. This view was spread not only by Dunning's writings but also by his many students and followers who came to dominate historical writing on the subject for at least the first half of the twentieth century. This view was also spread in textbooks as part of the general education of students in high schools and universities and was impressed upon the public in the form of popular culture. Thomas Dixon's virulently racist novel *The Clansman* helped popularize this point of view, as did director D. W. Griffith's 1915 film *Birth of a Nation*, which was based on the Dixon novel. This viewpoint probably reached its zenith in popular expression with the 1939 film *Gone with the Wind*, a movie classic whose popularity will doubtless continue well into the twenty-first century, perhaps even until its hundredth anniversary in 2039.

This discussion of how historians and artists came to view Reconstruction is important to our discussion of legislatures and courts and how they dealt with the constitutional demands of the Fourteenth and Fifteenth Amendments. Our sense of history, particularly recent history, informs our understanding of the past, to be sure. But our historical sensibilities do more: they invariably influence the way we think about contemporary issues. For American legislators and jurists at the beginning of the twentieth century, the tragic-era view of Reconstruction inevitably shaped their views of the Reconstruction amendments. Some argued forcefully that Reconstruction was evil and that the Fourteenth and Fifteenth Amendments were mistakes. Some even went so far as to propose their repeal. Others, less radical, argued that the amendments, the products of what they believed to be cynical power politics, could not have really intended to provide a robust guarantee of equal rights for blacks. So dominant was the tragic-era view of Reconstruction that even some champions of equal rights feared that the history lent little support to a strong egalitarian interpretation of the Fourteenth Amendment. They doubted that it could be a vehicle capable of providing a strong challenge to Jim Crow.

The emergence of social Darwinism also helped strengthen the emerging Jim Crow order in the South and elsewhere in the nation at the beginning of the twentieth century. Racism had long existed in the United States. There had also long been efforts to justify racial exclusions along scientific lines. Those efforts would increase with the coming of the twentieth century. If Charles Darwin's theories on evolution, conflict among species, and natural selection helped transform the biological sciences, those theories had no less profound an effect on social thought and the emerging social sciences. Scholars in academic disciplines like sociology, economics, and increasingly law readily adopted, or attempted to adopt, evolutionary models to their fields of study.

Pioneering English sociologist Herbert Spencer would add the notion of survival of the fittest in adapting Darwinian theory to the study of social relations. It was, he argued, nature's plan that the best and the fittest survive and that the weaker species perish. Why shouldn't that be applicable to the social world as well as to the biological? Why shouldn't weaker peoples or races perish in the great evolutionary competition that was life? This was a strongly held view in America at the beginning of the twentieth century. No less a figure than Supreme Court Justice Oliver Wendell Holmes, for example, was quite sympathetic to the eugenics movement, a movement that sought to improve the population by limiting the reproduction of those deemed inferior.

Many adherents of social Darwinism saw Afro-Americans in particular as an inferior people destined to naturally lose and perish in the competition between the races. In their view the new industrial society of the twentieth century had no place for the inferior Negro. If blacks had had a place in the simple agrarian South of the nineteenth century, they were surplus and dysfunctional in the modern twentieth century. Left to their own devices, they would be unable to survive. Many social commentators predicted the not too distant disappearance of African Americans from the South and the nation altogether.

Another social Darwinist who would have an important influence on legal thinking was sociologist William Graham Sumner. One of the pioneers of American sociology, he was elected president of the American Sociological Society in 1908. In his 1906 book *Folkways*, Sumner argued against any attempt to remedy racial inequality through legal mechanisms. In a way Sumner was reiterating the point made by Massachusetts Justice Lemuel Shaw in *Roberts* that racial prejudice was a strong part of American culture and that it was a part of the culture that could not be changed by the law. Sumner would take Shaw's point even further, questioning whether the very concept of equal status before the law was, even in theory, a good or workable idea.

The intellectual climate of the early twentieth century was not hospitable to a serious challenge to the developing Jim Crow order in the South. Ironically that order also seemingly received support by the most prominent black leader of the day, Booker T. Washington. Washington was a complex figure. A son of the South, who recounted his difficult early years and hard-won education in his autobiography *Up from Slavery*, Washington publicly accepted the segregation and disenfranchisement that were the order of the day at the start of the last century. He did so, it seems, in part to insure some measure of racial peace in a violent time and also to garner white philanthropy for his school, the

Tuskegee Institute. Privately Washington's views were considerably different. He financially supported lawsuits against various discriminatory measures. In any event, Washington's prominence—he had a close working relationship with President Theodore Roosevelt among others—and his seeming acquiescence to Jim Crow certainly aided those who supported segregation and disenfranchisement.

In the years before the First World War, a time called the Progressive Era by many historians, the social and intellectual climate was not supportive of constitutional challenges to racial discrimination. Yet, the Thirteenth, Fourteenth, and Fifteenth Amendments were still there, unerased despite the new atmosphere. How would the courts judge the constitutional provisions against the modern practices and thinkings that were the new realities of the new century? To what extent were the Civil War amendments still living parts of the Constitution, to what extent had they been effectively discarded?

<hr/>

Before the Bar: Race, the Civil War
Amendments, and the Supreme Court

The Supreme Court had a decidedly mixed record on racial issues in the era between its decision in *Plessy* in 1896 and the entrance of the United States into the First World War in 1917. The Court was certainly influenced by the segregationist climate of the times. This climate, it should be added, was considerably strengthened by the election in 1912 of Woodrow Wilson. Wilson was a strong champion of segregation who strengthened Jim Crow in the federal civil service and placed new restrictions on the ability of black men to enlist in the navy, among other discriminatory measures when he was president. Yet the Court was also faced with the stubborn facts of the Civil War amendments. They existed. They had not been repealed. There was a body of case law, including the recently decided *Plessy*, that indicated that these amendments could not be completely emptied of all meaning. How would the Court strike a balance between the prejudices of the day, shared by most of its members and the demands of the Thirteenth, Fourteenth, and Fifteenth Amendments—amendments that were crafted in a very different day? The way the Court threaded this needle often gave little relief to victims of racial discrimination at the time. But the Court's decisions probably preserved the possibilities for future challenges to racial discrimination.

An important issue touching on the Thirteenth Amendment and large numbers of southern blacks was the issue of peonage. For many Negroes in rural areas, the legal abolition of slavery did not mean the actual abolition of forced labor. The share-cropping system that developed in much of the South at the end of the nineteenth century left many poor black sharecroppers with little money and perpetually in debt. The common pattern was that black families would work on a small portion of a plantation, frequently the very plantation on which they or their families had been enslaved before the Civil War. The plantation owner would extend credit to the black family for seed, tools, food, and other essentials. The family was to pay the plantation owner back with a portion of the crop. Naturally the plantation owner had the records of how much had been lent, and not surprisingly black sharecroppers frequently found no matter how much they managed to pay to the plantation owner at the end of the year or at harvest time, they still owed more. They had a legally binding debt and were often forced to continue working. Naturally credit would be extended for next year's crop, increasing the indebtedness of the black family. In many southern localities, sheriffs and sometimes even local courts forced the black family to continue working on the plantation to pay off the debt.

This system of peonage was illegal. Congress in 1867 had passed an anti-peonage statute. It had been passed pursuant to Congress's power to enforce the Thirteenth Amendment prohibition on slavery and involuntary servitude. In 1904 the Supreme Court had an opportunity to look at a case that raised a constitutional challenge to the anti-peonage statute. The case, *Clyatt v. United States* (1905), involved an appeal to the Supreme Court of the conviction of a white defendant for violation of the anti-peonage statute. The defendant, Samuel M. Clyatt, had been charged with unlawfully forcing two black men, Will Gordon and Moses Ridley, to work for him under conditions of peonage. Clyatt had had Gordon and Ridley forcibly returned from Florida to Georgia under warrants for larceny. Once they had been returned to Georgia, they were forced to work for Clyatt to pay off their debts.

The Supreme Court ordered a new trial for Clyatt on the grounds that the trial court record did not have sufficient evidence for conviction. What is important for our purposes is that the Supreme Court rejected the argument made by Clyatt's attorneys that the Thirteenth Amendment did not give Congress the authority to legislate against the actions of individuals. You will remember our previous discussions concerning *Cruikshank* and the *Civil Rights Cases*. In both cases the Supreme Court held that Congress did not have the power to pass civil rights legislation under the Fourteenth Amendment that prohibited individuals from depriving people of their civil rights. In *Clyatt*, Clyatt's attorneys wanted that doctrine applied to the Thirteenth Amendment. In other words, Clyatt's attorneys asked for a ruling that would have, in effect, said that if a private individual subjected another private individual to involuntary servitude, only the state government, not the federal government, would have the authority to declare such action a crime and to prosecute alleged offenders. Needless to say, in the atmosphere of the early twentieth-century South, such a ruling would have greatly strengthened the system of peonage. With the passage of anti-peonage statutes left solely to unsympathetic state legislatures and enforcement left to local sheriffs beholden to plantation owners, mill operators, and other commercial interests in their communities, the Thirteenth Amendment could have become a virtual dead letter. The *Clyatt* decision helped prevent that.

If the Court was willing to take a reasonably robust view of the protection guaranteed by the Thirteenth Amendment, it was also quite protective of segregation and the right of state governments to erect a wall of separation between black and white. The Court's stated reasoning was that the police power, the authority to regulate in matters of safety, health, and morals, gave states broad powers to regulate in matters of race relations including legislation that mandated segregation. One of the more important cases in this area in the first decade of the twentieth century was the case of *Berea College v. Commonwealth of Kentucky* (1908). Berea College had admitted black and white students since the nineteenth century. In 1904 the state of Kentucky passed legislation forbidding schools from educating black and white students at the same facility. Berea College was a corporation and hence had the legal status of a person. The college was indicted for failure to comply with the mandatory segregation statute. It was convicted and sentenced to pay a $1,000 fine. Berea College officials ultimately appealed the ruling through the Kentucky state courts and then to the United States Supreme Court.

Berea College presented issues that went beyond the "separate but equal" doctrine that had been proclaimed in *Plessy*. *Plessy* dealt with legally enforced segregation on public transportation. Those facilities presumably had separate and equal sections for black and white patrons. *Berea College* involved the power of the state to require that a private institution maintain segregation. Here there was not a question of separate facilities; instead there was an issue of state-mandated total exclusion. There was one Berea College, and even though the statute said that a private institution might build a separate facility for Negroes, that of course was extremely unlikely. If the state could enforce segregation on private schools, it could exclude Afro-Americans from many of the available educational opportunities.

The argument in *Berea College* and the Court's decision in the case was not framed in terms of the Fourteenth Amendment and the issue of equal protection. Instead it was argued in terms of the property rights of Berea College and its officials. At the beginning of the last century, the Supreme Court was particularly concerned with protecting property rights and the right of individuals to have broad freedom to make contracts against state interference. Attorneys for the college argued that the Kentucky statute restricted the college's property rights.

The Supreme Court's decision rested on interesting ground,

somewhat removed from the issues of equal protection and stigmatization that had been so central in *Plessy*. The Court held that as Berea College was a corporation and as a corporation was the creation of a state statute, the state could have broad power to regulate the conduct of a corporation, broader power than it might for a private person. The Court acknowledged that such a statute might be unconstitutional if applied to an individual—on the grounds that it might violate the individual's property rights or freedom to contract. The Supreme Court indicated that it was only upholding the statute as to corporations and not individuals. The Court noted that the Kentucky Court of Appeals indicated that the statute would be applied only to corporations not individuals. Of course, it should also be added that the Court's holding that a corporation could be prevented from educating black and white students in the same facility in effect sanctioned a ban on most likely forms of integrated private education. Almost all schools of any appreciable size are likely to be run by corporations and not individuals. The Court's distinction between the two in *Berea* was, for practical purposes, of little importance in the field of education.

Separate but equal was revisited in *McCabe v. Atchison, Topeka and Santa Fe Railway Company* in 1914. In that case McCabe, a Negro living in Oklahoma, filed suit against the railroad. A state statute passed in 1907 permitted railroads to offer separate facilities for black and white passengers. The railroad did not offer sleeping cars or dining cars for African Americans, even though those facilities were available for whites.

McCabe filed for injunctive relief. A few words are in order before we move on. Two types of civil remedies are available in American courts: legal remedies and equitable remedies. The distinction between law and equity is part of our inheritance from English jurisprudence. Briefly put, legal remedies usually consist of monetary damages. If you own a dairy farm and a chemical plant accidentally pours pollutants into the stream from which your cattle drink, killing several of the cattle worth, say, $100,000, you would sue the owner of the chemical plant for $100,000, hopefully recover, and that would be the end of the matter. Now let us suppose that the chemical plant was regularly discharging pollutants into the stream, that polluting the stream was a regular part of the chemical plant's operation. Waiting for the plant's operation to kill your dairy cows and then going to court to seek a monetary recovery would not seem like an attractive idea. Especially if you are convinced that this harm will continue indefinitely—you would effectively be out of the dairy business. Instead you might seek equitable relief. You might go to court and seek an injunction requiring that the chemical plant cease discharging pollutants into the stream. This would allow you to prevent the harm rather than merely seeking recovery for damages after the fact. Equitable remedies—which usually require the courts to require certain behaviors from parties—are asked for when legal remedies are believed inadequate.

This brief discussion of equity will become more and more important as we go along because equitable relief is usually the kind of court assistance that plaintiffs in civil rights cases ask for. It was what McCabe asked for in *McCabe v. Atchison, Topeka and Santa Fe Railway Company.* McCabe based his argument on the Court's decision in *Plessy. Plessy* allowed separation but also said that the Fourteenth Amendment required that separate facilities must be equal facilities. Clearly a railroad company that failed to provide sleeping cars and dining cars for black passengers while it provided such facilities for whites was not providing equal facilities. McCabe wanted the Court to require equal facilities.

The Court agreed that the railroad had an obligation to provide sleeping cars, dining cars, and other facilities. It rejected the argument made by the railroad company that because few Negroes used such facilities, there was no requirement to provide them. The majority decision held that the right to equal facilities was not dependent upon how often such facilities were used. The Court nonetheless did not order the railroad company to provide such facilities. The Court's opinion held that equitable remedies were extraordinary remedies and would not be provided unless McCabe could show that legal remedies—monetary damages— would not be adequate. Here the Court presented another difficulty for those seeking broad relief from the discriminations of the Jim Crow system—the reluctance of the Court to use equitable remedies to remedy unequal treatment. Courts have traditionally viewed equity as an extraordinary remedy. Courts have done so because equity interferes with the freedom of a party who is under supervision of a court using its equity powers. Courts have also done so because it involves a more active role for the courts. And of course at the beginning of the twentieth century, racial attitudes strengthened the Court's traditional reluctance to use equity in cases involving racial discrimination. Courts at the time were quite willing to use their equitable powers when they felt that the cause was appropriate. One such area was in the use of labor injunctions, which were frequently employed against trade unions. Injunctions were frequently used to prevent or stop strikes. But using equity to prevent racial discrimination? That was another matter.

One case, *Buchanan v. Warley* (1917), did involve a victory against a statute requiring segregation. The 1917 case involved a Kentucky statute that prohibited white people from selling residential property to African Americans in blocks where the majority of residents were white. The Court struck down the statute largely on the grounds that it interfered with freedom of contract, principally the freedom of contract and the right to dispose of property of potential white sellers of residential property. The opinion, authored by Justice William Rufus Day, also indicated that the statute interfered with the contractual rights of Negro purchasers as well. *Buchanan* was also notable as one of the earliest cases that had an amicus brief filed by a new organization, the National Association for the Advancement of Colored People, which was founded in 1909.

Another major constitutional issue facing the Court in the first decades of the twentieth century was the increasing disenfranchisement of black voters in the southern states. The Fifteenth Amendment prevented the states from directly limiting the vote to whites, as had been the case before the Civil War. Nonetheless, a number of southern state governments had found what they hoped would be a series of legal loopholes around the constitutional requirement that black and white have equal access to the ballot box. A case that arose in Alabama in 1902 can illustrate how these loopholes worked. A new provision of the Alabama Constitution called for a new registration of voters. All voters registered in 1902 were to be registered for life. Those who registered in 1902 were required to take a relatively easy test to demonstrate their literacy and qualifications to be electors. After 1902 the literacy test was made considerably more difficult. In 1902 in Montgomery, Alabama, the registrar of voters simply refused to register black men, making them ineligible for registration under the easier standards. This brought about the case of *Giles v. Harris* (1903). Giles, a black man, filed on his behalf and on the behalf of five thousand other Afro-American men denied the right to register in 1902. Giles sought equitable relief, asking the courts to compel the registrar to register him and the other men.

The case was decided by the Supreme Court in 1903. In a majority opinion written by Justice Oliver Wendell Holmes, the Court denied Giles requested relief. The grounds for doing so was that the requested relief was equitable relief. The Holmes opinion indicated that the Court would be reluctant to give Giles an equitable remedy that would, in effect, require the Court to supervise the activities of state voting officials. Holmes expressed the view that this would be beyond the prerogatives of the Court and would heavily involve the Court in the political process of the state of Alabama. The Holmes opinion suggested that Giles's remedy was more likely to be a legal remedy—monetary damages for deprivation of his civil rights.

The next year the Court heard a case directly on that issue. Giles was back in the case of *Giles v. Teasley* (1904). This time Giles was asking for monetary damages in the amount of $5,000 for the refusal of the Montgomery County Board of Registrars to register him. The opinion of the Court, this time authored by Justice William Rufus Day, was something of a masterpiece of judicial double-talk. The Day opinion sustained the ruling of the Alabama Supreme Court. That court had said in effect that either the provisions of the Alabama Constitution under which the registrars operated were repugnant to the Fourteenth and Fifteenth Amendments, in which case they had no legal effect and hence no damages were owed Giles, or they were not repugnant to the Constitution, in which case the registrars were operating within the scope of their authority and no damages were owed Giles. The Giles cases left the Fifteenth Amendment a constitutional right without any effective remedy.

The Fifteenth Amendment fared considerably better a decade later in the case of *Guinn and Beals v. United States*, which was decided in 1915. That case involved a grandfather clause in the Oklahoma Constitution. That state's constitution provided for a literacy test for voters but exempted potential voters who were either eligible to vote or who were lineal descendants of those eligible to vote before 1866. Chief Justice Edward Douglass White, a native of Louisiana, authored the Court's unanimous opinion stating that the Oklahoma restrictions were repugnant to the Fifteenth Amendment. It should be noted that the opinion did not state that literacy tests as such were impermissible under the Fifteenth Amendment. This, combined with the Court's reluctance to use equitable powers to supervise local electoral officials, left significant room for discrimination in the registration of voters.

The Supreme Court had a generally dismal record on racial issues in the Progressive Era. During this period the Court was willing to give the Civil War amendments only a fairly limited effect. Part of this can certainly be attributed to the racial conservatism of the era. Most of the justices shared the prejudices of the day. Few were unconvinced of the essential soundness of the white supremacist view on which segregation and disenfranchisement were based. Even Justice Harlan, who wrote courageous and important dissents in a number of cases where anti-Negro discrimination was at issue, could be counted among the ranks of those who shared strong anti-Chinese prejudices.

Part of the Court's reticence with respect to the Civil War amendments can also be attributed to an institutional conservatism concerning the role of the judiciary. A vigorous enforcement of the Fourteenth and Fifteenth Amendments—even given the constraints of the separate but equal doctrine—would have required a vigorous exercise of the Court's equitable powers and an overstepping of traditional bounds of federalism. These were steps the Court was certainly not prepared to take before the First World War. They were definitely not prepared to take these steps in defense of a constitutional notion of racial equality that they deemed suspect at best.

It was in this atmosphere of strong local efforts to nullify the Civil War amendments and judicial reticence to vigorously enforce those amendments that the NAACP was born. They began from the beginning to play a role in attempting to spur the judiciary into a more vigorous enforcement of the Fourteenth and Fifteenth Amendments—the organization filed amicus briefs in *Buchanan* and *Guinn and Beals*. How they started and got into the business of civil rights litigation is the subject of our next chapter.

CHAPTER 3

The NAACP in the Interwar Years
The Struggle Renewed

The NAACP was formed to fight Jim Crow. Jim Crow was twentieth-century America's experience with petty and not so petty apartheid. It was, as we have discussed, a system of discrimination supported by the reigning ideologies and to a great extent the prevailing cultural mores at the start of the new century. We will have more to say about this cultural question later, but for now it is sufficient to say that the America of the early twentieth century was by and large a nation that was largely comfortable with the increased racial restrictions of the day.

That was largely true, but not entirely true. There was opposition to Jim Crow. Northern white reformers like Mary White Ovington, John Milholland, and Oswald Garrison Villard, the grandson of abolitionist William Lloyd Garrison, took public and courageous stands against the oppression of Afro-Americans, as did some white southerners like historian John Spencer Bassett. Black intellectuals including the eminent scholar and essayist W. E. B. Du Bois, newspaper publisher William Monroe Trotter, and crusading journalist Ida B. Wells-Barnett also fought against the growing regime of racial restrictions. Negro newspapers in both the North and the South took strong editorial stands against Jim Crow, as did such liberal northern publications as *The Independent*, *The Nation*, and the *New York Evening Post*. Organized opposition to Jim Crow included groups like the Constitution League, which pushed for legal challenges to the American caste system; Chicago's Equal Opportunity League; Trotter's National Independent Political League; Wells-Barnett's Negro Fellowship League in Chicago; the National Negro Political League; and not insignificantly, Du Bois's Niagara Movement.

The Niagara Movement had been formed in 1905. Its members were almost entirely well-educated Afro-Americans. The organization hoped to challenge discrimination through public agitation for civil, economic, and political rights. It also hoped to prick the conscience of the white community and to rouse the black population to greater action. The Niagara Movement had a short existence. By 1909 it was largely moribund. But that was the year the NAACP was founded. It would have the same aims as its predecessor, but it would have much greater staying power—and national impact.

From the start, the National Association for the Advancement of Colored People (NAACP) was interracial. Blacks and whites were among its early organizers. W. E. B. Du Bois was undoubtedly the most important of the organization's founders. Du Bois, who would serve as the NAACP's first executive secretary and as the editor of its official journal, *The Crisis*, was a pioneer in the study of Afro-American history and American race relations. Born in Massachusetts, Du Bois received bachelor's degrees from Fisk and Harvard University. He also received a Ph.D. from Harvard University and did advanced studies at the University Berlin. His accomplishments were almost unheard of for an African American before the First World War. These also included an appointment at a white university, the University of Pennsylvania in 1896. During that appointment he authored the groundbreaking historical and sociological study *The Philadelphia Negro*. Du Bois was a firm believer in a strong liberal arts education for what he termed "the talented tenth," those who by virtue of education and intelligence would be able to press the cause of equal rights and ultimately challenge and vanquish the segregation and discrimination of the era. It was a vision Du Bois imparted to the early NAACP and indeed the nation.

Du Bois's vision and that of the NAACP clashed with the public posture of the most powerful Negro leader of the era—Booker T. Washington. Washington's accomplishments were remarkable, particularly for a man who started life as a slave child in Virginia. He was president of the Tuskegee Institute, one of the nation's earliest colleges for Negroes. He was also the founder of the National Negro Business League and a frequent purveyor of national Republican patronage. Much of Washington's strength in the black community came from his emphasis on industrial training, economic development, and the accumulation of wealth. Washington publicly distrusted the kind of academic training for Negroes and public challenging of Jim Crow and disenfranchisement that were integral to Du Bois's philosophy and that of the NAACP. Washington achieved a strong measure of acceptance on the part of many whites, particularly white philanthropists, precisely because of his public acceptance of segregation and his rejection of liberal arts educations for black students. Du Bois had taken Washington to task in 1903 when he published *The Souls of Black Folk*, criticizing Washington's program and declaring instead that the way to the Negro's proper place in society was through equality in civil rights and social status, and the training of a black leadership class.

Under Du Bois's leadership, the NAACP would have a public posture remarkably different from that of Washington. Indeed the organization would often be in conflict with Booker T. Washington until his death in 1915. The NAACP would take the bully pulpit to push for the abolition of segregation and racial caste distinctions, and it would fight for open and equal access to education and employment for Negroes. The organization would crusade against lynching, and it would offer legal assistance that would defend black people mistreated in criminal court. It would advance the cause of equal rights under the law. Over time, the NAACP would become the nation's premier civil rights organization. It would do so in large part because the NAACP early on recognized that the courts, despite their racial conservatism, were a potentially potent weapon in the battle for racial change.

Before American entry into the First World War, cases like *Buchanan* and *Guinn and Beals* had shown that well-argued, well-prepared cases could put a constitutional brake on state-sponsored racial discrimination, even in an era when the law and the general culture were not especially encouraging to the notion of racial equality. There would be other legal victories. One came about after the First World War. The year 1919 was an especially violent year in the history of American race relations. It was a year that saw a number of lynchings, many of them of Negro doughboys returning from "the War to End All Wars." Horrific race riots scarred the nation North and South. One such racial conflagration occurred in Phillips County, Arkansas, in the fall of 1919. Official accounts indicate that as many as two hundred blacks and five whites lost their lives in a racial clash. Six Negroes were sentenced to death. The NAACP filed a writ of habeas corpus on behalf of the condemned men, alleging, among other things, that many of the prosecution's witnesses had been tortured into giving testimony against the defendants. The NAACP lost in federal district court, but prevailed in the Supreme Court in *Moore v. Dempsey* (1926). *Moore* again showed that the courts might be an avenue for racial remedy.

A bit of philanthropy also helped develop the NAACP's emphasis on litigation. The Garland Fund, named after its benefactor, Charles Garland, gave the NAACP $5,000 to conduct a study of public school financing in southern states. That study showed the significant disparities in spending on black and white students as well as the great differences in salaries paid to white and black teachers. Also, between 1925 and 1929 the NAACP received over $25,000 in grants from the fund to support legal action. These legal actions included challenges to racially restrictive covenants—clauses that were included in contracts for the sale of homes that specified that the homes could not be sold to Negroes, Jews, Asians, and other minorities. The grants also provided funds to challenge the state-sanctioned white primary in Texas. That was particularly important because by the 1920s, in many southern states politics was so totally dominated by the Democratic Party that if blacks could be kept from voting in the Democratic primary, they would be effectively disenfranchised even if they were still technically on the voter rolls.

The most dramatic case supported by the Garland grants involved the case of a Dr. Ossian Sweet, an African American physician. Sweet had moved into a previously all-white neighborhood in Detroit in 1925. He and his family, which consisted of his wife, his baby daughter, and his two brothers, Henry and Otis, found their home besieged by a white mob yelling "nigger" and threatening to storm the house. Fearing for their lives, Sweet and one of his brothers fired guns into the air to scare off the mob. A member of the mob was killed. Sweet and the other adults in the family were charged with murder. The NAACP intervened. The organization hired Clarence Darrow and Arthur Garfield Hayes, two of the most famous trial lawyers of the day, to defend the Sweets. After two trials Darrow and Hayes managed to secure acquittals for the Sweets. The importance of good lawyering and the possibilities of court victories even under extremely adverse circumstances were becoming clearer to the NAACP.

The relationship between the Garland Fund and the NAACP grew stronger. In 1930 the fund's board of directors—which included NAACP executive secretary James Weldon Johnson—approved a proposal for a grant of $100,000 to support legal action. Under the proposal, the NAACP would sponsor litigation against residential segregation, Jim Crow transportation, and discriminatory exclusion of blacks from grand juries. The NAACP also intended to institute a coordinated campaign in the most flagrantly discriminatory states of the Deep South—Alabama, Arkansas, Florida, Georgia, Louisiana, Mississippi, and South Carolina—to equalize expenditures on black and white schools. The $100,000 grant was never fully realized. Financial disagreements between the Garland Fund and the NAACP and the depletion of the fund's financial resources due to the Great Depression of the 1930s resulted in the NAACP actually receiving only slightly more than $20,000 of the promised gift. It was not as much as was expected, but the money was put to productive use. The NAACP would use it to hire Nathan Margold as its first staff attorney. The money would also be used to hire Charles Hamilton Houston and Thurgood Marshall. All three would play significant roles in developing the litigation strategy that led to *Brown*.

Nathan Margold wrote a report in May of 1931 that outlined a legal strategy with which to challenge school segregation.

Margold proposed a strategy in part direct, in part circumspect. It wouldn't do to attack school segregation under any and all circumstances. It could be done, but Margold recognized that given the temper of the times, such an approach would invite, in his words, "intense opposition, ill-will and strife." Instead Margold urged an attack on "the constitutional validity of Southern school systems as they exist and are administered *at the present time* [italics added]." *Plessy v. Ferguson* had given "separate but equal," a constitutional imprimatur. The Court had recently reiterated that doctrine in a case involving the racial classification of Chinese students, *Gong Lum v. Rice* (1927). There the Court had stated that it regarded the doctrine as "many times settled." A frontal attack on the doctrine would be legally futile, maybe even counterproductive. But there was an opening. It was clear that in the South, expenditures on black schools were significantly inferior on a per capita basis to those for white schools. The NAACP had the numbers from its earlier studies. Here the 1886 *Yick Wo* case might provide an answer. The way to unravel this Gordian knot was to focus on the actions of state officials. Focus on their actual behavior, their failure to give equal or nearly equal funds to black and white schools! Go beyond the assertion that they were providing separate but equal education! Force state officials to live up to *Plessy;* focus on the equal part of the separate but equal doctrine! State officials, according to Margold's strategy, would be forced into the Hobson's choice of having to greatly increase expenditures on the black schools or to think the unthinkable, providing one set of schools for all children.

Margold had a good strategy. Unfortunately it could not be implemented in the early thirties. Litigation is expensive, and the cash-strapped NAACP of the early depression years had little money to prosecute Margold's innovative litigation strategy. The decade of the thirties had started with an early victory. Margold had argued and won the case of *Nixon v. Condon* (1932) before the Supreme Court. In that case the Court agreed that the Democratic Party of Texas could not prevent Negroes from voting in the party primary. It was an important victory. The NAACP was ready to move forward with more cases, especially school litigation. But the financial resources were not there. Not yet.

There would not be sufficient money to implement Margold's strategy during his tenure at the NAACP. In May 1933, the newly inaugurated administration of Franklin Delano Roosevelt appointed Margold solicitor to the Department of the Interior. Charles Hamilton Houston succeeded Margold as the NAACP's chief attorney. Hamilton was a man of extraordinary brilliance. He graduated as a valedictorian from Amherst College in 1915 at the age of nineteen. For a short time afterward he taught in the English department at Howard University. With America's entry into the First World War, Houston and other young black men in the Central Committee for Negro College Men joined the NAACP in lobbying for the establishment of a program to train black officers for the wartime National Army. Houston was commissioned as a first lieutenant after attending a training camp for Negro officers in Des Moines, Iowa. Houston served in France with the all-black, rigidly segregated Ninety-second Division. In France he experienced some of the worst of the strident racism of the Jim Crow army of that era, including almost being lynched by a mob of white troops. Those wartime experiences left an indelible impression on the young Houston, creating, as he indicated, a determination to strike back at racial oppression: "The hate and scorn showered on us Negro officers by our fellow Americans convinced me that there was no sense in my dying for a world ruled by them. I made up my mind that if I got through this war I would study law and use my time fighting for men who could not strike back."

He did get through. In the fall of 1919 he entered the Harvard Law School. At Harvard he compiled a brilliant record, graduating in the top 5 percent of his class and serving as the first Negro editor of the *Harvard Law Review*. In 1922 he received the L.L.B., then the first degree in law at American law schools. A year later Houston earned the S.J.D., the highest legal degree offered in the United States. While at Harvard, Houston favorably impressed two important members of the Harvard faculty. The first of these was Roscoe Pound, an advocate of "sociological jurisprudence," the idea that judges should carefully weigh the social and economic consequences of judicial decisions. The second faculty member was Felix Frankfurter, to whom Houston was a virtual protégé. Frankfurter would later be part of the *Brown* court. After Harvard, Houston went on to study the civil law system at the University of Madrid.

Houston, who was a native of Washington, D.C., returned to the city after his legal studies. He practiced law with his father, William Lepré Houston, an 1892 graduate of the Howard University Law School. While practicing, the younger Houston taught law part-time at Howard. In 1929 he was named vice dean and associate professor at the school. It was then that Houston decided to make changes—changes that would profoundly influence Howard University's law school and the course of the nation's civil rights law.

Howard University first opened its law school in 1868. It had a precarious existence and small enrollments throughout the nineteenth century. It was one of the few law schools that admitted black students. Howard also was one of the first law schools to have women students. Still the Howard of 1929 was far from Houston's educational expectations. Houston was a product of the Harvard Law School and that law school emphasized, indeed pioneered, the study of law as a full-time academic endeavor. The Harvard model stressed that law should be the province of full-time students led through the rigors of legal analysis under the tutelage of full-time legal academics, individuals whose existence was dominated by teaching and writing about the law. When Hamilton became vice dean, much of the Howard faculty and student body consisted of part-timers, lawyers who practiced law during the day and taught at night, students who worked in government offices during the day and attended classes at night. It was a formula that worked, indeed often worked well at other law schools in Washington and other cities, but somehow it was not working at Howard. The school was not accredited by the American Bar Association (ABA), which at the time did not admit black lawyers. It was also unrecognized by the new Association of American Law Schools (AALS). And Howard's program was at

sharp variance with Houston's idea of what a good legal education should contain and what would be necessary to train effective civil rights advocates.

Houston made changes. He eliminated the night program. He
eased out many part-time professors, cut the size of the student
body, and imposed a demanding rigor on the teaching of
Howard's young lawyers-in-training. Houston's improvements
were noted with approval by the larger legal community. In 1931
both the AALS and the ABA formally accredited the Howard
Law School.

Houston had been a cooperating attorney with the NAACP
while in private practice. He continued this relationship while at
Howard. Convinced that the law could be an important tool in
the fight against racial repression, Houston began to give the
Howard Law School a strong civil rights orientation. He established the first course in civil rights law taught at an American
law school. Houston also made the law school library a deposi-
tory for files on civil rights litigation from around the nation.
These files could be accessed by attorneys involved in the fight
against racial discrimination. Howard became a clearinghouse
and research center for those involved in the fight against segregation. Students were not only exposed to the theoretical possibility that law could shape social change, but also had the
opportunity to actually work on cases that were changing the law
and the society as well.

When Houston became the NAACP's special counsel in 1933,
he reexamined Margold's litigation strategy. There would still be
efforts to equalize pay for black and white teachers, as well as suits
to equalize the facilities in the colored and white schools. These
suits could be won. But as Margold's report predicted, these suits
could pose problems for the long-term goal of eliminating segregation. Black teachers who agreed to act as plaintiffs in such suits
ran serious risk of being fired. This was a risk made all the more
severe by the desperate scarcity of jobs in America in the 1930s.
Still the NAACP was able to get support from some very courageous Afro-American educators who agreed to allow their names
to be used to press the complaints of discrimination in teachers'

salaries. Between 1936 and 1940, the NAACP had notable success in Maryland with lawsuits and negotiated settlements designed to equalize the pay of Negro and white teachers. The organization also won a case challenging unequal pay in Virginia. That case, *Alston v. School Board of City of Norfolk* (1940), was decided in the United States Court of Appeals for the Fourth Circuit.

Houston decided that the NAACP's campaign should shift to another, perhaps more promising, direction: segregation in higher education, specifically graduate and professional schools. Segregation in graduate and professional education was as common in the South as segregation in elementary and secondary schools. But there were far fewer graduate and professional programs, and fewer targets that could be the object of concentrated litigation efforts. A victory against a state's single law school or medical school would have positive reverberations across the state. Without the need to fight a long series of pitched battles with dozens of different school boards across the different counties and cities of a state, the NAACP could focus its efforts on one statewide professional program and achieve dramatic results.

Also it was easier to make the case that discrimination was occurring in professional schools. Boards of education that ran elementary and secondary schools had an arsenal of potential defenses for differences between white and black schools. Did the school for white children offer an academic curriculum while the school for Negroes offered a vocational program? Well, schools can't be expected to be identical; the schools were simply serving the different needs of their different constituencies. Was a new building constructed for the white school and not the black one? Perhaps, but the physical facilities were substantially equal, and besides the new building for the white school could help explain the differences in per capita expenditures for white and black students. These kinds of arguments could be challenged, of course, but they would involve the NAACP in long, often hard to prove, fact-specific litigation. The possibilities for long-term evasion of any reckoning over inequalities in education were clear.

But professional schools offered a more tempting target. Here the NAACP was not faced with the tedious prospect of trying to compare the buildings in the colored schools with those in the white, or trying to argue that a school with courses that stressed practical education, home economics, or shop was inferior to a school whose curriculum included Latin or French. Instead, with professional schools the NAACP was dealing with total exclusion; the state provided a law school or a medical school, but only for whites. Professional schools were also a tempting target for another reason: they carried less emotional baggage. In the atmosphere of the 1930s, and indeed for a long time after, any effort that seemed like it was directed at the integration of primary or secondary education would raise an emotional and political firestorm. Large numbers of white children attended the public schools. Racist demagogues were sure to charge that black and white children attending elementary and secondary schools together would lead to the dreaded scourge of race mixing. The political opposition would be intense, perhaps fatal.

But professional schools were another matter. Few people attended them. There would be even fewer African Americans eligible for admission. The students were mature. An attempt to get some good cases and set some decent precedents with regard to professional schools? That might work. Maryland looked like it might provide fertile ground for such an effort. The University of Maryland's law school was only open to whites. There was no state school for the education of Negro lawyers. Between 1933 and 1934, nine Afro-Americans had applied to the school in Baltimore and had been denied admission because of race. The NAACP looked around for a strong potential plaintiff.

Houston and his associates knew the importance of getting the right plaintiff. In 1933, the NAACP had taken the case of Thomas Hocutt, a student at the North Carolina College for Negroes. Hocutt had applied for admission as a transfer student to the School of Pharmacy at the University of North Carolina. Unfortunately, Hocutt was a weak candidate. His high school grades had been poor. From the NAACP's point of view, the case was a fiasco. Hocutt proved to be a poor witness on his own behalf. When cross-examined he was barely able to read his own high school transcript. It's not clear whether that was the result of nervousness or inability, but in any event the trial judge found that Hocutt had not proven his qualifications for admission. The NAACP did not appeal the case.

The NAACP was determined not to repeat that mistake in Maryland. They needed a strong plaintiff, and in Baltimore resident Donald Murray they found one. Like Houston, Murray was a graduate of Amherst College, and by any standard qualified for admission to the University of Maryland Law School. That is, he was qualified by any standard but one. His application was rejected. The rejection letter stated that the school "did not accept Negro students." His application evidently got more than routine notice and rejection. University of Maryland president Raymond Pearson informed Murray that while the University of Maryland did not accept black students, Howard University did. He indicated that Murray might attend Howard under the auspices of a scholarship for black students who could not attend state institutions.

The correspondence between Murray and University of Maryland officials allowed the NAACP to focus on the issue of segregation. Maryland was willing to provide a state-supported legal education for Murray, only not in Maryland and not at the state university. NAACP lawyers brought the case in state court. The question was simple: was Maryland's system of providing state-sponsored scholarships to schools outside the state equal to providing an education at the state's law school?

The trial judge said no, as did Maryland's highest court on appeal. Careful selection of the right plaintiff had paid off. This became clear in the language of the appellate opinion. Murray, the court noted, had been "denied admission on the sole ground of his color." The court was forced to confront the constitutional issue. It was clear to the court that to entirely deny blacks the opportunity for a state-sponsored legal education when whites were provided with one would violate the formula laid down by *Plessy*, but this was not the issue. The issue was whether the state had properly chosen the method by which equal treatment would be maintained.

The court found the state's method inadequate, not in theory but in fact. There was no separate law school for blacks, and there was no authority to establish one. The state legislature had passed a statute in response to Murray's lawsuit. The statute had provided only $10,000 for scholarships in the amount of $200 each for up to fifty black students seeking a professional education out of state. These were to be used to defray tuition only. By the time of the trial, only seventeen days after the scholarships became available, 380 African American students had asked for applications, 113 had returned them, and there were still twelve more days during which completed applications would be accepted. On these facts, the court found that there was inadequate funding for the large number of applicants and no guarantee that Murray would have been successful had he applied for a scholarship.

Even if he had received a scholarship, the court found that Murray would still be at a significant disadvantage. The court compared Murray's cost of attending Howard, the nearest institution that would accept Negroes, with the cost at Maryland. Although tuition at Howard was less than tuition at Maryland, the court also calculated commuting expenses between Baltimore and Washington or the cost of Murray's relocation to Washington. These expenses were considerably greater than they would have been if Murray had been able to attend the University of Maryland, which was located in his hometown.

The appellate opinion went on to consider the question of intangible differences between a law school education at Howard and one at the University of Maryland. Here it might be important to note that the decision in *Pearson v. Murray* (1936) might have been strongly influenced because the question involved law schools. Judges, of course, know a great deal about law schools and how to judge them. They are law school graduates, and they spend their professional lives working with law school graduates. They have an expertise in the subject matter far beyond that which they have in other kinds of cases. The *Murray* court noted that if Murray were barred from the University of Maryland's law school, he would miss the benefits of a state law school education, specifically gaining a familiarity with the courts of the state in which he intended to practice law. Houston's skillful cross examination of the dean of the University of Maryland's law school highlighted this point.

The court held that the state had failed in its Fourteenth Amendment obligation to provide an equal education. It might have complied with the Constitution by establishing a separate law school, but it had not. As the court put it, "Only an inadequate substitute has been provided." The court did not condemn the scholarship program as a matter of law. Instead the court relied on a close examination of the facts and concluded that Murray had not been provided with an equal opportunity. The court did not hold that another scholarship program would be unconstitutional.

Finally the Maryland court used the 1914 case, *McCabe v. Atchison, Topeka and Santa Fe Railway Company*. You will recall that in that case, the United States Supreme Court rejected the argument that the railroad company did not have to provide first-class cars for Negro customers who wanted them because the numbers who wanted them were relatively small. The *McCabe* court held that the right to equal treatment under the Fourteenth Amendment was personal, not dependent on the numbers who chose to exercise the right. The *Murray* court applied that view. Murray had a personal right to an equal opportunity at a legal education. It did not matter how few Afro-Americans were able to qualify for the University of Maryland; he qualified. As the scholarship program was demonstrably inadequate, Murray had an equal right to an equal education. And the court said he had a right to it immediately, not at some future point when the state might construct a Jim Crow law school. The court ordered Donald Murray admitted into the University of Maryland's law school.

Murray was noteworthy. It was the NAACP's first major victory in the campaign against segregated education. But the case was important for another reason as well. It was the first major case for a young attorney who would succeed Charles Hamilton Houston as NAACP special counsel—Thurgood Marshall. Like Donald Murray, Marshall was a Baltimore native. He too had applied to the University of Maryland's law school in 1930, and like Murray, Marshall was rejected. As a result, Marshall attended Howard's law school, just as Houston's reforms were beginning to take hold. Marshall graduated first in his class and passed the

Maryland bar in 1933. He immediately began the practice of law, representing the NAACP's interests in Maryland. When Marshall sat with Houston on Murray's case, Marshall must have taken no small amount of pleasure in attacking the Maryland law school's policy of discrimination. Houston no doubt took pleasure in seeing, in Marshall's commitment and performance, graphic evidence of the success of his policies at Howard.

With *Pearson v. Murray*, Houston and Marshall accomplished many things. They got Donald Murray admitted to the University of Maryland. They won a major victory, one that set an important precedent. While the case would not be binding precedent outside of the state of Maryland, it was binding in that state and might persuade courts in other jurisdictions. It also added, perhaps at that point only in small measure, to the NAACP's goal of expanding the black leadership class, Du Bois's "talented tenth."

Other cases and plaintiffs would follow. Soon after the victory in *Murray*, the NAACP would look at the case of Lloyd Gaines. Gaines was the president of the senior class at Lincoln University, Missouri's university for Negroes. He wanted to go to the state law school, but the University of Missouri, like the University of Maryland School of Law, did not admit African Americans. For the NAACP, Gaines's case presented somewhat different issues than had been faced in *Murray*. Under Missouri law, Lincoln University was authorized to establish a law school if there was sufficient demand. State law also required that the state pay tuition for Missouri's black students enrolled in professional schools in neighboring states if Lincoln University lacked the same program. Gaines would bring suit, and as had been the case with Donald Murray, the issue would boil down to the adequacy of the out-of-state tuition scholarship. But the facts were different—considerably different.

The case was first tried in the state courts. In *State ex rel. Gaines v. Canada* (1937), the Missouri Supreme Court found that the state's scholarship program satisfied the objections that had doomed the Maryland program. Scholarship funds were clearly available—there was adequate funding of the program. There were no hidden costs, as had been the case in Maryland. Gaines would have to pay room and board wherever he went. His out-of-state alternatives were the state law schools in the neighboring states of Illinois and Nebraska. There were some differences in the cost of transportation to each place, but the Missouri Supreme Court was unconcerned with that issue. The Missouri court stressed that financially Gaines was actually better off attending the universities in the neighboring states. Missouri would pay tuition for Gaines to attend Illinois or Nebraska. Students at Missouri had to pay their own tuition.

The case would be a tough one for the NAACP. Counsel for the University of Missouri, aware of the holding in *Pearson*, was prepared. There was no special advantage for a prospective Missouri lawyer to attend the state law school. The state school taught general principles of Anglo-American law. It did not specialize in Missouri law. It used the same casebooks, taught the same general principles as Illinois and Nebraska. Gaines would not be disadvantaged by receiving his legal education out of state. The Missouri Supreme Court agreed.

Houston argued the appeal before the United States Supreme Court. He framed the issue as one of whether an out-of-state legal education could be equal to a legal education at the state university. The state of Missouri responded by arguing that segregation in education was constitutional and that between Lincoln University and the out-of-state scholarship program, the state had met its obligation of substantially equal treatment for black professional students.

In 1938 the U.S. Supreme Court, by a six to two majority, reversed the Missouri court. It noted that Lincoln University did not have a law school and that the adequacy of Missouri's program depended on the adequacy of its out-of-state scholarship program. The Court's opinion, authored by Chief Justice Charles Evans Hughes, expressed some doubts about the adequacy of the funding of the scholarship program but deferred to the Missouri court's finding of sufficient funds. The Court then turned to the central question of whether the out-of-state program satisfied the constitutional requirement for equal protection, or whether the state of Missouri itself was obligated to provide equal opportunities: "The basic consideration is not as to what sort of opportunities other States provide, or whether they are as good as those in Missouri, but *as to what opportunities Missouri itself furnishes* to white students and denies to negroes [*sic*] solely upon the ground of color. The admissibility of laws separating the races in the enjoyment of privileges afforded by the State rests wholly upon the equality of the privileges which the laws give to the separated groups *within the State*" (italics added).

Commentary on *Gaines* was mixed. Some saw the case as a great victory that would give rise to an expansion of opportunity for blacks. *Time* magazine hailed the case as "a historic decision." Oswald Garrison Villard, writing in *The Nation*, opined that the case was not just "far reaching" but "epoch-making" and "a milestone." Legal commentators understood the extent and the limitations of *Gaines*, and depending on their point of view, either approved or did not. The author of a student note in the *Brooklyn Law Review* argued that the opinion did not go far enough. "The true spirit of the Fourteenth Amendment," he declared, "will find expression only when it is realized that segregation of the races is neither necessary or desirable." Another student in the *Cornell Law Review* declared that the case was "sound," "forthright," and "heartening." A review of the case in the *Georgia Bar Journal* was typical of the position of southern legal analysts, however, emphasizing the "practical" difficulties inherent to the Supreme Court decision and preferring "the opinion of the dissenting justices" for guidance as to how to deal with the southern states' preference for segregation.

No doubt the case's southern detractors as well as many of its proponents recognized the practical difficulties for southern legislatures. As the Margold report had foretold, funding truly separate but equal facilities, even at the graduate and professional level, would be an expensive proposition. Southern failure to undertake that expense would provide an opening to urge the courts to mandate desegregation. Segregation's supporters argued that that would be the first step toward social upheaval and societal ruination. Jim Crow's foes saw only possible change for the better.

Still, some feared that while *Gaines* presented possibilities for changes, those changes might be slow in coming and more nominal than real. White southerners were intransigent with respect to segregation. They could be expected to fight desegregation at every step and to retreat, but slowly. And they could also be expected to achieve support from some black educators who had strong institutional and personal stakes in segregated education—the fear that desegregation would lead to an elimination of black institutions. James Shepard, president of the North Carolina College for Negroes had, for example, opposed the NAACP during the Thomas Hocutt litigation, arguing against Hocutt's admission to the University of North Carolina. By the 1930s even NAACP founder W. E. B. Du Bois was among those who expressed skepticism concerning the NAACP's efforts against segregation. The NAACP was facing an uphill battle.

The *Gaines* decision also met with further resistance from Missouri officials. While the Hughes opinion did state that Gaines was entitled to admission to the university, it did so with an important qualification: Gaines was entitled to admission "*in the absence of other and proper provision for his legal training within the state*" (italics added). The opinion did not include an order of admission. Instead the opinion included an order that the case be "remanded for further proceedings not inconsistent with this opinion."

The *Gaines* decision was also notable for the strident dissent authored by Justice James Clark McReynolds. McReynolds was an egregious bigot known for going out of his way to be personally unpleasant to two Jewish justices, Louis Brandeis and Benjamin Cardozo, who served on the Court with him. During the oral argument in *Gaines*, McReynolds turned his chair around during Houston's presentation, keeping his back to Houston throughout Houston's argument. Suspicious of federal power and a supporter of segregation, McReynolds dissented from the Hughes opinion. He pointed out that there were a number of possibilities open to the state. In McReynolds's view, it was possible that the state would "abandon her law school and disadvantage her white citizens without improving petitioner's opportunities for legal instruction." An alternative, the one for which Gaines and the NAACP hoped, would be to "break down the settled practice concerning separate schools," but this was not the only one. The state might avoid desegregation and concomitant *"damnif[ication of] both races"* by "some other," unnamed course (italics added). This was the alternative Missouri chose.

The Missouri legislature, in response to the Gaines litigation, decided to increase the funding for the out-of-state scholarships as a way to bribe away potential litigants with the prospect of inexpensive professional educations. Also the state legislature changed the terms of Lincoln University's mandate. By statute the Negro university was to have courses of study equal to those provided by the University of Missouri. Lincoln's board of trustees ordered the establishment of a law school.

By 1939 Gaines's case was once again before the Missouri Supreme Court. Once again that state's highest tribunal rejected Gaines's claim. The Missouri court opinion held that the establishment of a law school at Lincoln University would satisfy the Supreme Court's constitutional requirements. The opinion assumed that Lincoln's law school would open on schedule in September of 1939, in time for Gaines to enroll for the forthcoming academic year. If Gaines were to find that the new law school was not equal to the one at the state university, the court held that Gaines was bound to follow "orderly procedures" and bring any new cause of action before a trial court. The effect of the Missouri Supreme Court's decision would be further delay in Gaines's attempt to enroll in the University of Missouri. He had begun his efforts some four years earlier and was faced with the prospect of yet more litigation.

The NAACP wanted to continue the struggle. There was, to be sure, some controversy within the organization over what to do. Houston, who had returned to private practice but who was still a cooperating attorney with the NAACP and still handling the Gaines case, was sensitive to the need to allow Gaines, the client, to make the decision whether or not to continue. He was also sensitive to the fact that the case was potentially delicate from a public relations point of view. If the NAACP did not accept

Missouri's offer of a separate law school for blacks, some would charge that the organization was less interested in expanding opportunities for African Americans and more interested in "creating problems for propaganda purposes." NAACP general secretary Walter White wanted to continue the struggle, arguing that the NAACP's fight was not simply to achieve equal facilities but instead to "end all attempts at segregation."

Meanwhile events had overtaken the litigation. While his case was in the courts, Lloyd Gaines had moved on with his life. He worked at temporary jobs, received a master's degree from the University of Michigan, and had finally moved to Chicago. And then mysteriously, Gaines disappeared. What happened to him remains a mystery to this day. By the end of 1939, the case came to an end, because without Gaines, the NAACP could not pursue the issue any further. How would the Missouri and United States Supreme Courts have further treated the case? The law school finally established at Lincoln University was not the equal to the one at the University of Missouri. The Lincoln school had a $200,000 allocation from the state. It had twenty-seven students, a ten-thousand-volume law library, a dean, and three professors. It was housed on the former site of a hair tonic factory and cosmetics school. The school shared its aged building with a hotel and a movie theater. The University of Missouri's law school was something else entirely. Located in a modern building, the law library had some forty thousand volumes. Unlike their counterparts at Lincoln, students and faculty at Missouri could engage in their legal studies uninterrupted by the sounds of matinee idols, cartoons, and newsreels.

What the courts would have done with these facts is not clear. Would the inequalities have been recognized, or would the courts have said that the facilities, despite differences, were substantially equal? We don't know. Nonetheless, it is clear that if Gaines had not been willing to engage in litigation, even the limited progress that the law school at Lincoln University represented would not have occurred. Overall, the Gaines cases were a victory for the NAACP. The Supreme Court's opinion that the state had to provide an equal educational opportunity in the state was an important one. But the victory was a qualified one. The Supreme Court depended on the lower courts to do the fact-specific work of determining whether or not programs available to blacks were the equal of those available to whites. The Supreme Court simply could not do that work on its own. But that reliance left more room for state officials to evade the Court's mandate. Getting state officials to act on the mandate would be difficult. Resistance would be strong.

The strength of that resistance would be shown in another Missouri case involving Lucille Bluford. Bluford was an editor at the Kansas City, Missouri, black paper, the *Kansas City Call*. She had earned her undergraduate degree at the University of Kansas under the out-of-state scholarship program. Like Gaines, Bluford had not applied to Lincoln University for a graduate degree, for the university had no graduate program in her chosen field, journalism. When she applied to the University of Missouri, she was turned down because of her race. Bluford filed suit in state court for a writ of mandamus to force her entry into the University of Missouri, and in federal court for damages. She lost in both venues.

The Missouri Supreme Court's opinion in *State ex rel. Bluford v. Canada* (1941) was marked by a somewhat contemptuous treatment of the U.S. Supreme Court's reasoning in *Gaines*. Consistent with its prior opinion, the court found that under the revised statutes governing Lincoln University, the university was required to develop new programs to satisfy the constitutional mandate for equal programs. That requirement would satisfy the state's obligation under the separate but equal doctrine. Lincoln University, according to the Missouri court's opinion, would have a reasonable time to develop new programs as demand developed. The fact that there was no journalism program currently available to Bluford was not constitutionally fatal according to the Missouri decision.

This reasoning flew in the face of the U.S. Supreme Court's decision in *Gaines*. Although the Supreme Court's reasoning in *Gaines* would have given Bluford immediate access to a state-sponsored graduate journalism program equivalent to that offered by the University of Missouri, the Missouri tribunal's decision left Bluford a right with no effective remedy. There was neither a journalism program at Lincoln nor any requirement that that university's officials develop one in the near future. What was perhaps more surprising than the Missouri court's treatment of Lucille Bluford was her treatment at the hands of the federal district court. The NAACP had brought parallel cases on Bluford's behalf. She sought equitable relief in the Missouri court (i.e., compelling her entrance into the University of Missouri), and she sought monetary damages or legal relief in the Federal District Court for the Western District of Missouri. In that latter case, *Bluford v. Canada* (1940), the district court ruled against her on the grounds that she had not applied to Lincoln University. This point had also been stressed by the Missouri Supreme Court. Both opinions explained why she had an obligation to do so even though Lincoln University had no journalism program. Both courts indicated that the absence of such a program was not fatal to her right to equal treatment. These decisions represented extraordinary feats of analytical legerdemain. Bluford appealed, but by then Missouri had established a journalism school at Lincoln. The appeal lapsed.

Missouri's reactions to Gaines and Bluford represented what would become a familiar formula for the frustration of desegregation efforts. The first part of this formula involved delay. Gaines had applied for admission to law school in 1935 and was last denied in 1939. The case might have gone on even longer had he not disappeared. Even so the case lasted long enough so that almost any plaintiff would have decided to get on with his life, go to another school, move, or change careers as indeed Gaines ultimately did. With Bluford, the state managed to delay long enough to make her application a moot point.

The second part of the formula involved the willingness on the part of recalcitrant lower court judges to overlook Supreme Court pronouncements, searching instead for loopholes that might allow the white South's preference for segregation to survive. Finally the formula depended on the cooperation of state legislatures. A timely authorization for new programs for the state's

Negro university could preempt a desegregation order, or at least delay it or provide the basis for a court to dismiss a suit for desegregation. *Gaines* and *Bluford* showed that lower courts would not look closely at the quality of programs provided. Delay, recalcitrant lower court judges, and timely legislation—these would defeat even the hardiest of litigants.

In spite of this tenacious rearguard action, the NAACP continued its efforts to achieve desegregation through litigation. The results were not altogether successful. In Tennessee the state Supreme Court heard the case of *State ex rel. Michael v. Witham* (1942). Six black plaintiffs had sued to attend graduate or professional schools at the University of Tennessee. Their request for an order of admission was denied. The legislature had made a provision that mandated that the state's black institutions, on request, would provide professional training equivalent to programs offered at the University of Tennessee. As in the Missouri cases, the *McCabe* present-right formulation posed no problem for the Tennessee court. The opinion indicated that the state had an interest and a right to "reasonable advance notice" before providing an educational program, and that notice had not been given. Similarly, a case involving admission to Louisiana State University's Law School was disposed of under the same reasoning.

Similarly, *Wrighten v. Board of Trustees of University of South Carolina* (1947) involved a demand for admission to the law school at the University of South Carolina. The South Carolina legislature had authorized a state law school for Negroes, but the school was not in operation. There, the trial court, the Federal District Court for the Eastern District of South Carolina, noted its impatience with the state officials, warning that "where the state does not make preparations in advance to furnish facilities to which its citizens are entitled, it runs the risk of being forced to share those facilities furnished to members of one race with another." Yet the court did not order the admission of the plaintiff, holding instead that if the new law school were, by the time of the new academic year six weeks away, "satisfactorily staffed, equipped, and a going concern and on substantial parity in all respects" with the state's white law school, constitutional demands would be met; if not, the plaintiff would be allowed to enter the University of South Carolina. Though the court's opinion contained little in the way of apologetic explanation of the need for "reasonable notice," the court did manage to give the state time to get the new school up and running. When the new school opened, it had poor facilities and only three professors and was clearly not the equal of the school at the University of South Carolina, but a year after it had issued its warning, the federal district court declared that the black school provided an opportunity equal to that provided to whites. Wrighten never attended the University of South Carolina.

None of this is to say that the NAACP litigation was without consequence. Although the litigation resulted in little in the way of actual desegregation, it did pave the way for increased graduate and professional opportunities for blacks. The most direct result of *Gaines* was the establishment of Lincoln University's law school and later its journalism school as well. But there was more. In 1935 before *Murray* and *Gaines*, none of the seventeen southern and border states had graduate or professional schools that admitted blacks. By 1938, seven states offered out-of-state scholarships and four authorized limited study at white institutions within state borders. By 1941 eight southern states authorized limited opportunities for Negroes to study at white institutions.

Statistics from a later period can help illustrate this point. By the 1947–1948 academic year, ten years after *Gaines*, there were nine state-sponsored graduate schools for blacks in the South. Seven of these enrolled some 438 students. There were also four state-sponsored professional schools enrolling some 134 students. Twelve states offered out-of-state scholarships to blacks, despite *Gaines*. Georgia offered scholarships to Atlanta University, a private institution. Maryland continued to admit Negroes to its law school. West Virginia admitted Afro-Americans to its graduate and professional schools. Delaware and Arkansas announced plans to do the same. By 1939 in North Carolina the legislature had authorized both out-of-state scholarships and the establishment of graduate and professional schools at the state's black colleges. A law school was opened at the North Carolina College for Negroes in 1939. It immediately closed for lack of students and reopened a year later. Well-funded out-of-state scholarships that included both tuition and travel expenses were available for the study of subjects unavailable at the state's black colleges, but the number of such scholarships that were needed by 1947 was smaller than it might have been in earlier years. By then, 70 black students were enrolled in graduate courses at the North Carolina College for Negroes, and 34 more at North Carolina Agricultural and Technical College.

Gaines helped spur significant improvements in graduate and professional opportunities for blacks during the following decade. Some of these educational opportunities were made available to African Americans for the first time. There was a significant increase in the numbers of black people in graduate and professional programs. If the opinion in *Gaines* was less than the NAACP had hoped for, it nonetheless did spur state officials into making improvements, if only to forestall desegregation efforts.

But lower courts and state education officials had given *Gaines* an exceedingly cramped and narrow interpretation, allowing the use of out-of-state scholarships and thoroughly inadequate segregated graduate and professional schools. One frequent contributor to the academic journals dealing with Negroes and higher education described advanced degree programs for blacks in 1943 as "pitifully small and inadequate." By 1947, another scholar evaluated library facilities, equipment, faculty, and staff in those graduate programs available to blacks and described them as "far short" of those in white institutions. Another in 1948 described graduate programs at black colleges as "makeshift" and "farcical," noting that the Association of American Universities had approved only one state-run black college as having a curriculum capable of training a student for graduate study, let alone to offer such study.

In a sense, the *Gaines* litigation had helped to create a Faustian bargain. Whites wanted to maintain segregation and blacks wanted to have greater educational opportunity. Both achieved some of what they wanted. On the one hand, blacks could accept the substitutes for entrance into the state universities, and these substitutes, inadequate as they were, did increase opportunities. Southern whites, on the other hand, could maintain segregation. It was a compromise many could accept. Many that is, but not the NAACP. To the organization's credit, the NAACP never gave up its fight to eliminate segregated education. It continued to seek for the black community a seat at the table instead of crumbs from the floor.

To be successful the NAACP realized it would have to convince the courts to take a much closer look at the equal side of the *Plessy* case, something the courts had been reluctant to do since *Gaines.* The alternative was to convince the courts that segregation was inherently unequal and that that inequality could be eliminated only by outlawing segregation itself. The NAACP attempted to convince the court to do both when it argued the case of Ada Sipuel.

Sipuel was a junior at Oklahoma's State College for Negroes in Langston, Oklahoma, when she became interested in attending the state's only law school, the University of Oklahoma. She sought the aid of the NAACP in accomplishing her goal. She applied to the law school and was rejected solely because of her race. She filed suit to have the school accept her. Her case was promptly dismissed. Thurgood Marshall himself would argue her appeal before the Oklahoma Supreme Court. The Oklahoma tribunal decided that Sipuel's real interest lay not in being admitted to the University of Oklahoma law school, but in having an opportunity for a legal education in the state. This, the court reasoned, could be accommodated by the creation of a separate black school. The court also reasoned that before a school could be created, there had to be demand. Sipuel had not done so. Therefore, the Oklahoma tribunal reasoned, her rights had not been violated.

Although the NAACP sought review of the Oklahoma decision before the U.S. Supreme Court, Marshall had not really expected the Supreme Court to take the case and was not enthusiastic when the Court did so. Because the case had been dismissed before trial, there was no factual record, and while Marshall anticipated that the Oklahoma court would be overturned, he feared an opinion by the Supreme Court that would reaffirm *Plessy*'s separate but equal doctrine.

In part for this reason, Marshall took a bold step. His brief before the Supreme Court included a frontal attack on segregation, marshaling sociological arguments against segregation. These arguments were given greater currency by the publication of Gunnar Myrdal's *An American Dilemma*, which had catalogued in great detail the extent to which America's black population was oppressed (see next chapter). This was not an argument the NAACP would make for the first time. As an amicus curiae, or friend of the court, the NAACP had supported Mexican American parents in Orange County, California, who had challenged the segregation of their children from whites in public schools. In its brief before the appellate court, the association had relied heavily on sociological arguments about the harm that was caused by segregation in and of itself. Though the Mexican American parents would win their appellate case, the court did not rule on the validity of the NAACP's arguments. Marshall thought it was time to raise these issues again.

This would prove not to be the case. In an unsigned one-page per curiam decision in *Sipuel v. Board of Regents of the University of Oklahoma* (1948), the Supreme Court explained simply that Sipuel had been denied a legal education that had been supplied by the state to whites, and that the state was under an obligation to "provide it to her in conformity with the equal protection clause of the Fourteenth Amendment and provide it as soon as it does for applicants of any other group."

Sipuel had been argued on January 7 and 8, and it had been decided in surprisingly quick fashion on January 12, with registration to begin at the law school on January 29. The *Sipuel* decision looked like good news for Sipuel and the NAACP, and they assumed that it meant the Court wanted her admitted to the school. But as in *Gaines*, the Court had ordered only that the case be remanded to the lower court "for proceedings not inconsistent with this opinion." This left room for the Oklahoma court to pull a fast one, both figuratively and literally.

The Oklahoma Supreme Court on January 17 ordered the opening of a substantially equal law school. On January 19, the board of regents established the new school, Langston Law School, to be located in the state capital. It was planned to have three professors, and it would have the use of the state supreme court law library. And significantly, if the school were not ready, any members of Langston's first-year class could attend the University of Oklahoma until such time as the new school was ready.

The board of regents invited Sipuel to apply to Langston, but she declined, and since it would not be possible for this hastily developed law school to open on January 29 when the University of Oklahoma's would, Marshall returned to the Supreme Court and petitioned for an order directing the Oklahoma court to order Sipuel's admission to the all-white school. But in *Fisher v. Hurst* (1948), the Supreme Court declined to issue such an order. Given that Sipuel, now Fisher after her marriage, could enter law school in conformity with the calendar at the University of Oklahoma whether or not Langston was open, the Oklahoma courts had complied with the Supreme Court's order. The question of whether the new school was the equal of the old one would be left for later determination at trial.

Ada Sipuel Fisher would never attend Langston Law School, and while its doors were open, Langston Law School would have only a single student. After the school closed in 1949, Fisher was admitted to the University of Oklahoma's law school, from which she graduated in 1951. The arguments Thurgood Marshall and the NAACP would make for the first time for one of their clients, however, that segregation was inherently unequal, that it inherently violated the equal protection clause, would later find currency. Marshall's argument would combine the new learning of the social sciences of the twentieth century with the central point argued by Charles Sumner on behalf of Sarah Roberts and Albion Tourgée on behalf of Homer Plessy in the nineteenth. Why did Marshall think that the courts might be more receptive to this argument in postwar America than they had been in the nineteenth century? That is the subject of our next chapter.

CHAPTER 4

From Scientific Racism
to Uneasy Egalitarianism
One Nation's Troubled Odyssey

The NAACP's efforts brought limited but nonetheless quite real successes in *Gaines*, *Murray*, and *Fisher*. Greater victories would come in 1950 in *Sweatt v. Painter* and *McLaurin v. Oklahoma State Regents for Higher Education* (see chapter 5), both of which also involved discrimination in higher education. To understand these successes, it is necessary to know something about the business of preparing a case and what influences judicial decisions. Ordinarily if you were to ask a group of lawyers what is important in preparing a case, they would doubtless clearly agree that an attorney must thoroughly know the relevant law. The lawyers would then go on at great length about the process of finding the law. One would note the importance of looking at the language of a statutory or constitutional provision. "First we must ask, what is the plain meaning of the provision?" Another might suggest a look at the legislative history: "What did the drafters intend?" Still another would stress the importance of the courts: "How have they interpreted the statute? What have they said about the constitutional amendment? What precedents have been established?" The conversation might quickly devolve into a discussion of somewhat arcane terms and concepts. The air would then be filled with such words as *dicta, concurring and dissenting opinions, binding and persuasive precedents*. There would also be discussions of how one federal district court has applied a rule that is disfavored by a given state supreme court or distinguished away in another federal circuit court of appeals. There might also be considerable speculation about the quality of a particular brief in an analogous case or the relevance of a law journal article or a legal treatise to the problem at hand. One or another of your attorney friends would inevitably raise a procedural issue or two, mumbling something or other about demurrers or motions for summary judgments or the possibilities of cross- or counter-claims or the like.

All of this is important—in fact, critical. It is the meat and potatoes of the lawyer's trade, the essence of routine litigation. Yet the outcomes of cases often depend on something more. It is difficult to say exactly what that something more is. It's not the lectures on anthropology that are delivered at Harvard—although they are a part of it. It's not the paperback novels sold at train stations—though they, too, are a part of this extra something. Nor is this something movie stars or sports heroes, popular tunes or opaque poems, dance crazes or statistical disquisitions in the social sciences. All of these are part of this extra something that can play a vital role in the process of making law and influencing court decisions. Probably the best word that can be used to describe this extra something is *culture*, a word that takes in the collective values, tastes, prejudices, sometimes even the reflexes that are common to particular societies at particular times. Are courts, are judges influenced by the broader culture? Of course they are! We can join a lively and long-standing debate over the extent to which jurists should be swayed by such nonlegal considerations as popular or elite opinion. There is certainly a strong case to be made that law, perhaps particularly constitutional law, was meant to act as a bulwark against the temporary opinions and passing passions of the day. But it would be hard to look at the legal history of the United States or indeed that of any other society without acknowledging the influence of contemporary culture on legal thought and judicial opinion. It must also be noted that the relation between law and the broader culture is symbiotic, a two-way street. Legal opinions, like literature and science, academic treatise and popular song, become part of the broader culture influencing the tastes and prejudices and indeed reflexes of the general public and selected elites.

This question of the symbiotic relationship between law and the broader culture is critical to our understanding of how the Supreme Court and the nation moved from *Plessy* to *Brown*. To understand that transformation, it is necessary to examine the change in racial attitudes that had begun to occur in America during the first half of the twentieth century. From our vantage point, at the start of the twenty-first century it is easy to forget how commonplace, even respectable, open expressions of bigotry were at the beginning of the last century. The United States in 1909, the year of the founding of the NAACP, was not only a land of strict legal segregation in the South—where nearly 90 percent of the black population still lived; it was also a society where whites often felt free, indeed encouraged to routinely assault the dignity, safety, and even lives of Negroes. The use of racial epithets, "nigger," "coon," "darky," "pickaninny," "jigaboo," and the rest was common. A black man, woman, or child might encounter such from a thug in the streets, or in the speeches or writings of a politician or a novelist. This attitude could even be encountered in popular songs; one tune, popular during that era, told of the great fun a white couple would have observing the antics of silly Negroes at the "Darktown Strutters' Ball."

There were other, more sinister expressions of the raw racism that infected early twentieth-century America. Towns posted signs warning Afro-Americans not to be found within town limits after sundown. Newspapers and prominent politicians defended lynchings in editorials and speeches. Race riots occurred during which white mobs terrorized black communities while police ignored the carnage or, even worse, assisted the mobs. One such riot, which took place in Atlanta in 1906, was described by Walter White, who would later become the general secretary of the NAACP. White, among other things, was a singularly American phenomenon. Although he was white by physical appearance—even down to his blond hair and blue eyes—he was classified by law and custom as a Negro, a classification he accepted with considerable pride. In his autobiography, *A Man Called White*, he told of his terrifying experiences as a thirteen-year-old boy facing the 1906 riot:

> Late in the afternoon friends of my father's came to warn of more trouble that night. They told us that plans had been per-

fected for a mob to form on Peachtree Street just after night-
fall to march down Houston Street to what the white people
called "Darktown," three blocks or so below our house to
"clean out the niggers." There had never been a firearm in our
house before that day. Father was reluctant even in those circumstances to violate the law, but he at last gave in at mother's
insistence.

Father told mother to take my sisters, the youngest of them
only six, to the rear of the house. . . . [F]ather and I, the only
males in the house took our places at the front window. . . .
There was a crash as Negroes smashed the street lamp . . .
down the street. In a very few minutes the vanguard of the
mob, some of them bearing torches appeared. . . . "That's
where the nigger mail carrier lives! Let's burn it down! It's too
nice for a nigger to live in!" In the eerie light Father turned his
drawn face toward me. In a voice as quiet as though he were
asking me to pass him the sugar at the breakfast table, he said,
"Son don't shoot until the first man puts his foot on the lawn
and then—don't you miss!" . . . In that instant there opened up
within me a great awareness; I knew then who I was. I was a
Negro, a human being with an invisible pigmentation which
marked me as a person to be hunted, hanged, abused.

But in the years before America's 1917 declaration of war on
Imperial Germany, raw racism was not the monopoly of the untutored mob or even the demagogic politician or tabloid editor;
it was instead the received wisdom of many of the most learned
men and also women of the day.

We have previously discussed scientific racism, eugenics, social
Darwinism, and the tragic-era view of Reconstruction. These intellectual currents are perhaps especially important for an understanding of the courts and how they reacted to legal
discrimination at the time. Judges are perhaps particularly sus-
ceptible to elite opinion, particularly elite opinion clothed in academic and scientific respectability. This was probably especially
true before the First World War. The legal profession, or at least
its most prominent members, were anxious about law's status as a

profession. The jackleg self-taught frontier lawyer of the nineteenth century, the man with little formal education who had learned the law by thumbing through his dog-eared copy of *Blackstone's Commentaries*, a popular treatise on the common law, had earned an enduring place in the folklore of the nation and indeed the legal profession—Abraham Lincoln's remarkable career insured that. But such an untutored avenue to the bar was increasingly being looked upon as something of an embarrassing anachronism by the legal profession's betters, especially the American Bar Association, as the twentieth century began. The law had to secure its place among the learned professions! To that end, it had to join the university. Lawyers had to be formally trained in a science of law! They had to be conversant or at least pretend to conversance in other fields of science, particularly the newly emerging social sciences. One school of legal thinkers, the legal realists, urged that courts had to frankly concern themselves with considerations of good policy, considerations that should rest on the best available scientific learning.

One early triumph of this school of reasoning came in the 1908 case *Muller v. State of Oregon*. In that case the United States Supreme Court found constitutional an Oregon statute that limited the number of hours that women workers could work. This was done despite a 1905 ruling by the court in *Lochner v. New York* that state limitations on wages or hours were unconstitutional because they violated freedom of contract. The key to the Court's decision in *Muller* was a brief filed by future Supreme Court Justice Louis Brandeis. The "Brandeis brief" presented evidence from the health and social sciences that argued for different treatment for women workers. The Court accepted the evidence. The twentieth-century marriage of jurisprudence and the behavioral or social sciences was beginning.

In an atmosphere where the bar was seeking academic and professional respectability and where courts were being urged to examine proffered evidence from the behavioral and biological sciences, the scientific wisdom of the day would have a tremendous influence on judicial opinion. And much of the wisdom of the day said that there was a superior but imperiled race of native-born whites of northern European ancestry, besieged by hordes of inferior immigrants from Eastern and Southern Europe and Asia, and of course by the presence of a large population of African descent. That population, the leading historians of the day agreed, should not have been granted equal rights or enfranchised by the Constitution. The courts noticed.

A few words about racism both popular and scientific and day-to-day relations between blacks and whites might be in order. The era before the First World War was a time of open and often raw racism. Does this mean that every encounter between blacks and whites was harsh and confrontational? Should we assume that there were no whites who recognized that Americans of African descent had legal and constitutional rights? Must we believe that every white man or woman was preoccupied with every twist or turn of Darwinian theory as it was applied to the putative evolutionary development of the races, or that every viewer of D. W. Griffith's *Birth of a Nation* agreed with his characterization of Negroes as inherently savage and bestial? No! There were whites who befriended blacks, even in the Deep South. Certainly there were white philanthropists who supported Negro institutions, colleges, churches, hospitals, and the like. While Jim Crow and disenfranchisement reigned in the South, there was a small but growing Afro-American population in northern and western states. In those states the formal barriers between blacks and whites were less strict. Schools were often integrated—or at least not segregated by law. The occasional black policeman or school teacher could be found. Residential segregation in the North before World War I was less pronounced than it would be later in the century. Blacks voted. They usually supported their historic allies in the party of Lincoln, but as more and more blacks moved into the cities of the North and Midwest, politicians in the Democratic Party were beginning to show increased interest in black voters. In a few northern states the black vote, combined with pressure from sympathetic whites, was strong enough to get *Birth of a Nation* banned.

Despite all of this, few white Americans were prepared to seriously challenge the view that had become deeply woven into the fabric of American culture: the belief that Afro-Americans were a separate caste, a group apart. Even in the relatively liberal cities of the North, black workers found little welcome in the newly developing factories or skilled trades that employed white workers, including immigrants. Residential segregation was on the increase. Racial violence, though less pronounced than in the South, was still common. And of course, many of the leading social thinkers of the day endorsed the view of the inherent biological inferiority of African Americans. This view was even held by many of the progressive intellectuals of the day. Upton Sinclair's sociological novel *The Jungle* is quite instructive on this score. With sympathy and passion Sinclair's novel portrayed the desperate plight of Eastern European immigrants caught up in the harsh working world of the Chicago slaughterhouses at the turn of the century. The same novel dismisses its Negro characters as semihuman hulking brutes.

But even before the First World War, there were countercurrents, individuals, and institutions that were challenging the conventional racism of the day. Among the more significant and unfortunately less recognized of these was the small group of African American scholars who early on began to challenge the received presumptions of Negro inferiority that dominated much of the American academy and American letters. Most prominent of these was W. E. B. Du Bois. Du Bois's pioneering 1899 sociological study *The Philadelphia Negro* set a standard for the use of census data, city directories, and other sources of vital statistics in an effort to analyze an Afro-American community that is still emulated by modern social historians. Du Bois, one of the founding members of the NAACP, would throughout his life employ his scholarly and literary talents in an effort to rebut much of the antiblack prejudice that existed in early twentieth-century academia. One of his most significant efforts in this regard would come in 1935 with the publication of his book *Black Reconstruction in America, 1860–1880*. In that study Du Bois directly challenged the precepts of "Dunning School" scholars that Reconstruction was a tragic mistake in American history.

Another important figure in this regard was pioneering Afro-American historian Carter G. Woodson. In 1915 Woodson founded the Association for the Study of Negro Life and History. That association would, for much of the twentieth century, provide an intellectual home for many black and also quite a few white scholars who believed that Afro-American history was a subject worthy of serious scholarly attention. From the beginning Woodson and his associates began to present the history of slavery, the Civil War, Reconstruction, and other topics related to Afro-American life in ways that were at radical variance with prevailing stereotypes popular and academic. Woodson and his associates would challenge the presumptions of Negro inferiority that dominated the American sense of the past in the latter part of the Progressive Era. In place of the moonlight and magnolia myth of a benign antebellum southern slavery, their work would document the cruelty in the antebellum South's "peculiar institution." Their work would also show the positive side of Reconstruction, public education for poor children of both races, universal manhood suffrage. Most of all the articles that appeared in the *Journal of Negro History* edited by Woodson documented histories of black achievement in the face of incredible adversity—an implicit and explicit refutation of many of the assertions of the scientific racists.

Did the early efforts of Du Bois, Woodson, and their followers have a major impact on American racial attitudes? Did they cause most historians and social scientists to reassess their views on the American past or on the biological determinants of racial ability? No, at least not right away. Black scholars in the 1910s and 1920s lived on the periphery of American intellectual life. Confined to teaching jobs at woefully underfunded black colleges, they were simply not taken seriously by white scholars at major universities or by journalists or novelists and others who shaped public opinion. White scholars who saw the history of the Negro as a subject worthy of respectful and serious study were subject to being dismissed as eccentrics or perhaps as misguided idealists. The efforts of Du Bois and Woodson and their followers black or white would have little impact on American thought on race—not immediately, at any rate.

America's participation in the First World War played a role, an indirect role, in changing racial attitudes. The army was strictly segregated; Jim Crow put on a uniform for the duration. The treatment of black troops was shabby for a nation that wanted Negroes to fight "to make the world safe for democracy." Most black soldiers were confined to work as menial laborers. The Marine Corps and Army Air Service excluded Negroes altogether. Afro-Americans could only serve as mess attendants—uniformed cooks and officers' servants in the navy. Opportunities for promotion were limited. The army frequently refused to give medals for heroism to Negro soldiers who had clearly earned them. Black troops were lectured, sometimes on the battlefields of France, not to expect political or social equality when they returned from "over there." But the army with all its discriminations exposed many Afro-Americans from the rural South to a very different way of life. They left their restricted communities. They were paid according to rank, not color. They saw black men in positions of authority, mostly corporals and sergeants, but also occasionally a lieutenant or captain. One of those World War I officers, Charles Hamilton Houston, would later transform Howard Law School and be one of Thurgood Marshall's mentors.

Despite often harsh discipline and demeaning segregation, the experience for some was oddly liberating. It fostered a new assertiveness, particularly among the two hundred thousand who had served with the American Expeditionary Force. It was a new assertiveness that was particularly unwelcome in the South. The year 1919 was a dangerous one for returning black doughboys, a number of which were lynched in uniform. That was not the reaction everywhere. In New York City a black National Guard regiment was welcomed home with a ticker tape parade. Chicago also held a parade for its returning Negro National Guard regiment, although that city would also be the scene of a bloody race riot in 1919.

World War I played an important role in helping move large numbers of Negroes from the rural South to the cities of the North and West, beginning what historians have called the "Great Migration." The increased need for factory labor and the fact that the war curtailed European immigration helped bring a growing number of Afro-Americans to the North. This helped heighten racial tensions in northern cities, but it also provided new opportunities for many blacks. Northern cities provided Negroes with better educational opportunities, better incomes, and the right to vote. All these would help strengthen the NAACP and other groups concerned with civil rights. The black presence in the cities would also strengthen the small but growing group of Afro-American academics, intellectuals, and writers—the people who were a vital part of the Harlem Renaissance and its counterparts in other cities. These people would also over time play a role in changing American thoughts on race.

From the point of view of evolving racial attitudes, no set of developments was more important than the changes in social science thinking that occurred after the First World War. At first, in the early twenties, it appeared that the scientific racism of the prewar years would not only continue but take an even firmer hold in the minds of the social science community. World War I had been the occasion of the first mass IQ testing of the American public. The army administered IQ tests to the large (nearly four-million-man) National Army that was mustered for the war. Those tests confirmed the preconceptions of the scientific racists —recruits of Northern European ancestry scored higher than recruits, usually recent immigrants or the sons of recent immigrants, of Southern and Eastern European ancestry. Whites scored higher than blacks, although champions of theories of inherent inferiority tended to downplay the fact that Afro-American recruits from the North scored higher than white recruits from the South. Princeton University psychologist Carl Brigham, a major figure in the development of standardized testing, argued in 1922 that the army tests demonstrated the inherent superiority of the "Nordic" races and the inherent inferiority of others.

But the intellectual ground was shifting away from the biological determinists. Increasingly, scholars in the social sciences, particularly the disciplines of anthropology and sociology, were becoming convinced and were convincing others that culture and social environment, not biology, were largely responsible for observable differences among groups. The most important figure in the intellectual battle against scientific racism was anthropologist Franz Boas. Boas, a naturalized American of German Jewish background, drew on his extensive ethnographic experience to argue against the then-popular equation of race with culture and the other staple assumptions of biological determinists. By the 1930s his arguments would gain increased acceptance in the behavioral science community.

The development of sociology as an academic discipline in universities would also have an important long-term influence on academic attitudes concerning race in American society. Clearly the most important sociology department in the nation between the two world wars was the department at the University of Chicago. The most important figure in that department at the time was Robert Ezra Park. Park, who had earlier worked with Booker T. Washington, strongly believed in the desirability and inevitability of the ultimate assimilation of minority groups. Park's views would have a major influence on the training of sociologists in the thirties, forties, and fifties and indeed beyond. Afro-American sociologist E. Franklin Frasier, a student of Park's, would have a major influence on the sociology of race relations, particularly in the 1940s and 1950s.

In the 1920s and 1930s, the scientific community began to move away from racism rooted in theories of biological determinism. But racism still had strong support in the popular culture. In the 1920s the Ku Klux Klan had a membership that exceeded three million. Demeaning portrayals of blacks and other minorities in books, films, and artwork continued just as it had before World War I. And in the 1930s a new medium, radio, provided another avenue for racial stereotypes. These could range from the buffoonish portrayal of Negro characters complete with outlandish dialogue in the popular *Amos and Andy* show, to the vicious anti-Semitic diatribes of Father Coughlin, the Radio Priest.

But by the 1930s, important changes were occurring. An increased percentage of the African American population lived in the cities of the North. They voted in increasing numbers, and more and more attention was being paid to them, not just by their traditional allies the Republicans but increasingly by Democrats as well. Franklin Roosevelt's New Deal was increasingly reaching out to this constituency with relief measures for those hit hard by the Great Depression of the thirties. It should also be quickly added that Roosevelt took great pains not to offend the segregationist order in the South. There was discrimination in the administration of New Deal relief measures. The Civilian Conservation Corps, a work relief program for unemployed youth, was largely segregated. Roosevelt was reluctant to support a national antilynching bill—a measure that was strongly urged by the NAACP. The president did little to alleviate the gross anti-Negro discrimination in the peacetime armed forces. Still the enfranchised northern Negro population was a constituency to be courted, and Roosevelt's administration did so. For the first time in American history, substantial numbers of black voters began to support the Democratic Party. And if Franklin Roosevelt was somewhat reluctant to embrace the cause of civil rights and Negro equality, his wife, Eleanor, had no such reticence. Hers was a public and vigorous championship of the cause of civil rights, often to the consternation of her more racially conservative husband. Her actions often had an important symbolic value that went far beyond the official powerlessness of her position as First Lady. When she arranged in 1939 for Marian Anderson to sing at the Lincoln Memorial after the Afro-American singer had been barred from performing at the concert hall of the Daughters of the American Revolution, it sent a powerful symbolic message to Americans both black and white.

The decade of the Great Depression brought other changes. Increasingly, although by no means unanimously, social scientists and historians were rejecting earlier notions of inherent racial inferiority. This rejection would be aided by the arrival in the thirties of a significant number of influential European scholars, many of them Jewish refugees from the Nazi regime of Germany and Austria who had devastating firsthand experience with the consequences of pseudoscientific racism. Two important contributions to the field of Afro-American studies, W. E.

B. Du Bois's *Black Reconstruction* (1935) and Melville Herskovitts's *The Myth of the Negro Past* (1941) began to suggest a richer and more complex African American past than had previously been presented by the American historical profession. Although both works had a rather muted influence at the time of their publications, the influence of both would grow after the Second World War. Another important development was the growth in popularity of Freudian psychology. If the field had little to say concerning race relations as such, it nonetheless introduced university-educated Americans to such concepts as unconscious and subconscious motivations for behavior. These concepts would later prove important in subsequent studies of racial prejudice and the effects of prejudice and discrimination on blacks and other minority groups.

Of course, relatively few people paid attention to changes in historiography or the development of psychoanalytical theory; these were the concerns of a small minority of the population. But if the elite culture was changing in the thirties, so was the popular culture. The American caste system certainly remained in place, segregation in the South was as rigid as ever, and in many ways the hard times of the depression made race relations in the North even harsher than before. Still there were some positive developments. A few black sports stars—Olympic runner Jesse Owens and boxer Joe Louis—became not simply Afro-American heroes but also American heroes in their competitions against Nazi-sponsored sports figures. Important changes also occurred in films. In many ways films would become the popular literature of the twentieth century, even more so by the 1930s when Hollywood added sound to the movies. With their lifelike representation of characters and action, films would become a powerful medium, probably the most powerful in history, for shaping public perceptions. By the 1930s, the major studios had begun to offer a new kind of stereotypical black character. This new Negro character was still inferior to whites. Shiftless and servile, comic and cowardly, the character was usually a simple-minded servant whose utterances managed at once to mangle both logic and English syntax. Still these characters were a far cry from the menacing savages, the Negro as brute more common in literature and film earlier in the century. Nowhere is this transformation better seen than in a comparison of the 1915 film *Birth of a Nation* with the 1939 movie *Gone with the Wind*. *Gone with the Wind* is an important film for students of American race relations. It undoubtedly did more to inform or, more accurately, misinform mid-twentieth-century Americans about the central drama of nineteenth-century southern history, slavery, the Civil War, and Reconstruction than all of the books and articles written by professional historians. The 1939 production retold a tale quite familiar to audiences that had seen *Birth of a Nation*. The movie told the South's story of chivalrous and kindly slaveholders, tragically forced into Civil War by the North's ignorance and cupidity. The film goes on to present the tragedy of Reconstruction and the glorious fight to regain (white) southern rule. In those themes *Gone with the Wind* was essentially indistinguishable from *Birth of a Nation*.

But thematically the 1939 production differed from the 1915 film in one significant way. The black characters had been transformed. In place of the bestial Negroes offered in D. W. Griffith's silent epic, *Gone with the Wind* offered depictions of black characters who were essentially decent and sympathetic human beings, albeit inferior and often wildly comic ones. Some of the characters, particularly Hattie McDaniel's "Mammy," were even portrayed as having an innate wisdom despite their lowly status and presumed intellectual inferiority. Although Hollywood and the national popular culture more generally at the end of the 1930s still supported traditional notions of caste, racial hierarchy, and separation, they did so with less of the raw racism that had existed just a generation before. Slowly the world of race and racial perception was changing.

That world would change with even greater rapidity during the Second World War. Even before the entry of the United States into the world conflict, the war helped bring about a new sophistication to black politics and civil rights advocacy. Walter White and other civil rights leaders were able to use the presidential election of 1940 to press for racial reform. In that election, in which Roosevelt ran for an unprecedented third term, both Roosevelt and his Republican opponent, Wendell Wilkie, had considerable support among black voters. Roosevelt, under pressure from White and others, promised to open up new opportunities for black men in the previously all white Army Air Corps and other branches of the expanding army. He also promoted Benjamin Davis to the rank of brigadier general in the army. Davis was the first Afro-American to hold that rank. In July of 1941, black labor leader A. Philip Randolph was able to use a threatened march on Washington to pressure a reluctant Roosevelt into signing a fair employment practices order barring racial discrimination in the expanding defense industries.

War was brought to the United States with a terrifying surprise on December 7, 1941. That war would help bring about profound changes in the racial thinking of many ordinary Americans, but not all at once. The army was still firmly committed to segregation. Blacks and whites were in separate units. The army largely planned to restrict Negroes to positions as uniformed laborers, reserving combat and technical positions for white soldiers. The Air Corps, under presidential prodding, had finally begun, reluctantly, to train Afro-Americans as pilots and in aircraft maintenance and other technical specialties, but Air Corps leaders wanted to severely restrict those opportunities, preferring also to keep black soldiers as uniformed laborers. The navy and Coast Guard were even more restrictive. They again wanted to confine Negroes to a servants' role as mess attendants, as those services had largely done in the First World War. The marines wanted to exclude African Americans altogether. They only reluctantly admitted their first black recruits in 1942, when required to by law.

The armed forces may have wanted a severely limited role for black troops, but the political pressure generated by the NAACP and other civil rights supporters helped open new opportunities for African American men and later women in uniform. But it was not just political pressure that forced new opportunities in the armed forces. The sheer scope of the military effort made unprecedented demands on manpower. Fighting occurred on every inhabited continent and in the adjacent oceans. American forces were stationed around the world. A popular song of the day, "They're Either Too Young or Too Old," might help us understand this. The song is a pledge by a young woman to her boyfriend in the service that she would remain faithful, in part because there were no young men left at home. Some of the lyrics give a sense of the worldwide nature of the American military effort:

> I'll never, never fail ya
> While you are in Australia,
> or off in the Aleutians,
> or out among the Rooshians
> and flying over Egypt,
> your heart will never be gypped
> and when you get to India,
> I'll still be what I've been to ya.

The unprecedented demands of global war helped throw a monkey wrench into the plans of those who wanted only a severely restricted role for Negroes in the armed forces. Personnel demands forced the armed forces to place black men and even black women in unaccustomed military roles. The army, often with considerable reluctance, found itself employing black men in combat roles in infantry, tank, artillery, and combat engineer units. Black men who had been mustered into the navy and Coast Guard to act as officers' servants could be found serving as members of antiaircraft gun crews engaged in deadly duels with Japanese Zeros and Kamikazes, or manning landing craft in amphibious assaults. The Air Corps, which had proclaimed before the war that blacks did not have the intelligence to fly planes, had all-black fighter squadrons. Those squadrons were formed into the 332nd Fighter Group, which saw action in the Mediterranean and European theaters. Three members of that group had the first confirmed kills of Luftwaffe jets over Berlin. Even the marines were forced to accept some twenty thousand Negro enlisted men during the war.

As had been the case in the First World War, the treatment of black men and women in the armed forces was often shabby. Units were segregated. Jim Crow custom was applied to mess halls and latrines, chapels and USOs. Negro MPs guarding German and Italian prisoners of war in the United States found that their prisoners could eat in restaurants reserved for whites, while they, the American soldiers guarding them, could not. Some Afro-American soldiers were lynched in uniform in southern towns near their training camps. In some overseas theaters of operation, racial tensions ran so high that black and white units even fired weapons at each other.

Nor were racism and racial discrimination confined to those in uniform. In 1942 Roosevelt signed an executive order forcibly removing and interning all people of Japanese descent, citizens and aliens, from the West Coast. The ostensible reason for the forced evacuation was military necessity—a dubious justification, since there was no mass internment of Japanese Americans in Hawaii, which had actually been under attack and was closer to Japan. A better explanation for the internment was long-standing animosities between whites and Japanese on the West Coast. Earl Warren, who was California's attorney general at the time of the evacuation, was a vigorous supporter of the internment. The United States Supreme Court upheld the constitutionality of the internments as a wartime necessity in two cases, *Hirabayashi v. United States* (1943) and *Korematsu v. United States* (1944). For black civilians the war years were a time of expanded economic opportunity but continuing racial tension. Jim Crow would remain strong throughout the South and in a good many venues outside the South as well. Race riots, often precipitated by cases of police brutality, broke out in a number of northern cities. Two of the more serious of these occurred in Detroit and New York. Jim Crow even came to blood banks. Although Charles Drew, an African American doctor, had played a leading role in developing procedures for collecting and storing whole blood, the Red Cross labeled blood by the race of the donor. This practice was followed in both civilian and military hospitals.

For those in uniform, despite the often strident racism found in the armed forces, the military experience would again provide a strange liberation for many of the more than one million Negroes who served in uniform during the war. As in the First World War, black men and now a few black women as well held positions of authority as noncoms and officers. They were limited to leading Negro units to be sure, but they had positions of authority that would have been inconceivable for black people in civilian life. Many learned advanced technical skills. More than half of the million who served during the war would serve overseas in the European and Pacific theaters. The war caused people whose world had been confined to the limited horizons of the rural South or the emerging ghettos of northern cities to experience a far broader world than the one in which they had been raised.

The war would also bring significant changes for African American civilians as well. The wartime economy created a great demand for industrial workers. Black men and women left sharecropping in the shadows of southern plantations to work in factories producing tanks in Detroit or plants producing aircraft in Los Angeles. The process of changing the Afro-American population from one that was largely rural and southern to one that was increasingly urban and located in the more liberal North and West accelerated during the war.

Military experience and the movement to the cities helped create a new awareness of and demand for rights on the part of blacks. Negro newspapers probably had the greatest influence in their history in exposing racism in their editorial battles against Jim Crow in the military. The *Pittsburgh Courier* was particularly effective in this regard. The NAACP and other groups were successful in opening every branch of the armed services to black recruits—albeit generally on a segregated basis. Black workers were able to use the wartime need for personnel to press against established barriers to industrial employment. Negroes of that generation spoke of a double *V. V* for victory against the Axis overseas and *V* for victory against racism at home.

And whites began to think about race differently because of the war. Many began to see the irony of a crusade against Nazi Germany with its racist ideology being waged by a nation with an entrenched caste system. Many began, slowly to be sure, to reassess long-standing prejudices. Again, the films of the era can help us understand this. During World War II, the Hollywood studios became a virtual arm of the War Department. Actors and directors received commissions in the army and navy and were assigned to military film units, often to make propaganda films designed to keep up the public's morale. The major studios all made patriotic war films designed to bolster public support and to sell war bonds. Studios had military advisers who, among other tasks, were there to insure that the armed forces and the war effort were depicted in positive lights.

The war helped bring about a new film image for the Negro. The shiftless comic of the thirties was out. The heroic Negro soldier was in. Under prodding from both the NAACP and the military services, movies began to show blacks as contributors to the war effort. Black servicemen even found an integration on film that was usually denied to Negro soldiers in the real armed forces. Black actor Kenneth Spencer was thus part of a squad that included Hollywood leading man Robert Taylor, movie tough guy Lloyd Nolan, and future sitcom star Desi Arnaz defending a doomed outpost in *Bataan* (1943). Ben Carter, an Afro-American actor, played a heroic navy mess attendant who accompanied a navy lieutenant, played by matinee idol Tyrone Power, on a somewhat improbable submarine-launched commando mission in *Crash Dive* (1943). Twentieth Century Fox, the producing studio, even ran the script of *Crash Dive* by the NAACP's Walter White for his approval of the film's portrayal of the black character. The War Department also got into the act producing short films designed to show the contribution of African American soldiers to the war effort. Hollywood director Frank Capra, a wartime lieutenant colonel in the Signal Corps, produced the film *The Negro Soldier* (1944), which presented to civilian and military audiences a sympathetic and heroic portrayal of black soldiers. The Air Corps produced the documentary *Wings for This Man* (1945), which depicted the training of black pilots and the combat operations of the 332nd Fighter Group. That documentary was narrated by actor turned Air Corps captain Ronald Reagan. His narration ended with a plea for fairness: "You don't judge a man by the shape of his nose or the color of his skin."

Did these cinematic depictions, civilian and military, provide audiences with a realistic portrayal of Negroes in the armed forces? No. Racism, segregation, and discrimination were not mentioned at all. The black soldier was depicted as contented and accepted, concerned only with performing his duties and defeating the enemy. Simplistic as these portrayals were, the films of the era were important. They provided Afro-Americans with a new and decidedly improved image with the white public. For the first time, a popular medium presented to millions of ordinary white Americans portrayals of Negroes as heroic, albeit often one-dimensional, characters.

If these wartime celluloid epics began to change the white public's image of Americans of African descent, new writings in the social sciences, spurred on in part by the life-and-death struggle with Nazi racism, were beginning to cause educated elites to view the dismantling of racial prejudice as a national and indeed moral imperative. Clearly the most important work written along these lines during the Second World War was Gunnar Myrdal's *An American Dilemma*. Published in 1944 by Myrdal, a Swedish economist and sociologist, *An American Dilemma* provided a massive sociological examination of prejudice and discrimination in the United States. *An American Dilemma* was particularly influential because it emphasized the contradiction between professed American ideals of democracy and equality and the stark harshness of black lives under America's Jim Crow regime. This theme would have a peculiarly strong resonance during the Second World War, a time when Americans increasingly came to see the nation not merely as a democracy but as a nation charged with the special mission of rescuing embattled ideals of democracy and freedom in a troubled world.

The idea of an American crusade against totalitarianism and the linkage of the Nazi dictatorship with racism helped contribute to the view that racism and racial prejudice should be viewed as psychological problems, perhaps even psychological abnormalities. *The Authoritarian Personality* authored by T. W.

Adorno and his associates was a significant breakthrough along these lines. The study, which began under the sponsorship of the American Jewish Committee in 1944, focused on anti-Semitism but also paid attention to the issue of antiblack prejudice. *The Authoritarian Personality* and other works that explored the psychology of prejudice were important because they started the process of asking an old question in a new and quite unfamiliar way. Americans had long been accustomed to social critics who posed the question: "What to do about 'the Negro problem'?" Adorno and others in the social sciences were informing university-educated audiences that the more important question was what to do about the problem of prejudice. This new perspective had a particular resonance in postwar America. Americans had been forced to take a hard, awful look at where racism could lead. That look began when ordinary men, GIs in the European theater, stumbled across not only the unbelievable but the inconceivable: killing grounds with names like Dachau, Buchenwald, Malthausen. These camps left an impression that would never be erased in the minds of the men who actually walked through them, including their commanding general, Dwight D. Eisenhower. The Nuremberg trials, as well as massive press coverage of Nazi atrocities, served to inform the wider American public of the horrors of the Third Reich's Final Solution. All of this would help make the kind of easy yet deep racial prejudice common earlier in the century far less respectable after the Second World War.

The postwar popular culture also played a considerable role in making racial prejudice less respectable. Jackie Robinson's 1947 move from the Kansas City Monarchs in the Negro Leagues to the Brooklyn Dodgers in what had been the previously all-white National League was a turning point in the history of American race relations that should not be underestimated. The American pastime's rigid segregation throughout the twentieth century had a strong symbolic importance to those committed to a Jim Crow America. Robinson's entry into the Dodgers was bitterly resisted. Robinson and Dodgers manager Branch Rickey, who had decided to integrate the team, were denounced by more than a few politicians and sportswriters. Robinson himself was subject to vicious taunts and threats on his life. His persistence and perseverance turned him into something of a folk hero for quite a few Americans, black and white. Hollywood even turned Robinson's story into a message movie about racial tolerance, *The Jackie Robinson Story* (1950), with the second baseman portraying himself.

Robinson's story wasn't Hollywood's only attempt to explore the issue of race. After World War II, Hollywood began to show a new and indeed unprecedented concern with the issues of race and racism. If the war itself had caused Hollywood to reassess the often grotesque racial caricatures of the prewar era, the aftermath of the war and some of the newer thinking on race caused filmmakers to take what were then bold steps in addressing the problem of racism in American society. The late 1940s were witness to a number of "message movies" designed to show and counter racial prejudice. One of the most important of these, *Home of the Brave* (1949), had actor James Edwards play a World War II Negro soldier who suffered psychosomatic paralysis as a result of his exposure to racism while on a reconnaissance mission with a white squad. The movie can and has been faulted for more than a little naïveté in its portrayal of racism—prejudice is depicted as the failing of a single individual. Institutional discrimination in the army is ignored. The widespread racial prejudices among whites in the 1940s is downplayed. Still, *Home of the Brave* and similar films of the era were bringing home to mass white audiences for the first time the fact that there was a serious problem of racial prejudice and that that prejudice often had devastating effects on sympathetic characters with whom white audiences could identify.

If social science studies and Hollywood movies were beginning to change, or perhaps reflect changes in elite and popular opinion with respect to race, national politics was beginning, slowly to be sure, to change law and public policy in the area. Roosevelt's successor, Harry Truman, would prove more receptive to the cause of civil rights than Roosevelt. Truman appointed presidential commissions on race relations. These commissions called for the elimination of segregation and discrimination in colleges and universities and other facets of American life. In

1948 Truman signed an executive order barring discrimination in the federal civil service. That same year Truman also signed an executive order barring discrimination in the armed forces. That order helped bring about the end of segregated units in the air force, navy, Coast Guard, and Marine Corps, although segregated units would persist in the army through the early stages of the Korean War. Truman's support for civil rights brought him into sharp conflict with southern Democrats. In his bid for election in 1948, he was opposed not only by Republican Thomas Dewey and Progressive Party candidate Henry Wallace but also by Strom Thurmond, a Democrat then running as the candidate of the Dixiecrat Party. Truman ran on a party platform that included strong support for civil rights. Truman's victory in that election was particularly significant because it proved that a Democratic candidate could win the presidency with strong southern opposition, something previously believed to be impossible. The election indicated to Democratic politicians that the votes of black voters in the North, coupled with those of whites who were supportive of civil rights measures, were at least as politically important as the votes of the once solid South. The political landscape on civil rights had changed and had changed significantly.

It was in this changed atmosphere in postwar America that Thurgood Marshall and his associates began searching for a way to make a frontal assault on Jim Crow in education. The America of the late 1940s and early 1950s was different from the America of 1909—the year of the NAACP's founding. Racism, discrimination, and Jim Crow were still very much alive. Lynchings still occurred; discrimination in employment and housing were everyday facts of life. In the South, White and Colored signs adorned water fountains and park benches, rest rooms and waiting rooms. But increasingly these practices were becoming an embarrassment to the nation. Those who shaped public opinion and indeed ordinary members of the public were becoming increasingly uncomfortable with the old certainties and traditional stereotypes about race. This discomfort was doubtless heightened by a new national self-image that had begun with the

Second World War. The United States was not merely a free nation but the guardian of freedom against totalitarian forces throughout the world. That self-image also helped to undercut what had been the previous widespread acceptability and respectability of racial prejudice.

American culture had changed. If strong local forces still pressed and pressed hard to maintain traditional patterns of discrimination and racial hierarchy, the even stronger national culture was less and less willing to grant these traditional practices the imprimatur of national law and policy. This changed national culture was reflected in the Supreme Court's decisions in *Sweatt* and *McLaurin* (see next chapter). It was also reflected in the 1948 case, *Shelly v. Kraemer*. In that case the Supreme Court decided it was a violation of the Fourteenth Amendment's equal protection clause for courts to enforce restrictive covenants, restrictions in deeds used to prevent Negroes, Jews, and others from buying homes in white neighborhoods. Slowly the law was beginning to reflect the changing national culture. Or was it leading the change? It is an argument as difficult and probably as futile as the chicken and egg controversy. Both were changing. Both the law and the culture were precipitating changes in each other. It was a moment in which Thurgood Marshall and the other members of the NAACP legal team could strike a telling blow against *Plessy*.

CHAPTER 5

Setting the Stage

America had changed, but *Plessy's* separate but equal doctrine still remained the law of the land. True, the NAACP had taken some chunks out of the doctrine. Starting with *Gaines* before the Second World War and continuing through to *Fisher* (see chapter 3) after the conflict, the NAACP was able to force southern state officials to either desegregate or offer alternative facilities for black graduate students. But at the end of the day, separate but equal remained entrenched, despite the NAACP's best efforts.

Still, even as the NAACP was butting its head against the seemingly impenetrable constitutional brick wall erected in *Plessy*, its attorneys were striking important blows against racial discrimination in other areas, making real differences in the lives of many people. They were also gaining valuable legal experience along the way. Blatant racism in the nation's police stations and criminal courts had long been a concern of the NAACP. The civil rights group had intervened in a number of criminal cases. In doing so they stopped a number of African American defendants from being railroaded, often to their deaths. *Chambers v. State of Florida* (1940), *Canty v. Alabama* (1940), and *Watts v. State of Indiana* (1948) were important cases where the NAACP managed to reverse convictions and have the U.S. Supreme Court confirm the basic principle that convictions based on forced confessions were invalid. In *Patton v. State of Mississippi* (1947), the NAACP was successful in convincing the high court to rule that a criminal court could not exclude Negroes from juries. During the war the organization had been particularly vigorous in preventing the mistreatment of Afro-American soldiers. They took up the case of three black soldiers who had been convicted of rape and sentenced to death in a federal district court in *Adams v. U.S.* (1943). These and other cases helped establish the NAACP as the premier place to turn when faced with racial injustice.

The organization's efforts extended beyond criminal cases. In the decade after *Gaines*, it would also achieve significant victories in the voting rights area. It was successful in having the Supreme Court strike down an Oklahoma statute that imposed a restrictive time limit on when Negroes could register to vote in *Lane v. Wilson* (1939). In *Smith v. Allright* (1944), the NAACP won a victory in the Supreme Court that finally put an end to the all-white primary in Texas. That issue had been the subject of continuous NAACP litigation since *Nixon v. Herndon* (1927) (see chapter 3). The NAACP's lawyers also struggled against barriers in public accommodations and the right to contract as well. In *Morgan v. Commonwealth of Virginia* (1946), the civil rights group represented a client who had been arrested when she refused to move to the back of the bus as was required by Virginia law. The NAACP won the case not on equal protection grounds but on the basis of the Constitution's commerce clause. The bus had traveled between Maryland and Virginia and was therefore part of interstate commerce. The Supreme Court held that the Virginia requirements put a burden on interstate commerce. *Morgan* might not have expanded the rights of Negroes under the Court's equal protection jurisprudence, but it did provide another tool with which the NAACP could attack segregation. Undoubtedly the NAACP's most important victory in protecting the right of members of minority groups against private discrimination in the immediate postwar period was *Shelly v. Kraemer* (see chapter 4).

Still the NAACP was looking for something more. In *Fisher* (see chapter 3) Marshall had attempted to use social science evidence to make the case that segregated facilities were inherently unequal. The Supreme Court had disposed of the case without addressing Marshall's argument. Marshall searched for another plaintiff who could help advance the issue. He found that plaintiff in Heman Sweatt. Sweatt was a letter carrier who lived in Texas. In 1946 he applied to the all-white law school at the University of Texas. He was immediately rejected. The rejection letter informed him that he could request that the state of Texas establish a law school for Negroes. The NAACP filed suit in state court on Sweatt's behalf. The results were familiar. The trial court opinion stated that state officials were under no obligation to admit him to the University of Texas. The opinion allowed state officials six months to establish a black law school. Just before the six months were up, the state presented the trial court with evidence that it had established the Jim Crow law school. The school was housed in two rented rooms in Houston. Administratively the school was part of Prairie View University, a Texas state university for Negroes, some forty miles away. The faculty consisted of two part-time instructors. There was no library.

Like the Lincoln University Law School in Missouri and Langston Law School in Oklahoma (see chapter 3), Prairie View's new law school was a poor excuse for equal education, indeed even for good education. Nonetheless the trial court found that the Jim Crow law school provided a legal education that was the equal of that provided by the University of Texas. Still state officials recognized that they were on shaky ground, that appellate courts would be more skeptical. The legislature moved to provide a more credible alternative. By the time an appellate court could hear the appeal, the legislature had appropriated $100,000 toward the establishment of a law school at the newly established Texas State University for Negroes in Houston. Until a new facility could be built in Houston, the new school would be housed in downtown Austin across the street from the state capitol. It was to have three rooms, a ten-thousand-volume library, access to the state law library in the capitol building, and three part-time faculty members. The part-time faculty members were professors from the University of Texas School of Law. Because of these changes, the case was remanded to the trial court to determine if the new school was equal to the one for whites.

Of course, the trial court found that the new school provided an education equal to that provided by the state university. The judge was the same judge who had held that the vastly inferior Prairie View school was equal. What was important was not so much the trial court decision as the record that was produced in the trial. That record included evidence related to the tangible differences between the black and white law schools, the differences in physical plant, financial resources, numbers of professors, books in the library, and the like. The trial court record also contained important evidence showing the qualitative, intangible differences between the two schools. The tangible differences were damning enough. The new law school's temporary facility in Austin turned out to be an office basement; the University of Texas had a permanent facility that housed a law review and a moot courtroom. The new law school had neither. Most of the library's books had yet to be delivered to the new law school, and there was no full-time librarian; Texas had over sixty-five thousand volumes. The entirely part-time faculty had no offices at the black school. Their offices were at the University of Texas. The white law school had sixteen full-time and three part-time faculty members and a student body of 850. The Negro university had only five part-time members and a tiny student body. The alumni of the University of Texas School of Law were large in number and wielded a great deal of power and influence throughout the Lone Star State and beyond. The new school had only one alumnus. By any concrete measure, the law school at the Texas State University for Negroes was a laughable substitute for the one at the University of Texas. It was, as lead counsel Thurgood Marshall stated, "an apology to Negroes for denying them their constitutional rights to attend the University of Texas," and, it should be added, not a particularly good one at that.

And there was more. If the tangible measures of inequality revealed stark differences in resources between the two institutions, there were harder to measure, intangible factors that also marked the black school's inferiority. The small size of the Negro law school's faculty meant that its curriculum lacked both breadth and depth. The absence of a law review or moot courtroom meant that critical cocurricular components of a law school education were not provided. The small number of students might have meant a smaller teacher-student ratio, but it also meant an inferior education; as one expert witness testified at trial, "a well-rounded, representative group of students" was necessary to enrich the learning atmosphere and to maximize the value of classroom discussion.

Beyond the comparison of tangible and intangible differences, Marshall also brought before the court the University of Chicago's Robert Redfield, an expert with doctorates in both law and anthropology. Redfield testified on the general effect of segregated education. He explained his view that segregated education gave its recipients a false education. It left blacks and whites ignorant of one another, "prevent[ing] the student from the full, effective and economical . . . understand[ing of] the nature and capacity of the group from which he is segregated." In effect, segregated education was bad education, for while education is meant to enlighten, segregation instead "intensifies suspicion and distrust between Negroes and whites, and suspicion and distrust are not favorable conditions for the acquisition and conduct of an education, or for the discharge of the duties of a citizen." Moreover, he continued, not only did segregated education produce negative effects, it also produced no positive effects. It had no basis in either educational or enlightened racial theory. Reflecting what had become the new thinking on race in the social sciences after the Second World War, Redfield further testified that scholars had recently become "compelled" to the conclusion that there were no "inherent differences in intellectual ability or capacity to learn between Negroes and whites," and that should any such differences be "later shown to exist, they will not prove to be significant for any educational policy or practice." Through Redfield, Marshall had made a record that would support a conclusion that segregation was irrational, and under the Fourteenth Amendment, no distinction that was not rational could stand muster. His use of Redfield's testimony also showed that social science could now be an important tool in the quest to vindicate the constitutional requirement of equal protection under the law.

The trial court ruled against Heman Sweatt and the NAACP, as did the Texas Court of Civil Appeals in *Sweatt v. Painter* (1948). The NAACP made essentially three arguments on Sweatt's behalf. The first of these was that there was "no rational basis for racial classification for school purposes," and that the practice of segregated education therefore violated the due process clause of the Constitution. In effect, this argument constituted an end run on the separate but equal formula under which previous cases had been litigated and decided. If the argument were accepted, questions of educational inequality under the separate but equal formula of *Plessy* would be irrelevant. For if racial classification itself were irrational and thus unconstitutional, then the establishment of a segregated school for blacks—even if it were equal —would be inconsistent with the Fourteenth Amendment's demand of due process.

The second argument presented in *Sweatt* was that it was "impossible" to have the equality mandated by the separate but equal formula "in a public school system which relegates citizens of a disadvantaged racial minority group to separate schools." Here, in essence, the NAACP was arguing that separate but equal was merely a "constitutional hypothesis" that was insupportable in real life. This argument, which had been made in the *Fisher* case, was still quite radical, but unlike the record in *Fisher,* the record in *Sweatt* was adequate to make this argument. It was in effect a full frontal assault on segregation.

The Texas appellate court rejected both arguments. The state's prerogative to segregate its citizens was "not now an open question," having been confirmed time after time in cases in direct line of descent from *Plessy.* For the court to hold otherwise would be "to convict the great jurists who rendered those decisions of being so far removed from the actualities involved in the race problems of our American life as to render them incapable of evaluating the known facts of contemporaneous and precedent history as they relate to those problems." Moreover, notwithstanding the testimony of NAACP experts and the data on which they based their opinions, the court found that the rationality of segregated education was not a fit subject for challenge: "The people of Texas, through their constitutional and legislative enactments, have determined that policy, the factual bases of which are not subjects of judicial review."

The Texas appellate court also rejected the NAACP's third argument, in effect its fallback position, that even if segregated education were not ipso facto unconstitutional in theory, it was "in fact and in practical administration . . . unequal and discriminatory." The faculty at the new school comprised members of the Texas faculty, and hence there could be no inequality. Given the smaller classes at the new school, there would be more personal attention from the professors. The school's temporary library, the library of the Texas Supreme Court, had forty-two thousand volumes, close enough to that at the University of Texas to be equivalent. None of this dealt with the intangibles that the NAACP had argued were important to the question of equality, but such arguments were too abstract for consideration, and as the court opined, it was "not dealing with abstractions but with realities."

By now it was February 1948, and Heman Sweatt's fight to pursue a legal education at the University of Texas had gone on two years. Yet, Sweatt refused to attend the law school at the Texas State University for Negroes. Both he and the NAACP refused to disappear. It would be another two years before the U.S. Supreme Court would hear and decide *Sweatt v. Painter* (1950), winning for him the right to attend the University of Texas. This would not occur before George McLaurin, another NAACP client, would bring another case, this one against the state of Oklahoma, a case that eventually would be decided on the same day as *Sweatt*, and with similar results.

In 1948 when he applied to the University of Oklahoma for the doctoral program in education, George McLaurin was a sixty-eight-year-old black man who already had a master's degree. He was a retired professor at Langston University, the state's Negro university. He was qualified for admission to the University of Oklahoma but was rejected. Race again was the reason. A state statute made it a criminal offense to operate a racially integrated school, or even to teach at such an institution, or for a white person to attend one.

By this time, the NAACP lawyers had rethought the practice of filing desegregation suits in state courts and allowing them to painfully wind their way through the judicial system with multiple, time-consuming appeals. These state court suits were often decided by judges who might not only be hostile to desegregation but who were also beholden to segregationist interests—interests who could block their reappointment or reelection to the bench. Federal courts are different. Under Article 3 of the Constitution, federal judges are appointed for life. Federal judges may—indeed do—have their personal faults and biases. Certainly the federal bench in that time contained its share of racists. But then, as now, federal judges have an independence often lacking among their state court colleagues. Keeping their positions is not dependent on satisfying different political constituencies. There was another advantage to try desegregation cases in federal courts. Ordinarily a federal case might take nearly as long as a state case. It would have to be tried at the district court level, and an appeal would then have to be taken to one of the courts of appeal. Finally the Supreme Court might exercise its discretion to take the case. But there was a special provision in the federal judicial code for those instances in which an injunction was sought against the enforcement of a statute or law on the grounds that it was unconstitutional. Such cases could go to a special three-judge court, and any appeal of its decision would go directly to the U.S. Supreme Court.

This was the route that NAACP lawyers decided to take on McLaurin's behalf. The legal issues were clear. Oklahoma did not provide a doctoral program in education at Langston University. In *McLaurin v. Oklahoma State Regents for Higher Education* (1948), the three-judge panel ruled that under *Sipuel*, "the plaintiff is entitled to secure a postgraduate course of study in education leading to a doctor's degree in this State in a State institution, and that he is entitled to secure it as soon as it is afforded to any other applicant." The state's options were limited. It was already October 6, 1948, when the court issued its opinion. Graduate registration closed on October 14. The state would have to either admit McLaurin to its flagship university, which was restricted to whites, or establish a doctoral program at Langston University—within a period of eight days. The state had already seen in the case of Ada Sipuel Fisher that the establishment of a new educational program was expensive and impractical, but this was downright impossible.

Oklahoma officials decided to admit George McLaurin to the graduate program. They also decided to keep him rigidly segregated within the program. Following the three-judge panel's decision, the state legislature amended the law to allow blacks admission to white universities when particular programs were unavailable in black institutions. But the legislature included a curious proviso that "said programs of instruction . . . shall be given . . . upon a segregated basis." McLaurin attended classes with his white classmates, but he was required to sit in an anteroom to the main classroom that housed white students. He could use the same library as his white classmates, but he was required to sit at a designated desk on the mezzanine level away from the main reading room. He was permitted to eat at the same cafeteria as white students, but at a separate time and at a separate table.

In a way McLaurin's experience with "integrated" education at the University of Oklahoma starkly illustrated the castelike nature of Jim Crow and the "untouchable" status of Negroes under that regime. McLaurin was put in constant isolation. After a while, the isolation took its toll. He complained of "mental discomfiture, which makes concentration and study difficult, if not impossible." He also said that the isolation affected his relationships with professors and with fellow students. He brought these complaints to federal court, again to a three-judge panel. He would not be so successful this time. The previous opinion had emphasized that the segregation laws of the state were not "incapable of constitutional enforcement." This was far from a blanket condemnation of Jim Crow education. The court opinion refused to make such a condemnation when presented with the new facts. The court opinion reasoned that while McLaurin experienced a separation from the other students, he nonetheless was "now being afforded the same educational facilities as other students at the University of Oklahoma." In this second case, the court found that separate was indeed equal, and that McLaurin's isolation was consistent with the equal protection clause.

It was now November 1948, less than a year from the time of his initial application, and McLaurin was in virtually the same position as Heman Sweatt. Both cases were ready for the U.S. Supreme Court, and the Court agreed to hear them. By the time briefs were submitted and oral arguments held, there had been changes in McLaurin's treatment. McLaurin now sat in the same classroom as his white classmates, but in a row of seats designated for black students. He continued to have a separate table in the library, but at least it was on the main floor. He could now eat at the same time as the white students, but only at a specially assigned table. In short, in terms of the concrete aspects of his education, McLaurin's experience was separate but equal, and this is what the Supreme Court found in *McLaurin v. Oklahoma State Regents for Higher Education* (1948). But the Supreme Court's analysis did not stop there. The state had set McLaurin apart from other students, and by doing so it had "handicapped [him] in his pursuit of effective graduate education." The state had inhibited "his ability to study, to engage in discussions and exchange views with other students, and, in general, to learn his profession," and in so doing, the state had imposed burdens on McLaurin, burdens that would affect him and those that he would teach in the future. Moreover, the state had deprived McLaurin of an opportunity that the white students all had—the opportunity "to secure acceptance by his fellow students on his own merits."

In one way the ruling in *McLaurin* was simple. The state could educate blacks and whites in separate institutions, but if it chose to educate them in one school, it could not conduct internal segregation. But *McLaurin* went beyond that. The Court touched on an area that had only been hinted at in *Murray* and *Gaines* and that had been avoided in *Fisher*. The equal portion of separate but equal must take into account intangible elements as well as those that were concrete and objectively measurable. This was a significant step. And in conjunction with *Sweatt v. Painter,* it represented a breakthrough of momentous proportions.

In representing Sweatt before the Supreme Court, Charles Hamilton Houston and Thurgood Marshall made the same three-part argument that had been rejected by the Texas Court of Civil Appeals. The first part of that argument was based on the equal protection clause. The segregated law school that Texas reserved for African Americans was unequal. Both the tangible and the intangible factors were inferior. The second part of the argument was also based on the equal protection clause. It was an argument that segregation inherently produced inequality. The NAACP pointed out in its brief and in oral argument that there was ample evidence of this. We believe that some modern scholars have missed the significance of the NAACP's argument in *Sweatt*. Terry Eastland and William J. Bennet in *Counting by Race* (1979) have argued that the NAACP lawyers "decided to stay within the confines of Plessy." Richard Kluger in *Simple Justice* (1980) has argued that "the NAACP continued to stress the consequences of segregation rather than its constitutional setting." But these arguments miss the point. The NAACP placed before the Court the predictable and unavoidable consequences of segregation: inequality. It did so in the hopes of dealing a fatal blow to segregation under the equal protection clause. In effect, the NAACP was making the argument it had made before the Texas court that the formula in *Plessy* was constitutionally malformed and that the 1896 case should be overruled.

The third prong of the NAACP's attack was based on the Fourteenth Amendment's due process clause. The Court had interpreted that clause to mean that no state action not grounded in a rational basis could stand constitutional muster. The NAACP argued that there was no "valid legislative end" that justified racial segregation, that segregation was arbitrary and irrational. This argument also concerned the equal protection clause, for a racial classification that was arbitrary and irrational could not satisfy the demands of the equal protection clause either. The NAACP also argued that racial segregation did not meet the more exacting standard that had been suggested by two cases decided by the Supreme Court during the Second World War. These cases, *Hirabayashi v. United States* (1943) and *Korematsu v. United States* (1944), involved the imposition of curfews, relocation, and confinement of Japanese Americans on the West Coast. Justice Robert Jackson in his dissent wrote that these actions had thrust the nation headlong "into the ugly abyss of racism," but the Court in *Hirabayashi* noted that racial classifications were "not wholly beyond the limits of the Constitution." In *Korematsu*, the Court stated that while "all legal restrictions which curtail the civil rights of a single racial group are immediately suspect [t]hat is not to say that all such restrictions are unconstitutional." Racial restrictions, even of the most damaging kind, might be upheld, though only under "the most rigid scrutiny." Now in *Sweatt*, the NAACP was arguing that segregation could not meet that high standard if it was irrational to begin with.

The Supreme Court's decision in *Sweatt* was unanimous in Heman Sweatt's favor. The Court ordered his immediate admission to the law school at the University of Texas. Simply put, the Court was "unable to find substantial equality in the educational opportunities offered white and Negro law students by the State." The Court saw significant differences between the University of Texas and the Texas State University for Negroes in the number of faculty, the breadth and depth of course offerings, the size of the student body, the size and scope of the library, and the availability of cocurricular offerings. In all of these tangible factors, the Court found the University of Texas superior. If the Court had ended its analysis there, the *Sweatt* case would have been just another case upholding the separate but equal doctrine—because the tangible facilities were not equal, Texas could not restrict Negroes to the Jim Crow school.

But the Court went beyond that. It examined the intangible characteristics of a legal education. What was "more important" than those factors capable of measurement were "those qualities which are incapable of measurement but which make for greatness in a law school. Such qualities, to name a few, include reputation of the faculty, experience of the administration, position and influence of the alumni, standing in the community and prestige." With respect to these factors, the University of Texas was the superior school, and the question, the Court said, was not even close. Moreover, just as black people were excluded from the University of Texas, the Texas State University for Negroes excluded the overwhelming majority, 85 percent of the population of the state, from which would be drawn most of the lawyers, judges and other officials, witnesses, and jurors in the state. Such an exclusion meant that the education at the separate law school for blacks was not the equal of the one received by whites. No matter how much money the state might spend at the black law school, how many faculty members the state might add, no matter how large the student body might grow or how large the library holdings might become, the qualitative differences in the intangibles associated with the two schools meant that to deny Heman Sweatt admission to the University of Texas was unconstitutional. In effect, the Court in *Sweatt* was saying that segregation in law school is inherently unequal. Once again, note that the Court was examining two different law schools and that the justices were familiar with legal education and from their own experience could see that the two schools were clearly not equal. These facts probably helped in influencing the Court's decision.

The Court had not overruled *Plessy v. Ferguson;* indeed, the Court was quite explicit on that point. There was no need. The Court had reiterated its frequent admonishment that it "will decide constitutional questions only when necessary to the disposition of the case . . . , and that such decisions will be drawn as narrowly as possible." But the Court had implicitly accepted the NAACP's first and second arguments in Sweatt, and though it had avoided the third, the due process claim, it had set a standard that was impossible for a segregated system of legal education to meet, for there would *always* be intangible differences in racially segregated schools.

An additional important point should be made. In *Sweatt* and *McLaurin*, the NAACP was no longer alone. The new postwar racial atmosphere helped bring the civil rights organization important allies who agreed with their stand. First among these was the United States government. Solicitor General Philip Perlman filed an amicus brief supporting the NAACP's position on behalf of the Truman administration. Perlman had previously filed an amicus brief in *Shelly v. Kraemer.* His actions were indicative of the new, more pro–civil rights attitude of the Truman administration. The motives behind the Truman administration's support for desegregation litigation were doubtless mixed. Certainly the growing importance of the Negro vote in northern cities played a role, as did the more liberal racial atmosphere that had developed in postwar America. Legal historian Mary Dudziak, in her studies of the relationship between the cold war and desegregation, suggests that often fierce foreign criticism of racial discrimination in the United States played a role in inducing the Truman and later the Eisenhower administrations to support desegregation efforts in court. We have discussed how the struggle against totalitarian regimes first in the Second World War and later in the cold war helped cause many white Americans to see the inconsistency between defending democracy abroad while supporting Jim Crow at home. All of these undoubtedly contributed to the new attitude on the part of the Truman administration and its willingness to support the NAACP's position in court.

The NAACP was also supported by others. In *McLaurin* and *Sweatt*, the NAACP also benefited from supporting amicus briefs filed by the American Federation of Teachers, the Committee of Law Teachers Against Segregation in Legal Education, the American Veterans Committee, the Congress of Industrial Organizations, the Japanese American Citizens League, and the American Civil Liberties Union. Social change had helped bring new allies to the fight against segregation.

McLaurin and *Sweatt* dealt segregated professional education a serious, perhaps fatal, blow. The Court's acceptance of the intangibles argument posed a virtually insurmountable obstacle for segregationist states. But the South was not prepared to capitulate. State courts and some lower federal courts were not prepared to faithfully follow *Sweatt* and *McLaurin*. In Florida, for example, in *State ex rel. Hawkins v. Board of Control* (1950), the state supreme court failed to cite *Sweatt* or *McLaurin* when it ruled that newly established schools for blacks in law, pharmacy, chemical engineering, and agriculture met the requirements of the equal protection clause. In *Epps v. Carmichel* (1950), a federal district judge found that there were educational advantages and disadvantages at both the North Carolina College for Negroes Law School and at the all-white University of North Carolina

Law School. The court's opinion stated that these advantages and disadvantages balanced each other out, and that notwithstanding *Sweatt*, "equality of opportunity in education can exist where segregation is practiced."

But *Sweatt* and *McLaurin* did have enough force to account in quick measure for an expansion of opportunities for blacks in higher education. Not more than three weeks after the decision in *Sweatt*, two black graduate students were admitted to the University of Texas, and Heman Sweatt, of course, became the first black person to enroll at the law school. By August 1950, the University of Delaware was ordered to admit blacks to its undergraduate campus because of the "woefully inferior" opportunities otherwise available to them. By the fall of 1950, the University of Maryland was forced by court order to open to blacks its graduate program in sociology. Louisiana State University had been ordered by a three-judge federal panel to admit black students to the law school, an order only three months later summarily affirmed by the Supreme Court. The historically white University of Tennessee also admitted black students to previously segregated programs, bringing the total of southern states doing so to six. By 1952, the number had grown to twelve.

Two things were left to the NAACP. The first was to apply the Supreme Court's new understanding of inherent inequality to elementary and secondary education, something that had long been a concern of NAACP strategists. The second was to see if cases could be brought that would coax the Supreme Court into doing what it had assiduously avoided doing in *Sweatt*: overturning *Plessy*.

Thurgood Marshall did not unilaterally make the decision to bring a direct challenge to *Plessy*. Although Marshall, after *Sweatt* and *McLaurin*, was the indisputable leader of the NAACP's fight against segregation, he could not act on his own. The NAACP's legal operation had grown considerably since the days when Marshall had taken over from Charles Hamilton Houston. First, the legal operation was technically no longer a part of the NAACP. It had been made into a separate corporation for tax purposes in 1940. The new organization, the NAACP Legal Defense Fund, was founded by Marshall. To be sure, the two organizations shared a common name and mission, as well as support staff, board members, and finances, but they were separate corporations. More important, the roster of NAACP lawyers had grown. In 1938, there had been just Marshall and a secretary. By 1950 the organization had a small brain trust of some of the nation's best attorneys, black and white. These included Franklin Williams, who would later become the staff director for the NAACP's West Coast office. Also in the group was Jack Greenberg, a 1945 graduate of Columbia College and a 1948 graduate of the Columbia University School of Law. Greenberg was only twenty-six. He would later succeed Marshall as chief of the Legal Defense Fund. Later in life he would return to his alma mater as dean of Columbia College and as a professor of law at the Columbia University School of Law. The legal staff was rounded out with Robert L. Carter, who had helped argue *McLaurin*, and Constance Baker Motley. Both Motley and Carter would later serve as federal district court judges. There was also a host of other cooperating lawyers around the country, including A. P. Tureaud in Louisiana, Louis Redding in Delaware, and in Virginia Spottswood Robinson and Marshall's Howard classmate Oliver Hill, who served as cooperating counsel. James Nabrit and Leon Ransom of Howard's law faculty, William Robert Ming Jr., an Afro-American professor at the University of Chicago School of Law, and Louis Pollack and William Coleman, both Wall Street lawyers and former clerks to justices on the Supreme Court, also served as advisers to Marshall. William Hastie, a former dean of Howard Law School, also advised Marshall even though he served as a judge on the federal Court of Appeals for the Third Circuit.

Unfortunately Houston was not to be found among this number. He had died just before the NAACP's triumphs in *Sweatt* and *McLaurin*. After leaving the NAACP, Houston continued his association with the organization. In addition to arguing *Gaines* before the Supreme Court in 1938, Houston also represented the NAACP before the high court in *Steele v. Louisville & Nashville Railroad* (1944), a case involving labor relations and racial discrimination, and in *Hurd and Hurd v. Hodge* (1948), the companion case to *Shelly v. Kraemer.* He also handled civil rights litigation before the lower courts. Houston had long been in poor health, suffering from time to time with tuberculosis, nervous exhaustion, and finally heart failure. At last, at the age of fifty-four, before the fruition of his work, he passed away.

Even without Houston, plenty of lawyers were eager to join Marshall. Forty-three joined with him and fourteen branch and local NAACP presidents at a conference after *Sweatt* and *McLaurin* in late June of 1950. Marshall had traditionally been cautious. He believed that cases involving segregated education were cases that the NAACP could not afford to lose, that they would set devastating precedents. Still he joined with the other conference members in agreeing to a resolution that declared that all future education cases would be aimed at a direct attack on segregation. The aim was to produce, in the words of the conference report, "education on a non-segregated basis and that no relief other than that will be acceptable."

The conference had mandated a frontal assault on *Plessy*. This was controversial. After all, after nearly half a century, the equal side of separate but equal was finally coming into prominence. *McLaurin* called into question the practice of seating blacks separate from whites on buses or railroad cars, and it had application in every area of public life in which black people were accommodated with whites. Because equality was being taken more seriously, states were being prodded toward making some progress in the equalization of schools, libraries, and recreational and other facilities. There were those who were pleased with the new progress and reluctant to give up what had been a successful campaign. But the new NAACP position did not require the sacrifice of the strategy that had brought victory in *Sweatt* and the other cases. The NAACP could continue to urge the courts to find segregation inherently unconstitutional. It could also offer the courts the alternative argument that even if the courts did not agree that segregation was inherently unconstitutional, it was nonetheless unconstitutional in actual practice. If a case that made a frontal assault on *Plessy* lost, it would be a blow to morale, but the NAACP could resume its current campaign to litigate equal protection under the new standards that had developed in *McLaurin* and *Sweatt*. Marshall and his associates knew they would have to choose their cases and their clients carefully.

CHAPTER 6

Arguing the Case

There was no shortage of potential cases; segregated elementary and secondary schools existed throughout the South and in other regions as well. Eventually, six cases involving segregation in elementary education would be consolidated. The challenge would not be undertaken in just one district. If that was done, it would be too easy for a peculiar set of facts, a shrewdly litigated defense case, or a clever and obstinate judge to thwart the NAACP's efforts. Instead different cases would be brought in several districts, in different regions of the South, and in other regions as well. Cases from across the country would be argued. Together these cases would collectively come to be known as *Brown v. Board of Education*. The NAACP was represented by different lawyers in these cases. No two of these cases were argued by the exact same legal team. The facts were somewhat different in each case, but the cases were all part of a coordinated strategy directed from the NAACP's headquarters in New York. They all had a common aim: the elimination of *Plessy v. Ferguson*'s "separate but equal doctrine."

One of these cases originated in Clarendon County, South Carolina. That county maintained a system of segregated schools. In the 1949–1950 academic year, there were 6,531 black students attending sixty-one schools. The annual expenditures for these schools were $194,575. There were 2,375 white students attending twelve schools. The annual expenditures for these were $673,850. Per pupil expenditures of public funds came to $43 per capita for black children and $179 per capita for white children. The average white schoolteacher earned two-thirds more than the average black one, and in contrast to its treatment

{ 119 }

of white children, the school board could not be troubled to provide a single bus for the transportation of black children.

When Negro parents in Clarendon County consulted the NAACP about filing a suit, Thurgood Marshall insisted on getting twenty plaintiffs to sign the petition. Late in 1948, Harry Briggs became the lead plaintiff among twenty in a lawsuit to desegregate the school system. The case known as *Briggs v. Elliott* (1951) was the first elementary and secondary education litigation taken on by Marshall. At the time Harry Briggs was a thirty-four-year-old father of five, including his oldest son, Harry Briggs Jr. Briggs was a veteran of the U.S. Navy who had served in the South Pacific during the Second World War. The son of sharecroppers, he worked at a gas station. His wife, Liza, was a chambermaid at a motel. It had not been easy to find these plaintiffs. A previous suit intended to force the provision of bus transportation for black students had been dismissed, but before then the plaintiff, a farmer, had been severely disciplined. White-owned stores and banks refused to extend him the credit he needed to operate. When he cut some timber to raise cash, the white-owned local sawmill refused to deal with him. When his crops ripened, no white farmer with a harvester agreed to bring them in. His crops rotted where they were in the field.

Briggs and the other plaintiffs expected that signing on to such a lawsuit would expose them to danger. They were right. On the day before Christmas, Briggs, who had worked fourteen years at a gas station, was fired. His severance package was a carton of cigarettes. When Harry Briggs refused to withdraw from the case, his wife, Liza, was also fired by the motel where she worked. Nor was the Briggs family the only one that suffered. Others were fired from their jobs, and one woman was also thrown off the land her family rented. One farmer could find no financing for needed farm equipment, and another almost had his mules seized for failure to pay a loan that was called in unexpectedly. White landowners put pressure on black sharecroppers not to patronize the funeral parlor of one plaintiff. The plaintiffs in *Briggs v. Elliott* found out, if they did not already know, that filing a lawsuit of this type took not only courage but also flexibility, resiliency, and financial reserves.

Marshall had a choice to file the case in state court, where in the past he had experienced a modicum of success in *Murray*, *Gaines*, *Sipuel/Fisher*, and *Sweatt*, or to go to federal court. The choice of going to federal court was easy, for the federal district judge in question would be Julius Waites Waring. Waring was a man of the South, a product of South Carolina's segregationist politics. Born at a time when racism and segregation were the orders of the day, Waring became involved in Democratic Party politics and Charleston city government and municipal politics. At one point Waring had served as campaign manager for Senator "Cotton Ed" Smith, a virulent racist and demagogue. In 1941, he became the beneficiary of Smith's patronage and was appointed to the federal bench. On the bench Waring became something of a surprise. He was vigorous in enforcing anti-peonage legislation. He also ended racial designations on the list of potential jurors. He even ended racially segregated seating in his courtroom and appointed a black man as his bailiff. When the NAACP in 1947 sued the state to provide a legal education for blacks, Waring found in favor of the NAACP. He ordered either the opening of a new school for Negroes or that Negroes should be admitted to the law school at the University of South Carolina. He did give South Carolina officials one other alternative: they could close the law school at the state university altogether. Perhaps more significantly, in another suit brought by the NAACP and decided on the same day, Waring ordered the end of South Carolina's all-white primary. Waring, in short, had a history of fair dealing on issues of race. If a judge in South Carolina could be trusted to deal with a case calling for the abandonment of *Plessy*, it was he.

But Marshall was bringing a case that called into question the very constitutionality of an entire body of law mandating segregation in South Carolina. This was a new area, not now-settled law like *Sweatt*. Because this was new ground, Waring would not decide the case alone. He would be part of a three-judge panel. The second member of the panel would be another district judge, George Bell Timmerman, who had proven already to be a staunch white supremacist. The third would be John Parker, the chief judge of the federal Court of Appeals for the Fourth Circuit. The NAACP had vigorously opposed and helped cause the defeat of his nomination to the U.S. Supreme Court in 1930, but since then, Parker had been a fair judge on racial issues, deciding matters in concert with Supreme Court precedents but unwilling to break new ground.

The likely outcome did not seem favorable. Marshall tried to finesse the issue in his initial pleadings. He did not directly challenge the system of segregation; instead he alleged that the black and white schools were not equal, by then a fairly standard allegation. But the relief Marshall called for was not the integration of a few black children into the white schools, but the dissemination of the white population among the black schools. This was a clever twist. The constitutionality of segregation would be put at issue, not directly but by implication. Were the black schools good enough for white children? Judge Waring rejected Marshall's efforts. Waring would only rule on bases that had been established in *McLaurin, Sweatt,* and the other cases. If inequality could be demonstrated, Waring was prepared to act. He was not prepared to go further. With Marshall's agreement, Judge Waring dismissed the suit without prejudice. Marshall filed another. He would go again before the three-judge court.

The key to *Briggs v. Elliott* and the other cases that presented direct challenges to segregated schools lay in the innovative use of expert testimony to establish the psychological harm that segregation inflicted on African American schoolchildren. In the early graduate school cases, the NAACP lawyers had proved that the South had not provided equal physical facilities and financial resources to their black colleges. Later, in *Sweatt v. Painter* and *McLaurin v. Oklahoma,* the lawyers established the importance to the educational experience of intangibles that were incapable of objective measurement. Among these was collegial interaction among graduate and professional students. According to *Sweatt,* this important aspect of the educational process could not be achieved in schools from which the opposite race was excluded. According to *McLaurin,* segregation internal to a desegregated institution interfered with the process as well.

The recognition of intangible factors as important to the calculation of equality allowed the NAACP to capitalize on a theory that Robert Carter had pushed in a case in the United States Court of Appeals for the Ninth Circuit. In that case, *Westminster School District of Orange County v. Mendez* (1947), Carter argued that sociological evidence could show that segregation in and of itself was unequal. If this theory were successful before the Supreme Court, it would render *Plessy v. Ferguson*'s formula outdated and unconstitutional. Indeed, the opinion by the district court in *Mendez* suggests that it bought the theory—"The methods of segregation prevalent in the defendant school districts foster antagonisms in the children and suggest inferiority where none exists"—but the appellate court decided the case on other grounds.

The theory would require the use of psychologists, social scientists, and other experts in the cases directly challenging segregation. The use of such experts accomplished a number of important goals. First, it demonstrated the psychological injuries that were caused by segregation. This made it clear that equalizing facilities would not remedy the harm that the black students were suffering. Second, it exposed the actual purpose of segregation, the perpetration of racial subordination, what Charles Sumner and Benjamin Roberts had recognized as a system of caste distinction even before the adoption of the Fourteenth Amendment. Third, the testimony of experts refuted widely held beliefs about the intellectual inferiority of Afro-Americans. The expert witnesses would force the judges to grapple with the realities of segregation. They could continue to engage in spurious rationalizations, or they could enforce the Fourteenth Amendment in a way that would make the constitutional provision meaningful. Jurists were placed in a moral and ethical dilemma. If they were intellectually honest, they could not, on the basis of the extensive evidence presented, rule that segregated schools were equal. The disparities were too obvious. At the same time, it was difficult for judges to break with long-standing social traditions and legal precedent. The jurists would be caught in a difficult analytical box from which there could be no escape.

Several social science and education experts aided the NAACP in the school desegregation cases, but one stands out for the simple but compelling test that demonstrated the psychological effects of discrimination on young children. In 1951, Kenneth Clark was a social psychologist at the City College of New York. Clark and his wife and fellow psychologist, Mamie Clark, developed a series of studies concerning the effects of discrimination on young children. The studies examined the psychological effects of segregated and racially mixed schools on black children. One of the studies, "Segregation as a Factor on the Racial Identification of Negro Pre-School Children," became the foundation for a critical element of the NAACP's evidence in the desegregation cases. In one of the tests, the Clarks used four dolls; two of them were brown and two others were white. The Clarks first asked the children, who were aged three to seven, to identify the race of the dolls. They then made a series of commands. These included:

1. Give me the doll you like to play with.
2. Give me the doll that is the nice doll.
3. Give me the doll that looks bad.
4. Give me the doll that is a nice color.

The experiments consistently showed that the participating black children preferred the white dolls. They picked the white doll when asked which was the "nice" one or with which doll they preferred to play. The black doll was selected when the children were asked which doll looked "bad." The Clarks also developed a coloring test. Black children were given crayons and a number of objects to color. The drawings included objects such as a leaf, an apple, an orange, and a mouse. If these objects were colored accurately, the study moved to a second stage. During this phase, the participants were given outline drawings of children and asked to pretend that they were the persons depicted. The children were then asked to select the appropriate color to fill in the drawings. Most of the medium-brown and dark-skinned children colored the drawings white, yellow, or irrelevant colors such as red or green. The Clarks concluded that these studies indicated self-rejection, one of the negative effects of racism on children at the early stages of their development. The Clarks' findings were corroborated by separate studies performed by other psychologists. Kenneth Clark was hired to provide expert testimony based on the doll studies.

The Clarendon County case was the first of the *Brown* cases to be argued. Appropriately, it received attention from the highest levels of state government—in particular, from the governor's office. South Carolina's governor, Jimmy Byrnes, a former Supreme Court justice and right-hand man to Franklin Roosevelt, was a savvy character. He was very much aware of the implications of the decisions in the graduate school cases, as well as the gross disparities in the educational facilities in South Carolina. Byrnes precipitated actions that he hoped would forestall the NAACP's attack. At the governor's request, the state legislature authorized substantial funding for a building program for black schools. This was coupled with ominous warnings from individual legislators that if the Supreme Court ordered desegregation, the state would discontinue its support for public education altogether and shut down its schools.

The Clarendon County school board retained Robert Mc-Cormick Figg to represent it in the *Briggs* litigation. During the planning of the school board's defense, Figg developed a clever ploy that was intended to deflate the NAACP's case. He decided to admit that the black schools were indeed unequal, and he based his defense on an argument that the state intended to equalize the schools within a short period of time. At the outset of the *Briggs* trial in Charleston, Figg "conceded that inequalities in the facilities, opportunities and curricula in the schools of the district [did] exist." He argued that the deplorable conditions of the black schools were the result of an impoverished rural economy but that the disparities were being corrected by the state's equalization program. He then asked the court to grant a reasonable period of time for the completion of the construction projects. A surprised Thurgood Marshall managed to retain his composure and responded that Figg's concession was irrelevant. The plaintiffs, he continued, intended to prove the inherent inequality of the segregated system. The issue was now squarely and irretrievably confronted. After Figg's bold move, there could be no return to an equalization strategy on the part of the NAACP. The trial proceeded with Marshall offering proof of the physical disparities between the black and white schools and the testimony of Clark and other experts establishing psychological injury.

The trial court's decision in *Briggs* was issued on June 23, 1951. The court accepted the state's concession that the black schools were inferior, but also declared that inasmuch as the state was in the process of improving the schools, the court held that there was no need to address the issue any further. On the question of the inherent inequity of segregation, the court found that the state laws requiring segregation were constitutional. In the court's view, "segregation of the races in public schools so long as equality of rights is preserved, is a matter of legislative policy for the several states, with which the federal courts are powerless to interfere." To support this conclusion, the court relied on *Plessy* and subsequent decisions in which courts had approved segregation.

Marshall had also argued that even if segregation were not inherently unconstitutional, the black schools were so demonstrably inferior that the court should "enjoin the segregation rather than direct the equalization of facilities." The court rejected this request based on its conclusion that the state's administration of the segregation law, rather than the law itself, produced the disparities that were shown during the trial. The NAACP had further argued that the rulings in *Sweatt* and *McLaurin*, in which the Supreme Court struck down segregation in graduate schools, supported its claims. The court responded that "segregation as applied to graduate schools is essentially different from that involved in segregation in education at the lower levels." Education at the lower levels was not a matter of choice, and the laws requiring segregation accommodated "the wishes of the parent as to the upbringing of the child and his associates in the formative period of childhood and adolescence."

Despite the several hours of testimony by the NAACP's experts, the court's opinion paid little attention to them. In a brief passage, the majority merely noted that some of the testimony indicated that mixed schools would provide better educational opportunities and that other witnesses stated that integrated schools would cause racial friction. These issues, the court found, were matters of legislative policy with which the court could not interfere. The court ruled that the black students were entitled to an order declaring the state's obligation to equalize its educational facilities, but they had not prevailed in their challenge to the laws requiring segregation. Segregation had been declared permissible by *Plessy*, and subsequent decisions had done nothing to alter the fundamental premise of that decision.

Judge Waring authored a passionate dissent. After criticizing the majority for failing to address the crucial issue presented in *Briggs*, Judge Waring expressed his views that the court was obligated to "face, without evasion or equivocation, the question as to whether segregation in education is legal or whether it cannot exist under our American system as particularly enunciated in the Fourteenth Amendment of the Constitution." Judge Waring contended that the weight of the legal authority supported a finding that legislative classifications could not be based on race, and *Plessy* did not prevent a finding that segregated education was unconstitutional. He cited the precedents from the graduate school litigation as well as several earlier NAACP cases involving housing, voting, and criminal law to support his sweeping assertion that *"segregation is per se inequality"* (italics added). Waring concluded that "the system of segregation in education adopted and practiced by the State of South Carolina must go and must go now."

It was apparent that there would be an appeal of this case to the Supreme Court, and South Carolina was pulling out all stops to defend segregation. Governor Byrnes prevailed on his friend and former colleague, John W. Davis, to represent the state before the Supreme Court. This reflected just how deeply the state feared the NAACP lawyers. The Democratic candidate for president in 1924, Davis had served for several years as the solicitor general of the United States, the government's advocate before the Supreme Court. He had also served as ambassador to Great

Britain and had argued more than a hundred cases in the Supreme Court.

Davis, in short, was the quintessential plutocrat. With his erect bearing, gentlemanly manners, and mane of flowing white hair, he looked every inch the part. Moreover, at the advanced age of seventy-nine, Davis was known as "the lawyer's lawyer" and was still at the peak of his influence. He was a named partner in a prominent Wall Street law firm that represented several of the most powerful corporations in America. The firm still carries his name on the letterhead. John W. Davis was by far the most formidable advocate that the legal establishment had to offer, and for the appeal of *Briggs v. Elliott*, South Carolina—and indeed the whole South—had him. Indeed, one of the NAACP's lawyers recalled years later that "when it was announced that John W. Davis of New York would argue for [South Carolina], Thurgood's knees appeared to buckle under him."

The case bearing the name by which the school desegregation cases are remembered began in 1948 when the Topeka, Kansas, branch of the NAACP petitioned the local school board to desegregate the public schools. After two years of inaction, the branch contacted the organization's headquarters in New York and requested assistance in filing a lawsuit. The lead plaintiff, Oliver Brown, was not a prominent figure in the local NAACP. He was an ordinary citizen who was angered that his daughter had to travel each day past a modern, fully equipped white school to a black school housed in a deteriorated building. There were several plaintiffs, but Oliver Brown's name came first alphabetically, and as a result, when the case was filed in the federal court on February 14, 1951, the case bore his name.

When Oliver Brown became the lead plaintiff in *Brown v. Board of Education of Topeka*, Topeka and the state of Kansas had a schizophrenic attitude about its Negro population. There was segregation, but it was not universal. Black people were only 7.5 percent of the state's population, and though they were in general relegated to the lowest rung of the economic ladder, they were allowed in some of the same civic organizations as whites. Restaurants and hotels were segregated, but bus and train station

128   { *Brown v. Board of Education* }

waiting rooms were not. Five of the seven movie theaters were relegated to whites only, and a sixth was for blacks; the seventh allowed both races, but blacks were consigned to the balcony. The state put no barriers in the way of higher education, for the University of Kansas had long been open to black people, and so had Washburn University. And the state did not mandate segregation in elementary schools, but for localities above fifteen thousand in population, the state specifically allowed school segregation as an option.

Thus, Topeka had a limited option to have desegregated schools, and the city took it. Elementary schools were segregated, as the junior high schools had been until 1941 litigation ended the practice. Senior high schools were integrated, but they had separate teams in basketball, swimming, wrestling, golf, and tennis, as well as separate pep clubs, separate cheerleaders, and a separate assembly at which black students were urged to keep to their place. Though the separate elementary schools for black children were older, they were in fact the rough equivalent of their white counterparts, and when *Brown* was decided at the trial level, the court found as much.

Robert Carter and Jack Greenberg were the NAACP's point men for *Brown*. Carter was lead counsel. Carter and Greenberg were further assisted by John Scott, Charles Scott, and Charles Bledsoe, local counsel from Topeka, Kansas. The NAACP's attorneys were unable to bring together the same cast of experts that had served as experts in *Briggs*. For one, it was unclear exactly how effective the testimony of sociologists and psychologists would be until after the trial in *Briggs*, and that trial ended little more than a month before the trial in *Brown* was scheduled. For another, the *Brown* trial was to begin on June 25, and due to the vagaries of the academic calendar and the schedules of university professors, it was harder to bring in experts in the summer than it otherwise might have been. Nonetheless, Carter and Greenberg were able to find experts whose opinions would help the NAACP's case.

One of these experts, Hugh Speer, head of the Department of Education at the University of Kansas City, testified that he had examined the public schools in Topeka and found in each case that the white schools were newer or otherwise physically superior to the black schools. Speer also stated that the educational experience in the black schools was deficient because although the same courses were offered, black students were denied the opportunity to associate with white students. Another expert, Horace B. English, was a professor of psychology at Ohio State University. English testified that learning ability was unrelated to race, but societal expectations had a significant effect on learning. He testified that legal segregation diminished the learning expectations of black students and was prejudicial to their educational efforts. English's testimony was corroborated by another expert who stated that segregated education caused black children to believe that they were inferior, and another who testified that segregated education lowered the ambitions of black students. Another one of plaintiffs' experts, Lisa Pinkham Holt, was a psychology professor at the University of Kansas. She testified that legally sanctioned segregation was interpreted by both races as denoting the inferiority of the black group. She also testified that the resulting stigmatization adversely affected African American students.

The three-judge court's judgment in *Brown v. Board of Education* was entered on August 3, 1951. With respect to measurable qualities and characteristics of segregated education, the court found that "the physical facilities, the curricula, courses of study, qualifications of and quality of teachers, as well as other educational facilities in the two sets of schools are comparable." Oliver Brown had testified that his daughter had to leave home each morning at 7:40 A.M. and walk through railroad yards to wait for a bus, which transported her to school. Brown emphasized that the black school was less attractive than the well-equipped white school, which in turn was much closer to his home. Brown stated that the disparities in the black and white schools prompted him to sue the school authorities. The testimony of the seven other plaintiffs proceeded along the same lines. But in truth, the NAACP had not put much emphasis to the equalization argument, and the court recognized that the NAACP had put most of its eggs in the basket of intangibles that *Sweatt* and *McLaurin* had explored and about which the experts had testified in *Brown.*

Equality with respect to concrete matters would decide the case, however, in spite of the Supreme Court's pronouncements in *Sweatt* and *McLaurin*, and in spite of the Court's apparent leanings:

> If segregation within a school as in the *McLaurin* case is a denial of due process, it is difficult to see why segregation in separate schools would not result in the same denial. Or if the denial of the right to commingle with the majority group in higher institutions of learning as in the *Sweatt* case and gain the educational advantages resulting therefrom, is lack of due process, it is difficult to see why such denial would not result in the same lack of due process if practiced in the lower grades.

The district court, however, noted an important distinction between *Sweatt* and *McLaurin* and the current case involving Brown and the other plaintiffs. The Supreme Court in *Sweatt* and *McLaurin* had made it clear that it was confining itself to graduate education. This case involved elementary education. It also came with pleas to *Plessy*, something the Supreme Court had specifically declined to do in the higher education cases. Despite NAACP victories, *Plessy* was still the law of the land, and the three-judge court was bound by it.

Despite its finding of physical and instructional equality, the district court entered a separate finding on the issue of the damage caused by state-enforced segregation, a finding that would resonate through the litigation before the Supreme Court:

> Segregation of white and colored children in public schools has a detrimental effect upon the colored children. The impact is greater when it has the sanction of law, for the policy of separating the races is usually interpreted as denoting the inferiority of the negro group. A sense of inferiority affects the motivation of a child to learn. Segregation with the sanction of law, therefore, has a tendency to restrain the educational

and mental development of negro children and to deprive them of some of the benefits they would receive in a racially integrated school system.

For the NAACP, this was a going-away present of major proportions. The opinion was written by Tenth Circuit Court of Appeals Judge Walter August Huxman, a former governor of Kansas who along with two other judges had been especially empaneled for the Topeka case. His opinion put the NAACP in a good position for appeal. Trial court decisions consist of findings of fact and conclusions of law. Unlike conclusions of law, with which appellate courts are free to disagree depending on the court's interpretation of a given legal principle, findings of fact must be sustained unless the reviewing court finds that they are "clearly erroneous," meaning not supported by the evidence. This is an extremely difficult standard to satisfy and cannot be met unless there is virtually no evidence to support the trial court's conclusion. Thus, the finding of fact on the damage question was critical because it obligated the Supreme Court either to reach a conclusion of law consistent with the lower court's factual determination or to remand the case for additional evidentiary proceedings in the lower court. The Supreme Court could conceivably have ruled that the factual findings were erroneous, but this would have been difficult given the extensive amount of evidence that supported the trial court's ruling.

Another important aspect of the Kansas court's ruling involved its finding of equivalency in the black and white schools. In none of the other cases that would be argued before the Supreme Court under the case name *Brown v. Board of Education* did the trial courts find that the black schools were physically equal to the white schools or provided a comparable level of instruction. These other cases would leave open the possibility of a Supreme Court ruling in the NAACP's favor on the equality issue without a resolution of whether segregation itself violated the Constitution. The ruling in the Kansas case foreclosed this option. A grant of certiorari in the Kansas case meant that the Supreme Court could not avoid the critical question of whether segregation itself was permissible under the equal protection clause of the Fourteenth Amendment. The Supreme Court would be on the spot, and the federal district court had meant to put it there.

The South Carolina and Kansas cases would also be joined by two separate cases that were filed in Delaware: *Gebhart et al. v. Belton et al.* (1952) and *Gebhart v. Bulah* (1952). *Belton* arose in Claymont, a suburb a few miles north of Wilmington. The combination grade school–high school in Claymont served about four hundred white students. It occupied a fourteen-acre site. The school was well equipped, and the grounds were beautifully landscaped. Black children, in contrast, were required to travel by bus to Howard High in Wilmington, the only black high school in the entire state. It was surrounded by factories and warehouses. The student-to-faculty ratio was three times higher at Howard than at Claymont. Sixty percent of Claymont's faculty held master's degrees, compared with 40 percent at Howard. Claymont offered several extracurricular activities that were not available at Howard.

The second case was filed by Sarah Bulah, a white woman in Hockessin, Delaware, who had adopted a black child several years earlier. When her adopted child reached school age, Bulah became annoyed when she was required to drive past the well-equipped white school to reach the dilapidated one-room schoolhouse that served black students. Louis Redding, a black civil rights lawyer, represented the plaintiffs in the Delaware cases. Redding was a graduate of Brown University and Harvard Law School and was admitted to practice in Delaware in 1929. He was still the only black attorney in Delaware when the desegregation cases were filed more than twenty years later. When Redding requested the NAACP's assistance, Jack Greenberg was assigned to assist him.

The Delaware cases were originally filed in the federal district court, but the state attorney general argued that the cases involved state law and should be heard first in state court. The NAACP refiled in state court, knowing that the cases would be heard by Chancellor Collins Seitz, a judge who had ruled in Louis Redding's favor in an earlier desegregation case involving the University of Delaware. During the trial of the Delaware cases, the NAACP attorneys introduced the testimony of fourteen expert witnesses. One of them, Columbia University's Otto Klineberg, testified that Negro students had the same innate learning abilities as white students. Ohio State's George A. Kelly, a psychologist, testified about the fatiguing and otherwise punitive effects of the long bus rides. Harvard psychologist Jerome Bruner explained that segregation produced feelings of frustration, apathy, and hostility in black children. Kenneth Clark described the findings of his doll studies.

This time, the experts measured the effects of segregation on white children. The studies indicated that segregation tended to reinforce prejudice. In response to questions about how they felt about black children, some of the white students stated that they wanted to tie the hands of black students and force them to work. Others thought that black students should work when white students were allowed to play. During the cross-examination, the state's witness, George R. Miller, was forced to acknowledge that he had authored a doctoral thesis that concluded that unequal educational facilities placed black students at a disadvantage. After three days of testimony, Chancellor Seitz visited the schools to observe the conditions and to compare the facilities. On April 1, 1952, the Delaware court issued a ruling in *Gebhart v. Belton* and *Gebhart v. Bulah*. Relying on the undisputed testimony concerning the psychological harm, the court found that "State-imposed segregation in education itself results in the Negro children, as a class, receiving educational opportunities which are substantially inferior to those available to white children similarly situated." Despite this determination, the court went on to hold that it was compelled by binding legal precedent to issue a conclusion of law that was inconsistent with its fact findings.

The court concluded that it was obligated by *Plessy* to hold that segregated schools did not violate the Fourteenth Amendment, "because by applying the separate but equal test, the Supreme Court has said in effect that inequality arising from segregation itself is not that type of inequality which violates the Constitution of the United States." If *Plessy* were going to be reversed, the

Supreme Court would have to do so. The court then turned to the question of whether Delaware had complied with *Plessy's* equality requirement, finding ultimately that the black schools were inferior. As the state had failed to comply with the equivalency requirement, the court entered a judgment for the plaintiffs. Unlike the courts in South Carolina and Virginia, the Delaware judge did not let the school boards off with a promise that equalization would be achieved at some point in the future. He ordered the white schools to allow the black students to enroll. If the school boards equalized the facilities at some time in the future, they could petition the court for a modification of its desegregation decree. The state immediately appealed the decision, but the decision was affirmed by the Delaware Supreme Court on August 28, 1952.

As these events were unfolding, a protest was being organized in a remote area in rural Virginia. It was a protest that would ultimately reach the Supreme Court. In April of 1951, a group of students at Moton High School, a black school in Prince Edward County, Virginia, organized a strike to protest the shoddy conditions at their high school. The students intended to remain on strike until the local school board agreed to construct a new school. Eventually, the students sent a letter to the NAACP's special counsel for the Southeast region. Two Richmond lawyers, Oliver Hill and Spottswood Robinson, served in that capacity. Both were graduates of Howard Law School and were trained during the years that Charles Houston served as dean. They were Thurgood Marshall's contemporaries and personal friends.

Hill and Robinson traveled to Prince Edward County, where they met with the striking students. The isolated community would not have been their choice for the location of a desegregation suit. The lawyers preferred urban settings, but they were impressed by the students' resolve. After a few meetings, Hill and Robinson decided to aid the students but to condition their representation on an agreement that the strikers would become the plaintiffs in an action seeking to desegregate schools. At a meeting held at a local church, the parents agreed to proceed with the case. On May 23, 1951, Spottswood Robinson filed a suit in the federal district court in Richmond, Virginia. It was known as *Davis v. County School Board of Prince Edward County* (1952).

Prince Edward County was represented by Archibald Robertson, a partner at a distinguished Richmond law firm, Hunton, Williams, Anderson, Gray, and Moore, along with James Almond, the Virginia attorney general. After a visit to Prince Edward County, Almond concluded that it would be impossible to defend the case on equivalency grounds. The racial disparities were too obvious. The lawyers eventually decided to admit that the black schools were deficient but to defend the state laws requiring segregation. The Virginia lawyers had monitored the proceedings in South Carolina. Detecting what they believed to be a flaw in South Carolina's defense, they decided to hire an expert to rebut the testimony that the NAACP would present.

The trial in the Prince Edward County case commenced on February 25, 1952. The NAACP's tack in the Prince Edward case was the same as it had been in the other cases: the development of an evidentiary record showing that the buildings and other facilities that housed the black schools were inferior to the county's white schools. After physical inequality was established, experts would be called to establish the harmful effects of state-sponsored segregation. When the trial commenced, the NAACP lawyers proceeded with their witnesses.

The school board's lawyers mounted an intense cross-examination, attacking the NAACP's evidence at every turn. When the school board presented its rebuttal evidence, the witnesses attempted to explain away the disparities in the black and white schools. Witnesses for the school board emphasized their belief that "custom" could not be legislated. One of the school board's experts testified that Kenneth Clark's studies were subject to varying interpretations and that segregated schools were not injuring black students. The state's star witness, Dr. Henry Garrett of Columbia University, challenged Clark's testimony. Garrett offered an opinion counter to Clark's—that in his view, segregated education, if equal, would not adversely affect black students. The five days of tense proceedings concluded with threats posed by the lawyers representing Prince Edward County. During closing statements, they flatly asserted that the county would not obey a desegregation order if one were issued. Virginia would close down its schools rather than comply with a desegregation order. The decision in *Davis v. County School Board of Prince Edward County* was issued on March 7, 1952. The court entered a judgment for the school board. It held that the policy of racial segregation was not arbitrary or capricious, as the plaintiffs had contended, but was "one of the ways of life in Virginia. Separation of white and colored 'children' in the public schools of Virginia has for generations been a part of the mores of the people. To have separate schools has been their use and want."

In the court's view, the expert testimony had been inconclusive. The NAACP's evidence supported the view that segregation was harmful, but the school board's experts offered equally weighty opinions that indicated that "given equivalent physical facilities, offerings and instruction, the Negro would receive in a separate school the same educational opportunity as he would obtain in the classroom and on the campus of a mixed school." On the equivalency issue, the court found, as the defendants had conceded, that the buildings and other facilities at the black schools were inferior to the county's white schools and ordered the defendants "to replace the Moton buildings and facilities with a new building and new equipment, or otherwise remove the inequality in them."

While the Prince Edward County case was pending, a separate case was filed in the District of Columbia. Compared with most other cities, Washington's black community was well educated and well off. A third of the city's Afro-American population was employed by the federal government. In 1950 there were 300 Negro physicians, 150 African American lawyers and judges, 150 black college professors, and 2,500 African American schoolteachers residing in the District of Columbia. Despite the relative affluence of its black community, Washington was as segregated as any city in the Deep South. Public facilities, public transportation, housing, and public schools were all rigidly segregated. Furthermore, because of the rapid growth in the city's black population during World War II, housing conditions in poor communities were deplorable, and the black schools were inferior to white schools.

The District of Columbia's desegregation case began when a local barber, Bishop Gardner, organized the Consolidated Parents Group. Gardner's group initiated a boycott of a black high school that was overcrowded and in a state of severe disrepair. As a result of class divisions within the African American community, Gardner's group formed separately from the school's PTA, which was dominated by middle-class blacks. The boycott was not supported by the local NAACP branch. In February of 1948, Gardner visited an NAACP meeting at a Methodist church where Charles Houston was delivering an address. After the meeting, Gardner introduced himself and met with Houston later that night. After Gardner explained the problems with the high school, Houston agreed to represent Gardner's group in a suit that would seek to equalize Washington's schools. Houston's health, by this time, was declining rapidly. He had been hospitalized after one heart attack and was incapacitated again after a second one. Houston summoned Gardner to his hospital bed and urged him to ask another lawyer, James Nabrit, to assume responsibility for the case. Gardner agreed and hired Nabrit.

The District of Columbia was federal territory and hence not subject to the Fourteenth Amendment's language, which makes the amendment applicable only to the states. The legal arguments in the state cases were based on the equal protection clause of the Fourteenth Amendment. This meant that the lawyers in the Washington case had to develop a different legal theory. They eventually fashioned an argument that the due process clause of the Fifth Amendment guaranteed equal protection of the law in the same manner as the Fourteenth Amendment. Gardner's case, *Bolling v. Sharpe*, was filed in 1951. Nabrit did not include any equalization claims but decided instead to rest his entire case on the inherent inequity of segregation. Nabrit was among the first to argue what has become known as the strict scrutiny test, namely that laws that treated groups differently on the basis of race were required to have a compelling justification and that there was none in this case. Despite Nabrit's innovative legal arguments, the trial court dismissed the case because a recent decision, *Carr v. Corning*, had found that segregated schools in the District of Columbia were permissible.

By mid-1952, the cases challenging school segregation were beginning to reach the Supreme Court. On May 10, 1952, the NAACP lawyers filed a new statement of jurisdiction in *Briggs* in the Supreme Court. On June 9, 1952, the Supreme Court noted probable jurisdiction in *Briggs* and *Brown* and set them down for argument during the fall term, which would begin in October. On July 12, the appeal of the Virginia case, *Davis v. Prince Edward County*, was filed. On August 28, the Delaware Supreme Court upheld the trial court's decision in *Gebhart v. Belton* and *Gebhart v. Bulah*. On October 8, the Supreme Court postponed the arguments in *Briggs* and *Brown*. It noted jurisdiction in the Virginia case and scheduled it for argument with the other cases on December 8. After the October postponement, the clerk of the Supreme Court took the unusual step of telephoning James Nabrit and asking him to petition the Court to hear *Bolling v. Sharpe*, which was still pending before the court of appeals. On November 13, the Delaware attorney general applied for a writ of certiorari in the two Delaware cases. All five cases were scheduled to be heard together on December 9, 1952.

By this time, some of the strain of Marshall's hectic schedule was beginning to show. His face displayed signs of middle age. There were dark circles under his eyes. His wavy hair was flecked with gray strands. He had gained weight, and his suits were slightly rumpled. Marshall continued to be lighthearted and jovial in meetings, frequently cracking jokes and telling entertaining stories to lessen the tension that the NAACP's team often felt. However, some of the lawyers and others who worked closely with Marshall noticed signs of increasing irritability and sour moods when others were not around. Despite the constant stress, Marshall and the other NAACP lawyers performed remarkably, especially given the weight of the responsibilities that they bore. They were not merely representing clients in individual cases. They were the advocates for an entire race and advocates for an idea—the idea of a caste-free America.

For the final preparations, Marshall rented a large hotel suite in Washington. Following a custom established years earlier, practice arguments were presented in the moot courtroom at Howard Law School, where students and professors acted as judges in grueling practice sessions. Dozens of volunteers—professors from some of the nation's leading law schools, historians, sociologists, and other scholars—were on hand to provide encouragement and assistance. In the end, it came down to Thurgood Marshall and a small group of dedicated but underresourced lawyers pitted against the best legal talent that the South could buy.

On December 9, 1952, at 1:35 P.M., the arguments commenced in the school desegregation cases. The first argument was presented by Robert Carter, who appeared on behalf of the black students in the Kansas case. After summarizing the circumstances of *Brown*, Carter directed the Court's attention to the trial court's finding of physical and instructional equality in the Topeka schools, emphasizing that the issue presented involved a challenge to the constitutionality of segregation itself. Carter also argued that the decisions in *Plessy* would not, as the lower courts had found, prevent a finding of illegality in the school cases. Attorney General Wilson appeared next on behalf of the state of Kansas. Wilson contended that racial segregation was constitutionally permissible.

At 3:15 P.M., the arguments began in the South Carolina case, *Briggs v. Elliott*. Thurgood Marshall appeared first, presenting the arguments for the Clarendon County schoolchildren. By the time of this argument, Marshall was a seasoned Supreme Court advocate, his style relaxed and confident. In contrast to the formality of less experienced advocates, Marshall's exchanges with the justices seemed more like a conversation among acquaintances than a historic argument before the nation's highest tribunal. But there were some dramatic moments. Like Carter, Marshall emphasized that *Briggs* involved a direct challenge to the constitutionality of segregation. This was not, Marshall stated, a case seeking equality of facilities. After making his position clear, Marshall focused on the expert testimony concerning the harm inflicted by state-supported segregation. Marshall then attacked the trial court's reasoning in *Briggs* and its failure to accord any weight to the experts' testimony. Marshall also contended that *Plessy* was not controlling precedent. The rulings in the more recent *Sweatt* and *McLaurin* cases supported a finding against school boards.

After Marshall finished, John Davis presented South Carolina's case. Proceeding with poise and confidence, Davis stressed South Carolina's claim that the schools had been equalized; that the state had a right to enact legislative classifications based on race; and that the NAACP's arguments addressed the wisdom of the legislative policy rather than the issue of constitutional rights. Davis then began to recite some of the details of South Carolina's equalization efforts. Before he could finish, the arguments were adjourned and reconvened on the following morning. When Davis resumed, he argued that the framers of the Fourteenth Amendment intended to allow racial segregation. Davis went on to stress his view that the Constitution had long been interpreted by courts and other governmental institutions to allow segregation. He then launched into an attack against the NAACP's experts, claiming that the evidence was generally lacking in probative value and had, in any event, been refuted by other experts. After responding to a number of questions raised by the justices, Davis completed his presentation.

Marshall's rebuttal addressed Davis's main points. During this phase of his argument, Marshall pointed out that most of the materials Davis cited had not been presented during the trial, but he conceded that the Court could take scholarly works into account in reaching its decision. Moving on, Marshall reiterated the points he had made during his initial argument, stressing again that there was no legal justification for South Carolina's legislative classification based on race.

On the afternoon of December 10, 1952, Spottswood Robinson commenced his argument on behalf of the students in *Davis v. County School Board of Prince Edward County*. Robinson began by summarizing the facts of the Virginia case and describing the trial court's decision. He argued that Virginia's segregation statute violated the Fourteenth Amendment of the Constitution.

Robinson's reserved and scholarly manner contrasted sharply with Marshall's relaxed and conversational style. Taking a slightly different approach from that of Marshall and Carter, Robinson suggested, in an indirect reference to *Plessy*, that the Court was not "irrevocably bound" to prior determinations "when error has been demonstrated" or "when it is plain that the conditions of the present are substantially different from those of the past." Robinson stressed that an injunction based on mere inequality of physical plants would be an inadequate remedy, since that would permit the state to resegregate the schools after the facilities were equalized. Echoing Marshall and Carter, Robinson stressed that the Virginia case challenged the constitutionality of segregation itself.

After Robinson concluded, the lawyers for the school board responded. Justin Moore stated that the schools in Virginia had been equalized. He also pointed out that during the trial, the state proffered expert testimony that refuted the NAACP's evidence of psychological harm. Moore argued that segregation at the elementary school level was different from segregation in graduate schools. As a consequence, the reasoning of *Sweatt* and *McLaurin* did not apply. When Moore completed his presentation, J. Lindsey Almond argued on behalf of Prince Edward County. Almond contended that when Virginia's segregation statute was enacted during the Reconstruction era, the legislators had given careful consideration to the question of whether the public schools should be operated on a segregated or integrated basis, but had chosen segregation. He also repeated the earlier assertion that the schools in Virginia were being equalized. After Almond concluded, Robinson used his rebuttal time to respond to the school board lawyers. The arguments in the District of Columbia case, *Bolling v. Sharpe*, followed the Virginia case. They were presented by George E. C. Hayes and James Nabrit. Milton Korman represented the District of Columbia. The Delaware cases, *Gebhart v. Belton* and *Gebhart v. Bulah*, were the last to be presented. H. Albert Young argued for Delaware. Jack Greenberg and Louis Redding argued for the students. The arguments in the Delaware and District of Columbia cases did not cover any new ground, except the Washington case relied on the

Fifth, rather than Fourteenth, Amendment, based on the District of Columbia's unique status as federal territory. The arguments concluded on December 11, 1952, at 3:50 P.M.

Several months later, the Court issued an order setting the cases over to the next term for reargument. The Court also directed the parties to submit briefs addressing the following questions:

1. What evidence is there that the Congress which submitted and the State legislatures and conventions which ratified the Fourteenth Amendment contemplated or did not contemplate, understood or did not understand, that it would abolish segregation in public schools?

2. If neither the Congress in submitting nor the States in ratifying the Fourteenth Amendment understood that compliance with it would require the immediate abolition of segregation in public schools, was it nevertheless the understanding of the framers of the Amendment:
    (a) that future Congresses might, in the exercise of their power under section 5 of the Amendment, abolish such segregation, or
    (b) that it would be within the judicial power, in light of future conditions, to construe the Amendment as abolishing such segregation of its own force?

3. On the assumption that the answers to questions 2(a) and (b) do not dispose of the issue, is it within the judicial power, in construing the Amendment, to abolish segregation in public schools?

4. Assuming it is decided that segregation in public schools violates the Fourteenth Amendment:
    (a) would a decree necessarily follow providing that, within the limits set by normal geographical school districting, Negro children should forthwith be admitted to schools of their choice, or
    (b) may this Court, in the exercise of its equity powers, permit an effective gradual adjustment to be brought about from existing segregated systems to a system not based on color distinctions?

5. On the assumption on which questions 4(a) and (b) are based, and assuming further that this Court will exercise its equity powers to the end described in question 4(b),

    (a) should this court formulate detailed decrees in these cases;

    (b) if so, what specific issues should the decrees reach;

    (c) should this Court appoint a special master to hear evidence with a view to recommending specific terms for such decrees;

    (d) should this Court remand to the courts of first instance with directions to frame decrees in these cases, and if so what general directions should the decrees of this Court include and what procedures should the courts of first instance follow in arriving at the specific terms of more detailed decrees?

The order setting down a second argument was a rare event. It added immeasurably to tensions many thought could not have been greater. Some of the NAACP lawyers took the order as a positive sign. Others believed that it was an ominous signal. In the end, there was nothing that anyone could do except to make preparations to respond to the Court's questions. To research the original intent question, Marshall enlisted John A. Davis, a professor of political science at Lincoln University, a predominately Negro university in Pennsylvania. Davis obtained the assistance of Horace Mann Bond, who was, at that time, the president of Lincoln University. Davis also solicited the assistance of C. Vann Woodward, who was well on his way to becoming one of the preeminent historians of the South, and John Hope Franklin, the leading expert in Afro-American history in the postwar era. William Coleman, a young African American lawyer who had graduated first in his class at Harvard and had clerked for Supreme Court Justice Felix Frankfurter, agreed to coordinate research in the various states.

During the next several months, the lawyers, historians, law professors, and other academics assisting the NAACP lawyers grappled with the research concerning the original intent of the framers of the Fourteenth Amendment. Records in state archives

Davis emphasized that during this entire Reconstruction period, the public schools in the District of Columbia, which were under the direct supervision of Congress, were segregated. This, in Davis's view, made it clear that Congress condoned segregated schools. Davis argued further that segregation was so firmly established that it was beyond the power of the Supreme Court to alter. He pointed to several post-*Plessy* cases in which the Supreme Court had approved segregation and numerous instances in which state courts had endorsed the practice. In a particularly forceful invocation of stare decisis, the doctrine that courts should stick with established precedent, Davis argued that somewhere, some time, to every principle there comes a moment of repose when it has been so often announced, so confidently relied upon, so long continued, that it passes the limits of judicial discretion and disturbance. Proceeding with the precision and confidence of a seasoned veteran, Davis concluded, stating that South Carolina had not come before the court in a "sack cloth and ashes" but was confident that its segregated schools were a permissible exercise of the state's authority. The Supreme Court, he continued, should not end the southern way of life "on some fancied notion of racial prestige." Davis was followed by Justin Moore, the Virginia attorney general. Moore emphasized that his state was in compliance with the trial court's order to equalize the schools. During Moore's argument, the Court recessed for the day and resumed on the following morning. When the Court reconvened, Moore described the circumstances surrounding the adoption of the Fourteenth Amendment. This line of argument proceeded along the same lines as Davis's argument. Lindsay Almond followed Justin Moore. Almond focused on the type of decree that should be entered if the petitioners prevailed, arguing that the cases should be remanded to the trial courts for the development of appropriate decrees.

After Almond completed his presentation, Marshall presented his rebuttal. It was a memorable display of Marshall at his best. Annoyed by the condescending tone of Davis's argument, Marshall urged the Court to consider the reasoning of *McLaurin*, in which it found that segregated education violated the Fourteenth

Amendment. The rationale of *McLaurin*, he believed, was directly applicable to lower-level schools and was dispositive of the issues raised in these cases. Responding directly to Davis, Marshall stated that the desegregation cases were indeed about "racial prestige," but not in the trivial manner that Davis implied. The "prestige" at stake involved a recognition of the fundamental constitutional rights of African Americans. Marshall urged the justices to remember that equality under the law was the critical issue and, contrary to the suggestions of his opponents, "the world will [not] fall apart" if segregation were declared unlawful. In a dramatic conclusion, Marshall issued a challenge to the justices, stating "the *only* way that this court can decide this case in opposition to our position . . . is to find that for some reason, Negroes are inferior to all other human beings" (italics added).

Assistant Attorney General J. Lee Rankin followed Marshall. James P. McGranery, attorney general under Truman, had filed an amicus brief in support of the NAACP's position. The McGranery brief spoke to the Court of the international consequences of racial discrimination in the United States: "It is in the context of the present world struggle between freedom and tyranny that the problem of racial discrimination must be viewed. . . . The existence of discrimination against minority groups in the United States has an adverse effect upon our relations with other countries. Racial discrimination furnishes grist for the Communist propaganda mills, and it raises doubts even among friendly nations as to the intensity of our devotion to the democratic faith." Herbert Brownell Jr., attorney general in the new Eisenhower administration, continued the federal government's support of the NAACP's position. Rankin represented the government in oral argument. He stated that the legislative history of the Fourteenth Amendment was inconclusive but that the overall import of the Fourteenth Amendment precluded the states from maintaining segregated schools. While Rankin's argument was significant, what was more significant was that his presence demonstrated the new administration's continued support for desegregation, at least before the Supreme Court. After Rankin concluded his presentation, the arguments proceeded in the Kansas case.

While the cases were pending before the Supreme Court, the Topeka school board voted to desegregate its schools. Robert Carter argued that the Kansas case had not become moot because the state claimed that it retained the authority to operate separate schools in districts that elected to preserve segregation. Carter was followed by Kansas Attorney General Paul Wilson, who affirmed that the Topeka school board had voted to end segregation. Wilson confirmed that Kansas believed that it retained the power, under the Fourteenth Amendment, to operate segregated schools should it wish to do so.

James Nabrit's arguments in *Bolling v. Sharpe* followed. Unlike the fact-intensive presentations in the other cases, Nabrit's argument was grounded entirely in legal theory. Relying on what became the "strict scrutiny" standard, Nabrit emphasized that the southern states did not have a compelling justification for classifying on the basis of race. The second round of arguments concluded with Louis Redding and Jack Greenberg's presentation of the Delaware cases. The Court recessed on December 9, 1953, at 2:40 P.M. The lawyers turned their attention to other matters. For the next five months, the entire nation waited for the Court's decision.

The decision in the school desegregation cases was announced on May 17, 1954, to an overflowing courtroom. Chief Justice Earl Warren read the opinion for a unanimous Court. Given the events that led up to *Brown*—trials lasting several days in Kansas, South Carolina, Virginia, Delaware, and the District of Columbia; testimony presented by dozens of witnesses; and several days of intense arguments in the Supreme Court over a two-year period—the opinion in *Brown* is remarkable in its brevity and simplicity. It was written in a straightforward style that could be understood by the most unsophisticated reader.

The opinion commenced with a recitation of the history of the cases from the trials to the arguments in the Supreme Court. The Court found, as a threshold matter, that the original intent of the framers of the Fourteenth Amendment on the question of segregated schools was not clear. The Court then traced the evolution of the separate but equal doctrine from *Plessy* through

McLaurin. After describing the importance of education to a democratic society, the Court framed the issue as whether "segregation of children in public schools solely on the basis of race . . . deprives the children of the minority group of equal educational opportunities." The Court found that it did, concluding that "to separate [black] children from others of similar age and qualifications generates a feeling of inferiority as to their status in the community that may affect their hearts and minds in ways unlikely ever to be undone." Relying heavily on the foundation developed in *Gaines*, *Sweatt*, and *McLaurin* as well as the social science evidence presented by Dr. Clark and others, the Court held that "separate educational facilities are *inherently* unequal" (italics added). With this pronouncement, America stood at the dawn of a new era in race relations.

CHAPTER 7

Anatomy of a Decision

Two Chief Justices, Eight Associate Justices, One Clerk, and a Special Assistant to the Attorney General

That new era in race relations was not inevitable. After the briefs, the oral arguments, the death of Chief Justice Vinson, the installation of Chief Justice Warren, and the extraordinary rearguments came the work: the decision making of the Court. How would the Court rule? That, of course, is always a mystery. The Supreme Court keeps, or at least tries to keep, its inner workings a secret. Its members do so in part to safeguard the Court's image as an impartial body whose decisions are based solely on the law and the arguments put before the Court. It would not do to show the extent to which the opinions of the nation's highest tribunal, like all other human endeavors, are the result of internal politicking, logrolling, and the peculiar interactions of distinct personalities. Today we know a fair amount about the behind-the-scenes workings of the Court in *Brown*. The surviving papers of different justices, particularly those of Justices Burton and Frankfurter combined with later reminiscences, tell us a good deal about the Court's deliberations between December 10, 1953, after the final oral arguments, and May 17, 1954, when the unanimous opinion was finally handed down. But the inclinations of the different justices were not all that well known when Thurgood Marshall first decided to represent the children of Harry Briggs in South Carolina. How did Marshall, Jack Greenberg, Robert Carter, Constance Motley, Spottswood Robinson, James Nabrit, and the others view their prospects for success before the high court in their fight against segregated schools? For that matter, how did John W. Davis and his associates see the Court? Could they have been confident that separate but equal would survive in the new atmosphere?

Both sides of course would have looked at the recent cases involving segregation in higher education. The NAACP had won important victories in 1950 in *Sweatt* and *McLaurin*. But these victories involving state universities in Texas and Oklahoma did not directly challenge the separate but equal doctrine that had developed in *Plessy* and that was now nearly half a century old. The Court had not yet faced the hard question; the day of reckoning was still postponed. What would the Court say regarding the central issue? Was state-mandated school segregation unconstitutional? Were segregated facilities inherently unequal? Neither side could be confident of the Court's answer. Both approached the question wondering what combination of their arguments and the differing judicial philosophies and personalities on the Court would win or lose the day in this high-stakes litigation.

If you were Marshall or Davis or any of the attorneys on either side of the six cases commonly referred to as *Brown*, your first act would probably have been to try and handicap the Court. Who were the justices? What kinds of arguments were they responsive to? What were their backgrounds, their biases? What was likely to convince them? Which arguments did they consider persuasive; which were sure losers? Attorneys on both sides would have recognized the importance of knowing the justices. We are going to try to do the same—at least briefly. It is crucial to understanding the decision. And we have the benefit of hindsight and more information than the *Brown* attorneys.

At first blush Marshall and his associates might have believed that they had cause for worry. Four justices—Hugo Black of Alabama, Tom Clark of Texas, Stanley Reed, and Chief Justice Fred Vinson, both of Kentucky—hailed from the Jim Crow South. Of course, Marshall and his associates knew that there were many white people from the South who questioned Jim Crow. Marshall had worked with white southerners in the fight against Jim

Crow. One white man from the South, Texas-born Columbia University law professor Charles Black, had played a major role in writing the NAACP's briefs in *Brown*. To believe that a man was a bigot simply because of where he was from, because of the accident of geography, was an unreasonable prejudice. Still . . .

Of the four southern justices, Hugo Black was perhaps the most enigmatic. He was an unlikely supporter of racial justice. Born to a middle-class Alabama family, Black's father was a store-keeper and a veteran of the Confederate army. He was a 1906 graduate of the University of Alabama's law school where, by all accounts, he was a brilliant student. Black's career included terms as a police court judge in Alabama and later as senator from that state. As a politician in Alabama, Black was not at all above play-ing the racial politics common to the state in the interwar years. In the 1920s he had been a member of the Ku Klux Klan. As a member of the Senate he took part in a filibuster against anti-lynching legislation in 1935. But there was another side to Hugo Black the politician. In the Senate he was a strong supporter of Roosevelt's economic reforms. Still, economic liberalism did not always translate into racial liberalism. Many populist southern politicians who supported protections for labor or relief from economic hardship also supported segregation. Nonetheless, Black had caught the eye of the NAACP's Walter White, who said of the Alabama senator, "He seemed to be an advanced guard of the new South we had dreamed of."

Black's support for the New Deal led Roosevelt to nominate him to the Supreme Court in 1937. On the Court Black proved to be a strong civil libertarian. He advocated what is called total incorporation, the view that the Fourteenth Amendment made every provision of the Bill of Rights applicable to the states. But Black also authored the majority opinion in the 1944 case *Kore-matsu v. United States*, a case that upheld the internment of Japanese Americans. Despite this, Black proved generally willing to strike down state practices involving discrimination against Negroes. As a member of the Court, he supported the decision in *Gaines*. He also voted with the majority to outlaw Oklahoma's grandfather clause in *Lane v. Wilson* (1939).

Chief Justice Vinson, who had been appointed by Truman in 1946, was less predictable on racial discrimination cases than Black. He had written the Court's unanimous opinions in *Sweatt*, *McLaurin*, and *Shelly* in 1948. Yet in 1953, Vinson would be the sole dissenter in *Barrows v. Jackson*, which held that a property owner could not sue in state court for damages when another had sold neighboring property to blacks. Earlier, in *Steele v. Louisville & Nashville Railroad* (1944), Vinson had joined with the Court in holding that under federal labor laws, an all-white union could not by contract force management to discriminate against blacks. But in 1952, Vinson, joined by Justices Reed and Minton, had dissented from the Court's majority opinion in *Brotherhood of Railroad Trainmen v. Howard* (1952) when it ruled that under federal law, a union could not demand that an employer fire black employees and replace them with white ones. Most observers agreed that Chief Justice Vinson's vote was a major question mark going into the *Brown* litigation.

Vinson's Kentucky colleague, Stanley Reed, might have seemed a bit more promising to Marshall and his associates. True, there is evidence of some private bigotry on his part, and he was generally considered conservative on civil rights and civil liberties issues. But he had voted to outlaw Texas' all white primaries in *Smith v. Allwright* (1944). He also voted with the Court's majority in *Morgan v. Commonwealth of Virginia* (1946), a case that held that the state of Virginia could not require segregated seating on interstate buses that were passing through the Old Dominion. Reed had also joined the Court's opinions in *Sweatt* and *McLaurin* and had also voted in *Henderson v. United States* (1950) to outlaw the practice of requiring black passengers in railroad dining cars to eat behind curtains, separated from other passengers. And in *District of Columbia v. John R. Thompson Co., Inc.* (1953), Reed had voted to uphold a Reconstruction-era municipal statute outlawing racial discrimination in restaurants. His vote in *Thompson* came despite some reported private misgivings. He is reported to have commented on the case, "Why—why, this means that a nigra [*sic*] can walk into the restaurant at the Mayflower Hotel and sit down to eat at the table right next to Mrs. Reed!"

The fourth southern justice, Texan Tom Clark, had been a member of the Court for three years when *Brown* was argued the first time. He was appointed by Truman in 1949. Clark tended to support desegregation. As attorney general under Truman, he had the Justice Department file an amicus brief supporting the NAACP's position in *Shelly v. Kraemer.* On the bench Clark joined the pro-desegregation majorities in *Sweatt, McLaurin,* and *Henderson.* Marshall and his colleagues might have expected a sympathetic hearing from Clark.

If the southern justices were hard to read, one of the justices from the Midwest might have looked promising to Marshall and his associates. Justice Harold Hitz Burton had been nominated by Truman to the high court in 1945. Burton had served as mayor of Cleveland and senator from Ohio. He had received a good deal of support from black voters and the NAACP during his Ohio political career. As a senator, Burton supported a constitutional amendment to abolish the poll tax and legislation to establish the Fair Employment Practices Commission, designed to prevent employment discrimination. Burton had been born in Boston. A Republican from a Massachusetts family, Burton was a graduate of Bowdin College and the Harvard Law School. We can easily imagine Marshall hoping that Burton, a Republican from Massachusetts, was steeped in that party and region's Yankee abolitionist tradition, a tradition that harkened back to Charles Sumner and the antebellum fight for equal rights. True, Justice Brown of *Plessy* had also been a Republican with a New England background. And Oliver Wendell Holmes, also a New England Republican and a veteran of the Union army, regularly voted to uphold Jim Crow legislation joining with the Court's majorities in *Berea* and *Giles,* among others (see chapter 2). Still, Burton's party and his native region might have given some grounds for encouragement. And Burton had voted to support desegregation in the major postwar cases, *Shelly, Sweatt, McLaurin,* and *Henderson.*

Moreover, Burton had demonstrated a willingness to use the Fourteenth Amendment to police state action in a way that was somewhat ahead of his contemporaries on the Court. In 1947

Burton had authored an important dissent in *Louisiana ex rel. Francis v. Resweber, Sheriff, et al. Francis* involved the case of Willie Francis, a sixteen-year-old African American youth in Louisiana who had been sentenced to die in the state's electric chair. On the original occasion of Francis's scheduled execution, the electric chair failed to kill him even though the executioner had pulled the switch and electricity did pass through Francis's body. Francis appealed that a second execution would be cruel and unusual punishment. A majority of the Supreme Court agreed with the state of Louisiana that the state had a right to reschedule the execution. Burton dissented. He argued for a strong reading of the Fourteenth Amendment, one that would make the state of Louisiana respect the Eighth Amendment's prohibition on cruel and unusual punishment. His dissent also argued the cruelty of the repeated execution. Burton's strong reading of the Fourteenth Amendment probably seemed like a favorable sign to the desegregation advocates. At the very least, he was not likely to be overly responsive to the states' rights argument when he believed the states were violating rights guaranteed under the Fourteenth Amendment.

Despite all of this, Burton was not an automatic vote for desegregation. Early in his career on the high court, he had disappointed civil rights supporters as the only dissenter in *Morgan* (cited earlier). Burton argued in his dissenting opinion that Virginia's requirement for segregated seating on buses did not unduly burden interstate commerce, the basis for the majority decision. He also expressed the view that if national law should prohibit segregation on interstate buses, that law should result from congressional legislation, not judicial decision. In all, although Burton had a record that was generally sympathetic to civil rights, the posture of the case, the way the legal issues were framed, and a reluctance to go beyond what he saw as the proper judicial role could cause him to vote to uphold segregation.

Sherman Minton was from downstate Indiana, not exactly a hotbed of racial liberalism. Minton, who had studied law at Indiana and Yale Universities, had served a term in the Senate between 1935 and 1941. A strong supporter of the New Deal,

Minton was appointed to the Seventh Circuit Court of Appeals by Roosevelt in 1941. In 1949 Truman nominated him to the Supreme Court. Minton had supported desegregation decisions in *Sweatt, McLaurin, Henderson,* and other cases. But Minton had also authored the dissent in *Brotherhood of Railroad Trainmen v. Howard.* In that case Minton argued that as a private organization, a railroad union had the right to discriminate against Negroes. How might Minton vote on the difficult question of school desegregation?

The next justice that both sides might have considered was Robert Jackson. From New York, Jackson held the distinction of being the last justice of the Supreme Court to have become a lawyer by "reading" the law. He learned the law in a manner that was common in the nineteenth century (see chapter 4): by clerking for an attorney and reading law in his spare time. A longtime supporter of Franklin Roosevelt, Jackson was appointed solicitor general in 1938. Roosevelt nominated him to the Supreme Court in 1941. Jackson took a leave of absence from the high court to serve as chief U.S. prosecutor during the Nuremberg trials. Jackson had voted with pro-desegregation majorities in *Sweatt, McLaurin, Henderson,* and the other postwar cases.

Marshall and his associates might have felt some confidence that they would get the support of William O. Douglas. Douglas, who was from the state of Washington, had studied law at Columbia University. A brilliant legal mind, Douglas practiced law at the blue-chip Wall Street law firm Cravath, Swaine, and Moore after law school. His later career then took him to teaching positions at Columbia and Yale law schools. Roosevelt appointed him as chairman of the Securities and Exchange Commission in 1937. Roosevelt later appointed him to the Supreme Court in 1939. Douglas tended to take a strongly liberal view on questions of economic regulation when they appeared before the Court. On cases involving race, he tended to be a reliable vote in favor of desegregation.

Felix Frankfurter, as we will see, would end up playing a pivotal role in *Brown.* Yet, it might not have been totally clear at the beginning of *Brown* how Frankfurter would come down in the tough and controversial case. Let's be clear: Frankfurter was a foe of racial discrimination. He had been a counsel for the NAACP and a teacher and patron of Charles Hamilton Houston. He was on a first-name basis with the NAACP's Walter White. As an associate justice, Frankfurter had appointed the first black law clerk to the Supreme Court, William T. Coleman, for the 1948–1949 term. Furthermore, Frankfurter had voted with pro-desegregation majorities in the postwar cases that led up to *Brown*. For Frankfurter racial discrimination was a violation of the very idea of American democracy.

Yet, Frankfurter had a certain reticence about the use of judicial power. Some students of Frankfurter's life have argued that that reticence might have stemmed from a feeling of being something of an outsider in American society. That feeling was reinforced in the WASP-dominated, often genteelly (and occasionally not so genteelly) anti-Semitic world of the early twentieth-century elite bar. Frankfurter and his parents were Austrian Jews who had immigrated to the United States in 1894. Frankfurter attended New York's City College and the Harvard Law School. Frankfurter taught at Harvard between 1913 and 1939 and was known as both a brilliant legal mind and a legal scholar well versed in history and other disciplines that might illuminate the law. Roosevelt nominated him to the Supreme Court in 1939. Frankfurter's strong advocacy of judicial restraint in part dovetailed with the New Deal philosophy. Roosevelt's New Deal had initially been hampered by the Supreme Court, which pronounced much of the early New Deal economic legislation unconstitutional. Many supporters of the New Deal consequently came to be advocates of judicial restraint, giving legislatures broad latitude to develop policy. That was certainly Frankfurter's view. In *Francis*, the case involving the faulty electric chair (cited earlier), Frankfurter had expressed the hope that the Louisiana governor would commute the youth's death sentence. But his opinion also indicated that the Court should not intervene.

Whether Frankfurter's relative judicial conservatism resulted from a sense of being an outsider, or whether it might be attributed to New Deal liberalism, it was an important part of Frankfurter's life on the bench. It influenced his view, for example, that the Fourteenth Amendment only applied parts of the Bill of Rights to the states, not all of the Bill of Rights as Justice Black believed. In fact, Frankfurter and Black had an often strained relationship, fueled in part by their different constitutional visions. Frankfurter saw judicial restraint as necessary in a democracy. Observers of his life have noted how the justice contrasted American democracy favorably with the aristocratic Austria he had observed in his childhood. A private letter to a Baltimore attorney, Reuben Oppenheimer, may have best indicated the associate justice's views on the role of courts in a democratic society: "The essence of democracy, as you are the last person who needs to be told, is the antithesis of the *Fuhrer Prinz*. Democracy does however imply that the good sense and decency of the mass of mankind must be actively evoked."

For Marshall and his associates, Frankfurter must have caused some anxiety. Which Frankfurter would prevail in the *Brown* litigation? Would the decision be made by the staunch foe of discrimination, the associate justice who had given legal advice to the NAACP and who had taken the unheard of step of hiring a Negro clerk? Or would the decision be made by the reluctant jurist, who felt that courts should have a circumscribed role in a democratic society?

The final member of the Court was Earl Warren. President Eisenhower appointed the former California governor to fill the vacancy left after the death of Chief Justice Vinson. Frankfurter represented the law's intellectual side, a life lived at the Harvard Law School amid the great legal minds of the day—First Amendment scholar Zechariah Chafee or Roscoe Pound, the proponent of sociological jurisprudence. Earl Warren was of a different stripe. He was from the rough-and-tumble world of state politics, a pragmatic world of give and take, deals and compromises. Warren was a graduate of the law school at the University of California at Berkeley. A former California attorney general and governor, he ran for vice president on the Republican ticket with Thomas Dewey in 1948. In 1952 he helped Dwight Eisenhower get the Republican nomination for president. Eisenhower first offered Warren the post of solicitor general as a reward for his support. That offer was made in August of 1953. With Vinson's death in September, Eisenhower instead nominated Warren as chief justice.

How did Warren look to the litigants? He was going to take part in the decision—the reargument insured that. Where did he stand on civil rights? Warren, as we have mentioned, supported the internment of Japanese Americans during the war. Early in Warren's political career he had been a member of an organization called Native Sons of the Golden West, an avowedly anti-Asian organization. Still, West Coast prejudices were different from those of other regions. There were certainly whites on the West Coast with strong anti-Asian prejudices who seemed comfortable with the notion of equal rights for Afro-Americans. Warren seems to have been of this stripe. He would remark, in his later years, that as a child he went to school with Negroes and that neither he nor his parents objected. As early as 1938 he wanted to appoint a black attorney to the state attorney general's staff. And Governor Warren supported antidiscrimination legislation. Toward the end of World War II, Warren also warned Californians that they would have to accept the returning Japanese Americans. In all, Warren probably looked favorable to Marshall and his associates.

All in all, the Court might not have looked too bad to Marshall and his colleagues. The Court had given the NAACP important victories in *Shelly*, the higher education cases, and other cases involving desegregation. The justices did not appear to be hostile, at least not flagrantly hostile to desegregation claims. Nonetheless, *Brown* was different. To accept the NAACP's view, the justices would have to be willing to take the radical step of taking on *Plessy* and doing it in a highly sensitive area, one involving the nation's children. Would the justices have the courage to do so, or would they blink when confronted with such a challenging constitutional and social dilemma?

Ordinarily we would end our discussion of court personalities here with these brief descriptions of the justices. But two other individuals who played an important role in the *Brown* deliberations deserve mention. The first is Alexander Bickel, who served as a clerk to Justice Frankfurter. Clerks are recent law school graduates who act as research assistants to judges. Those who serve as clerks to Supreme Court justices are invariably an elite among the elite, top graduates of the most selective law schools, almost invariably former editors of law reviews. By dint of their law school records and their service as Supreme Court clerks, they are destined for eminence in the legal profession, partnerships in major firms, professorships in elite law schools. Not a few of them will return to the Supreme Court itself in later life as justices; three of the current justices are former Supreme Court clerks. What do they do? It varies. Some justices have scarcely used their clerks at all. There is, for example, an apocryphal story that Justice Oliver Wendell Holmes believed that the chief function of his clerks was to accompany him on his afternoon walks, his constitutional if you will. At the other extreme, it is an open secret that some clerks have played major roles in writing decisions. Certainly most justices have recognized that the extremely bright and well-educated individuals who get Supreme Court clerkships can serve as more than simple research assistants. They can help frame the debate on cases, act in the role of devil's advocate, presenting the strongest possible legal or policy arguments for one side or the other in a particular legal controversy. And they can bring their considerable intellects and training to bear in an attempt to answer unique questions posed by particular controversies. That, as we will see, was the role played by Alexander Bickel.

Bickel came from a background not unlike Frankfurter's. Born in Romania of Jewish parents, Bickel would follow Frankfurter's path: an undergraduate education in New York's City College, law school at Harvard. Bickel was editor of the law review at Harvard and was hired as Frankfurter's law clerk in 1952. Bickel would play a critical role in *Brown* and later go on to a distinguished career as a legal scholar, teaching first at Harvard and later at Yale Law School. He would remain in close contact with Frankfurter, his mentor and friend, for the rest of the justice's life.

Philip Elman was another person who played an important behind-the-scenes role in the Court's deliberations on *Brown*. At the time *Brown* was argued, Elman was a special assistant to the attorney general in the solicitor general's office. Elman authored the federal government's briefs supporting desegregation in *Brown*. From 1941 to 1942 he had been Justice Frankfurter's clerk. Like Frankfurter, a product of City College and Harvard Law School, Elman would remain close to the justice long after his clerkship. Indeed Frankfurter would refer to Elman as his "clerk for life." Because of his close relationship with Frankfurter, Elman was able to play a role in influencing the decision in *Brown*. His role was little known at the time but has become, as we shall see, more controversial in recent years.

———

Seventeen Long Months:
The Dance of Deliberation

After the first set of oral arguments in December of 1952, Frankfurter would emerge as the key figure on the Court in shaping the high court's deliberations and ultimately the final opinion that would be handed down by the new chief justice, Earl Warren, in May of 1954. A word of caution might be in order here. Historians are prisoners of their sources. We see the past through the eyes of those who left the best records. The best discussion of the reactions of the different Supreme Court members to the *Brown* litigation comes from records left by Justice Frankfurter. These are augmented by records and subsequent discussions by his two former clerks, Bickel and Elman. These records reveal the pivotal role played by the Harvard professor turned associate justice. Might he have magnified his role somewhat? We cannot say definitively. We do know that the record clearly indicates that Frankfurter played an important part in giving his brethren on the Court a history of the Fourteenth Amendment that provided more support for a judicial role in desegregation than had previously existed. Frankfurter was also instrumental in getting supportive amicus briefs from the Truman and Eisenhower justice departments as well as playing a major part in getting the second round of briefs and oral arguments in *Brown*. Probably more than any other member of the Court, Frankfurter was responsible for the ultimate unanimous decision in the case.

From the beginning, Frankfurter strongly believed that a decision in favor of school desegregation, one that would take the radical step of in effect overturning *Plessy*, should be unanimous; the Court should speak with one voice. Anything less would invite uncertainty, recrimination, indeed virtual rebellion from the segregationist South. If Frankfurter hoped for unanimity, the early signs were not at all promising. Although there was no formal vote after the first round of oral arguments, Frankfurter was convinced that at least four of his colleagues, Chief Justice Vinson and Justices Reed, Jackson, and Clark, would have sided with the states and voted against desegregation. An order for desegregation with four dissenters would, Frankfurter feared, be a disaster.

The four likely dissenters all had their different reasons. In an initial conference held on December 12, 1952, right after the first set of oral arguments, Vinson made it clear that he would vote to uphold the right of states to maintain segregated schools. Notes by Justices Jackson and Burton indicate that the chief justice had three reasons for his position. First he noted that Justice Harlan's dissent in *Plessy* had not mentioned school segregation. He also argued that separate but equal had been a long-standing precedent and that even Congress supported it with a statute requiring segregated schools in the District of Columbia. Finally Vinson had a political concern. If the NAACP's position was accepted, southern legislatures would call for the complete abolition of public schools in the South rather than allow integration.

Justice Reed indicated that he, too, would vote against desegregation. In the December 12 conference, Reed's racial bias had shown through. He argued that the South needed more time to adjust to the idea of integration. Reed also argued that Negroes were not thoroughly assimilated and that the framers of the Fourteenth Amendment did not intend to require school integration. While Reed was also willing to concede that the definition of equal protection could expand beyond the sensibilities of the framers, he also argued to his colleagues that since seventeen states had school segregation, the spirit of the times did not require a new reading of the Fourteenth Amendment.

Both Justice Clark and Justice Jackson were reluctant to have the Court enter the desegregation fray. Clark noted that the states had relied on the *Plessy* decision. They had built up their institutions, including public schools, on the assumption that they could maintain separate schools for the different races. The justice from Texas argued that it would be unfair to change the rules, by judicial edict at this point. He also expressed fear of virulent protest in the South should the Court rule in favor of school integration. Jackson indicated that he, too, was reluctant to overturn a stable body of law that had developed following *Plessy*. To do so would fly in the face of stare decisis, the view that established legal precedents should be allowed to stand. Jackson also expressed the view that the political issue of national desegregation was better resolved as the result of congressional legislation, not judicial opinion. Notes by Justice Burton also indicate that Jackson was largely unimpressed with the social science evidence that had been offered in support of school desegregation.

Frankfurter initially had four allies—Justices Burton, Black, Douglas, and Minton—who supported outlawing school segregation. Justice Burton wrote little about his position at the first conference. He did indicate, however, that he was inclined to reverse the lower court cases in *Brown* that had sustained the right of states to maintain segregated schools. He also noted that he wanted *Bolling v. Sharpe*, the District of Columbia case, to be reargued. Jackson's notes give us a bit more detail on this, suggesting that Burton's view was that desegregation should be accomplished in as easy a way as possible.

Justices Black and Douglas were strongly in favor of an immediate ruling ordering desegregation. The two justices were often personally at odds with each other, but in the school segregation cases, they formed an early alliance. Theirs was an uncompromising position. Segregation should be ended immediately. *Plessy* should be overruled. So strong was their position that Frankfurter feared that both justices were impractical radicals who would have rushed ahead with a decision supporting school integration regardless of how slim the majority or whether or not it was politically sustainable. Philip Elman would even claim later, in a 1987 interview with legal historian Norman Silber, that Douglas and particularly Black would have been just as happy if the Court had confirmed *Plessy*, sustained school segregation, and allowed the two to be the new Justices Harlan, the great dissenters. According to Elman, Black was torn between his view that the Fourteenth Amendment did not permit segregation and his fear of violent southern reaction to a pro-integration decision. Whatever the accuracy of Elman's observations, clearly Frankfurter, at the initial conference in December 1953, must have felt the need to rein in Black and Douglas's enthusiasm every bit as much as he saw the need to change the votes of the justices inclined to uphold segregated schools.

If Burton was a quietly reliable and unproblematic vote for desegregation and Black and Douglas were the imprudent wild men who had to be restrained until the appropriate time, Minton turned out to be a bit of welcome relief. Although Minton had generally supported desegregation, he did dissent in *Brotherhood of Railroad Trainmen*. Another potentially troubling vote was his dissent in *Terry et al. v. Adams et al.* (1953), another Texas white primary case. Although the dissent was made on fairly narrow technical grounds, it was still potentially troubling. Nonetheless, on *Brown*, Minton clearly supported the NAACP's position. He believed that the arguments of Marshall and his associates had clearly undermined *Plessy*'s foundation and that the 1896 case should be overruled.

With four likely dissenters, Frankfurter realized that an early decision in *Brown* would be a weak pro-integration decision, at best. It would lack the moral and political authority necessary to stand up to the political firestorm that would surely follow. Such weakness would invite defiance from the states. It might even invite a lack of enforcement from the entering Eisenhower administration. Surely Frankfurter the legal scholar was keenly aware of the Court's ultimate institutional impotence. At the beginning of the Republic, Alexander Hamilton had reminded the American people that the Court lacked both the sword and the purse.

It could determine the law, but it depended on Congress and the president to provide the money and the police power necessary to enforce the law. A premature, divided Court could provoke national resistance. Frankfurter wanted more time. Fortunately, none of the justices was pushing for a quick vote.

Frankfurter took advantage of the judicial delay to draft a set of questions that might be used in a reargument. His colleagues accepted these with little change. *Brown* was restored to the calendar for reargument in October 1953. Some have argued that the new questions were primarily used as a delaying tactic to give Frankfurter more time to persuade his colleagues. Bickel would later note that that was Frankfurter's motive. Warren Burger, an assistant attorney general in 1953, believed that the reargument was intended to allow the Eisenhower Justice Department to have a say on what would surely be the most important Supreme Court decision of the former supreme commander's administration. Chief Justice Vinson believed that Frankfurter's additional questions and call for reargument were delaying tactics, but Frankfurter denied the charge in a note to Vinson, arguing that the rearguments and the new questions were necessary to allow the new Eisenhower Justice Department to state its position. Frankfurter noted this was especially important because the new administration would be in charge of the enforcement of any desegregation ruling that would come from the Court. In any event, the Court accepted Frankfurter's suggestions and indicated its interest in his five questions for reargument. These questions would later be put before the parties and amici in the case (see chapter 6). These questions reflected Frankfurter's concerns with the issues of the original intent of the Fourteenth Amendment with respect to school segregation. The questions also reflected Frankfurter's concern with the issue of implementation or remedy.

Frankfurter's questions betrayed his unease with what was then the conventional wisdom concerning the Fourteenth Amendment. He was concerned with the intentions of the drafters of that constitutional provision and what the amendment had to say concerning school integration. The justice also had another concern. Did the framers of the Fourteenth Amendment intend the courts or Congress to be the branch of government most concerned with enforcing the amendment? This was an issue of particular importance if Frankfurter were to persuade Justice Jackson to sign on to an opinion supporting school desegregation.

What was the source of Frankfurter's unease? We have mentioned earlier the cynical tragic-era view of Reconstruction, which had become the dominant view of that historical era in the early twentieth century (see chapter 2). That view certainly influenced the justices. Justice Black, for example, reportedly believed that Claude Bowers's *The Tragic Era,* one of the more vivid of the anti-Reconstruction tomes, was one of the best works of history that he had read. It did not stop Black from supporting desegregation in *Brown,* but it certainly cast the framers of the Fourteenth Amendment in an extremely unfavorable light. More worrisome, from the point of view of the school desegregation litigation, was a 1908 study, Horace Edgar Flack's *The Adoption of the Fourteenth Amendment.* At the time *Brown* was being litigated, Flack's study was the standard reference work on the legislative history of the Fourteenth Amendment. It was considered the authoritative treatment of the subject and frequently cited in the Court's opinions and in briefs in constitutional cases. *The Adoption of the Fourteenth Amendment* incorporated much of the cynical or tragic-era view of Reconstruction in its pages. The Fourteenth Amendment was seen largely as a vehicle to enhance the power of the northern states. What was perhaps most unsettling, from Frankfurter's point of view, was that the Fourteenth Amendment was seen largely as a grant of power to the Congress to enact civil rights legislation. The idea that the amendment created a strong legal principle of equality before the law was, at best, understated in the volume. With Flack as the reigning authority on the history of the Fourteenth Amendment, it would be hard to persuade the doubting justices to rule in favor of desegregation.

Frankfurter gave Alexander Bickel the task of doing original research on the legislative history of the Fourteenth Amendment. Bickel spent a good part of the summer of 1953 doing research in the *Congressional Globe* (which had the records of the Thirty-ninth Congress), examining the debates over the proposed amendment. Bickel produced a major study on the subject, which would later be published as an article in the *Harvard Law Review*. What he found was helpful. Bickel's study stressed that the Fourteenth Amendment was meant to insure the equality of the different races as a matter of law, thus giving emphasis to judicial remedies for unequal treatment, a contrast with Flack's emphasis on congressional power. Bickel's research also helped shape an idea that would play an important part in the ultimate decision in *Brown*, the notion that the framers had used broad language that might adapt the amendment beyond the terms of the 1866 debates. Bickel expressed this view in an August 1953 memo to Justice Frankfurter:

> Little regard was had for language by a Congress not notable for the presence in its membership of very many brilliant men. A blunderbuss was simply aimed in the direction of existing evils in the South, on which all eyes were fixed. There were a few muted warnings that the language was broad, but in the hurry of it in the end no one cared much. The dangers to which broad language might lead were distant anyway. It was preposterous to worry about unsegregated schools, for example, when hardly a beginning had been made at educating Negroes at all.

Some of Bickel's historical discussion would ultimately find its way into the Warren opinion.

Frankfurter's questions showed a concern not only with historical justification for an overruling of *Plessy;* the justice was also concerned with the question of practical implementation and how the issue of implementation or remedy would affect the votes of the other justices. If the Court ruled in favor of school desegregation, would it have to order immediate integration, or could there be some period of gradual adjustment? This question would be one of major concern to the NAACP. Their previous successes had hinged in part on the conception of constitutional rights as both personal and present rights. The Court, in essence, would be asking, if the plaintiffs in *Brown* should win, could there be a remedy that would permit substantial delay in the desegregation of schools? Indeed, depending on how lacking in immediacy the remedy would be, the question was whether these rights were really personal. If the remedy were too gradual, the children in whose names the suits were brought might live out their school-age years before desegregation would ever take hold.

This suggestion of the separation of constitutional right and remedy was a new view urged in the 1952 amicus curiae on behalf of the United States. The brief was authored by Philip Elman, who would later note that he borrowed the notion from the use of equitable remedies in antitrust law, a branch of law dealing with monopoly and unfair trade competition. In later life Elman would say of his suggestion, "It was entirely unprincipled, it was just plain wrong as a matter of constitutional law, to suggest that someone whose personal constitutional rights were violated should be denied relief." Nonetheless, Elman maintained that the bifurcation of right and remedy made the unanimous decision in *Brown* possible.

Elman's activities went beyond his brief writing and his introduction of the notion of a bifurcation between right and remedy. He was evidently in active consultation with Frankfurter during the course of the case. The two men were professionally and personally close and discussed the case. During 1953, as Elman was helping to draft the Justice Department's supplemental brief for the *Brown* reargument, he was in regular contact with Frankfurter, discussing the case and the reactions of the different justices to the arguments that had been advanced. This sort of ex parte communication is considered a violation of legal ethics. It is looked upon, and indeed in this case was, an attempt to influence the Court outside of regular channels. In later years, when Elman's role became better known, it would generate considerable controversy about Elman's role and indeed Frankfurter's conduct. In his 1987 interview with Norman Silber, Elman justified his departure from the conventional ethical standards of the legal profession:

I didn't consider myself a lawyer for a litigant. I considered it a cause that transcended ordinary notions about propriety in a litigation. This was not a litigation in the usual sense. The constitutional issue went to the heart of what kind of country we are, what kind of Constitution and Supreme Court we have; whether, almost a century after the Fourteenth Amendment was adopted, the Court could find the wisdom and courage to hold that the amendment meant what it said, that black people could no longer be singled out and treated differently because of their color, that in everything it did, government had to be color-blind. I don't defend my discussions with Frankfurter; I just did what I thought was right, and I'm sure he didn't give it much thought. I regarded myself, in the literal sense, as an amicus curiae.

From his conversations with Frankfurter, Elman gained some valuable insights. He learned that the justice and some of his colleagues were uneasy with the way the NAACP's lawyers had framed the case. Marshall and his associates had put the case before the Court as an all-or-nothing proposition. The NAACP's issue was direct: Can separate facilities be equal? Framed in such a way, the case lacked the middle ground, the wiggle room that some of the justices were seeking. Elman also had the benefit of Frankfurter's knowledge that there was only a bare majority for desegregation. Elman would later argue that his idea of separating right and remedy was an astute move that capitalized on the internal politics of the Court and on the confidential musings of its members.

It would be fair to say that Elman had a highly egotistical personality, and it is difficult to know the extent to which he inflated his role in *Brown*. He is almost undoubtedly correct in stating that the separation of right from remedy helped pave the way for the ultimate unanimous decision. Other participants have disputed the extent to which Elman could take credit for this development. In the 1990s, Herbert Brownell, who had been Eisenhower's attorney general during the *Brown* litigation, indicated that Elman had overstated his role in developing the bifurcation. Still, Justice Frankfurter gave great credit to his former clerk: "Elman was the real strategist. . . . [He] block[ed] the leaders of the colored people who proposed a remedy which not only would not have succeeded with the Court [and] would have had disastrous consequences. . . . Phil . . . proposed . . . that the Court should not become a school board for the whole country, that . . . non-discrimination . . . should be left primarily to the local school boards [and] . . . any dissatisfaction with their plans should go to the local federal courts."

Frankfurter's role went beyond his request for Bickel's historical research and his conversations with Elman. During the 1953 term, Frankfurter took a number of steps designed to move his more reluctant colleagues toward a favorable vote. In July of 1953 he requested that Helen Newman, then the Supreme Court's librarian, gather information on the voluntary school integration in Phoenix, Arizona, presumably to show his colleagues that that effort was working well. Frankfurter also played a key role in getting the new Eisenhower Justice Department to file an amicus brief in the case. In the summer of 1953, both Chief Justice Vinson and Justice Black expressed doubts about inviting the attorney general to submit briefs for the rehearing. Vinson argued against the invitation on the grounds that doing so was simply a matter of public relations or tactics—a continuation of his contention that Frankfurter was trying to steer the case in a pro-desegregation direction. Black feared that bringing in the Justice Department would further enmesh the case in national politics. But Frankfurter noted on June 8, 1953, "The reason for having the government appear was not a matter of tactics or 'public-relations.' The Conference agreed with the point which Bob Jackson made very early in our deliberations, that the new Administration, unlike the old, may have the responsibility of carrying out a decision full of perplexities; it should therefore be asked to face that responsibility as part of our process of adjudication."

Frankfurter prevailed. The new administration was invited to provide a new amicus brief for the United States. Frankfurter's actions and those of the other members of the Court during the summer of 1953 were done with the anticipation of reargument in October. Chief Justice Vinson's death in September and the appointment of Earl Warren as chief justice in October further delayed proceedings. Oral arguments for the rearguments would finally begin on December 7, 1953, a year after the original oral arguments.

The arguments proceeded. For three fateful days in December 1953, the lawyers had argued the two sides of the six cases, two consolidated into one from Delaware, and one each from Kansas, South Carolina, Virginia, and the District of Columbia. The lawyers were sharp, the questions by the justices tough. It would have been difficult to predict the outcome based on the questions. To illustrate this point, South Carolina's counsel Robert Figg estimated from the questions that Justices Black and Douglas would vote to overturn *Plessy*, that Justices Frankfurter, Jackson, and Reed would vote to uphold segregation, and that if push came to shove, Justice Clark would go along. John Davis thought that only Justices Black and Douglas were lost causes.

If Davis and Figg could have attended the conference held right after the oral arguments, they would have been disheartened. Once again we do not have official minutes, but we do have surviving notes from Justices Burton and Frankfurter. They reveal much concerning the mood of the justices. The new chief justice wanted to directly overrule *Plessy*. Segregation was based on the notion that black people were inferior to whites, a notion to which the Court could no longer give expression. Warren was concerned about being sensitive in fashioning a remedy, but Warren's views were clear: segregation must go. Douglas agreed. He also expressed the view that the Court should move quickly and settle the constitutional issue. Douglas believed that the Court could be flexible with its remedy. Justice Minton supported Warren's position. Separate but equal had to go, but the remedy had to be flexible and account for local circumstances. Perhaps surprisingly, Justice Clark was willing to go along with the abolition of school segregation, so long as the question of the remedy involved local flexibility. Justice Black's views had not changed; he was for ending the formula of separate but equal and the practice of school segregation immediately.

Justice Reed was just as certain that the rule of *Plessy* should survive. Separate but equal was a perfectly workable formula if the courts and the governmental agencies they sometimes over-saw would take the equality portion of the formula seriously. So long as there was real equality, there could be no denial of liberty.

Justice Jackson still argued that the principle of stare decisis counseled against overruling *Plessy*, for there was insufficient historical evidence to support that conclusion. Nonetheless, he was in favor of overruling *Plessy* as a political matter, but if the Court were to overrule *Plessy* on that basis, he would insist that the Court be open about it. Moreover, he thought that if the Court were to decide *Brown* this way, it should do it in one fell swoop, and the remedy should be decided, too, and not left for another day's decision.

Justice Frankfurter agreed with Jackson that history did not resolve the question of how the framers of the Fourteenth Amendment felt about segregated schools, and like Jackson, he wanted to overrule *Plessy*. In this conclusion, his position was un-changed from his position after the first argument in *Brown*. Nonetheless, perhaps because of his desire to see the Court rule with as close as possible to one voice, he counseled caution and deliberate decision making. There was no need to make a deci-sion quickly.

The unanimity that Frankfurter sought remained elusive. The Court was still not speaking with one voice. Although Burton's opinion at this first conference was not recorded, he presumably still held to his earlier view that *Plessy* should simply be over-turned. Warren, Douglas, and Minton were in favor of overrul-ing *Plessy* but also wanted to allow for local flexibility in fashioning remedies. Clark had come around to support a ruling for desegregation, but only if there were local flexibility on the remedy. Black was for outlawing segregation, but if his views had not changed, he was not in favor of local flexibility. Jackson was willing to outlaw segregated schools but only if the Court were to proclaim that the decision was not grounded in principle but instead the Court's own view of right and wrong. He did not favor local flexibility. Frankfurter wanted to end the rule of *Plessy* but thought it necessary to be gentle with the public, and Reed wanted to hold out in favor of *Plessy*. If this was not a potential mess, it was certainly potential confusion. It was probably just as well that the Court decided to wait, to flesh out the issues, to let them simmer before rendering a decision.

Frankfurter made efforts to achieve a more workable consensus on the part of his brethren. On January 15, 1954, the justice circulated a typewritten memo to the rest of the Court. Frankfurter evidently typed it himself to insure the utmost secrecy. In that memo he urged the separation of the constitutional principle that the state could not maintain segregated schools from the question of how desegregation should be implemented. It was a memo calling for the separation of right and remedy, perhaps reflecting his conversations with Elman. In the memo Frankfurter noted how, in the area of antitrust, the courts employed a balancing of considerations examining the alleged wrongs done to a plaintiff, presumably a victim of unfair competition, against the public consequences of remedies that were too immediate. Frankfurter also cautioned that simply declaring a practice unconstitutional would not be a magic wand, that there were physical, educational, and budgetary considerations that had to be examined. Frankfurter suggested that perhaps the Supreme Court could employ special masters empowered to oversee the gradual integration of formerly segregated school systems.

The question of how integration might be implemented also occupied Justice Burton, among others. Burton had his clerk James R. Ryan, a 1951 graduate of the University of Pennsylvania Law School and a native of Oklahoma, draft a memo on the question of implementation. Ryan's memo suggested a short desegregation decision, leaving implementation up to local school boards. The Ryan memo also noted some potential ways that states might try to thwart a desegregation decision. These included withdrawal of financial support from school districts that were desegregating and even abandonment of public education as a state function. Ryan's memo would prove prophetic (see chapter 8).

It would be five months before the give-and-take of deliberation would come to a close. The new chief justice joined Frankfurter in the effort to fashion an opinion that could get unanimous support.

If the decision to end segregation would not be unanimous, Warren hoped at least that he might gain a consensus on remedy. Justice Jackson wanted to take the Court in another direction. His memorandum rejected the NAACP's social science evidence. He argued instead for reading the Fourteenth Amendment as a document of a general nature and one with commands that could change with changing times. The Jackson memo argued that Negroes themselves had changed since the adoption of the Fourteenth Amendment. They were no longer a client race, but were ready to stand alongside their white brethren. Because they were ready, they should be treated as ready, particularly with respect to something as important as education. In this way, the Court might justify what Jackson maintained was an essentially political decision.

When the Court finally voted on *Brown* sometime in late February or early March 1954, it was clear that the decision would be in favor of ending school desegregation. What was not clear was how many opinions would be written. Justice Reed still did not agree that segregation should be overruled, and it was unclear whether Justices Jackson and Frankfurter might issue concurrences. What was clear is that Chief Justice Warren had taken on the task of writing the opinion for the anticipated majority, that there was general agreement that segregation would be declared unconstitutional, and that the opinion would not order the immediate desegregation of schools.

It would take until May 7 for Chief Justice Warren to circulate a draft of his opinion in *Brown*. There were actually two opinions, for *Bolling v. Sharpe*, involving the District of Columbia, could not be decided on precisely the same grounds as the state cases. There was not a good deal of disagreement with it, and indeed, the only quarters from which Warren anticipated trouble were in the persons of Justices Frankfurter, Jackson, and Reed. Frankfurter would turn out to be little trouble, as he had recognized all along the dangers of a divided Court. It was known that Jackson was preparing a concurring opinion, but his efforts had been compromised by a heart attack on March 30 and a long period of hospitalization. Moreover, when the draft made its way to the hospital, Warren's efforts seemed acceptable to Jackson, for he made only two suggested changes; Warren accepted one of these, and Jackson accepted Warren's draft. Thus, if there were to be a real problem, it would be Justice Reed.

Just as Warren had been preparing the majority opinion while Jackson worked on a concurrence, Reed had been preparing a dissent. Like Justice Jackson, he had released a memorandum to the Court in February outlining his views. The memorandum put in writing Reed's view that the case law following *Plessy* had established the principle that separate was required in fact to be equal, not that separate could not ever be equal. In Reed's view, the government's job more generally and the Court's job more specifically was not to amalgamate segregated schools, no matter how slowly, but to be sure that the demands of true equality were met. This memorandum was to have been the basis for a dissent by Reed, but it was never released to the public. Sometime after he had been assured of the assent of the other seven justices, Chief Justice Warren approached Reed, displayed a concern with the sensitivities of the South, and wondered aloud whether the country's interests were better served by unanimity in the face of predictable opposition, rather than an individual opinion that might encourage southern recalcitrance. Reed conceded, agreeing to join the majority. Later on, Frankfurter would thank Reed for making the decision unanimous: "As a citizen of the Republic, even more than as a colleague, I feel deep gratitude for your share in what I believe to be a great good for our nation."

Chief Justice Warren's opinions in the *Brown* case were finally approved at a conference of the Court on May 15. Two days later, on May 17, 1954, the Supreme Court issued its opinions in *Brown v. Board of Education* and *Bolling v. Sharpe*. The day had already been punctuated by one extraordinary event, the return to the Court of Justice Jackson seven weeks after his heart attack. While a seven-week recuperative period following a heart attack may be long by our standards at the beginning of the twenty-first century, it was quite short in 1954. The announcement of the decision in *Brown* would be not a simple piece of punctuation but a giant-sized exclamation point.

Separate But Equal Has No Place

The opinion in *Brown*, written by the new chief justice for a unanimous Court, was simple and yet rich. First, Chief Justice Warren explained the high-stakes nature of the gamble the NAACP and the states had taken in their appeals to the Court. In none of the cases was the issue of equality before the Court. Lower courts had found that the educational facilities in question were already equal or in the process of being equalized. In the university cases, *Gaines, Sweatt, McLaurin*, and the others, the Court had been able to avoid the question of whether or not segregation itself was inherently unequal. That ended with the *Brown* opinion. By explaining what he called "the common legal question" that drew these cases together, Warren confirmed that the Court would treat the issue as the NAACP had framed it, whether "segregated public schools are not 'equal' and cannot be made 'equal,'" and thus whether segregated public schools violated the Fourteenth Amendment's command of equal protection of the law.

Next Warren explained why the Court could not simply follow the original intent of the framers of the Fourteenth Amendment. On its face, the Court's request for a reargument in 1953 was, in part, motivated by a desire to learn more about the original intent and understanding of the equal protection clause. Lawyers on both sides had briefed the question fully and argued it ferociously, and reargument had been devoted in large measure to the history surrounding the framing, adoption, and ratification of the amendment. Nonetheless, the Court found itself in agreement with Bickel. The history seemed to be "at best . . . inconclusive."

How could this be? First, the debates on the equal protection clause were not at all one-sided. The most radical proponents intended for the clause to be read at its most expansive, "to remove all legal distinctions among 'all persons born or naturalized in the United States.'" The most obdurate opponents of the amendment intended for it to have as little effect as possible. Moreover, the Court found that what other members of Congress who proposed the amendment and of the state legislatures who ratified it may have intended could "not be determined with any degree of certainty."

Second, there had been little attention given to the issue of segregated public education during the debates on the Fourteenth Amendment. This was entirely understandable, the Court explained. The movement toward universal free public education had not yet taken hold in the South. Education for white children was largely a matter of private concern. For black children it was largely nonexistent. Even in the North, public education was but a distant cousin to what could be found in 1954. Compulsory attendance was "virtually unknown," and the curriculum was "usually rudimentary." Rural areas commonly had ungraded schools, and in many states the school year was a scant three months. "As a consequence," the Court explained, "it is not surprising that there should be so little in the history of the Fourteenth Amendment relating to its intended effect on public education."

If the history underlying the Fourteenth Amendment was not dispositive, nor was the jurisprudence interpreting the equal protection clause. *Plessy* itself had concerned transportation and not education. The Court had heard only seven cases involving equal protection and education. *Berea College v. Commonwealth of Kentucky* (1908) had merely declared the practice of separate but equal to be "many times decided." *Cumming v. Board of Education* (1899) and *Gong Lum v. Rice* (1927) were cases in which separate but equal as a doctrine had not been challenged. The NAACP had challenged the doctrine in *Gaines, Sipuel/Fisher, McLaurin,* and *Sweatt,* but in each case the Court had granted relief and yet had been able to avoid examination of the *Plessy* formula. Thus, the previous cases would not decide the issue presented by *Brown.*

The Warren opinion continued. If the Court would not resolve *Brown* by an appeal to the intentions of the framers of the Fourteenth Amendment in 1866, or by following *Plessy,* decided in 1896, it would be necessary to view equal protection and its role in public education in light of modern circumstances. Public education would be considered not in light of its role in the nineteenth century but instead "in the light of its full development and its present place in American life throughout the Nation."

Education was now "perhaps the most important function of state and local governments." Education, the Court recognized, is that which acculturates the young to good citizenship and enables their performance of basic public responsibilities. Education, the Court found, imposes cultural norms, awakens understanding of one's environment, and opens the door to economic participation in the society at large. Indeed, the Court said, "it is doubtful that any child may reasonably be expected to succeed in life if he is denied the opportunity of an education." True, the Court recognized, the states were under no obligation to provide at all for public education, but having done so, they were under an obligation to do so on equal terms, irrespective of race.

Warren presented the question clearly: "Does segregation of children in public schools solely on the basis of race, even though the physical facilities and other 'tangible' factors may be equal, deprive children of the minority group of equal educational opportunities?" He answered that question succinctly: "We believe that it does." *Brown*'s discussion of intangible factors was not written on a complete tabula rasa. In *Sweatt*, the Court had relied on intangible factors in determining that education at the segregated Texas law schools was unequal. In that case, the Court had compared "those qualities which are incapable of objective measurement but which make for greatness in a law school." *McLaurin*, too, had been a case in which the Court had measured intangible considerations, such as McLaurin's "ability to study, to engage in discussions and exchange views with other students, and, in general, to learn his profession."

Such intangible considerations, the Court found, "apply with added force to children in grade and high schools," for the effect of segregated education on black children was such as to "generate a feeling of inferiority as to their status in the community that may affect their hearts and minds in a way unlikely ever to be undone." The Court quoted with approval the finding of the three-judge panel that had held for the school board in Kansas:

Segregation of white and colored children in public schools has a detrimental effect upon the colored children. The impact is greater when it has the sanction of law; for the policy of separating the races is usually interpreted as denoting the inferiority of the negro group. A sense of inferiority affects the motivation of a child to learn. Segregation with the sanction of law, therefore, has a tendency to [retard] the educational and mental development of negro children and to deprive them of some of the benefits they would receive in a racial[ly] integrated school system.

The Court recognized that this finding was quite contrary to the one in *Plessy v. Ferguson*—that any connection between segregation and inferiority was merely in the minds of black people. The *Brown* Court explicitly noted that the *Plessy* Court had been without the benefit of modern science that supported the finding of stigmatization. Among such authorities were sociologists E. Franklin Frazier and Gunner Myrdal and a host of psychologists, including—for all the criticism of his doll test made by the lawyers for the states in the *Brown* case—Kenneth Clark.

The Court concluded "that in the field of public education the doctrine of 'separate but equal' has no place. Separate educational facilities are inherently unequal" and thus were in violation of the equal protection clause of the Fourteenth Amendment. As momentous as this statement was, and for all the implications it had for the future (Thurgood Marshall was heard to crow, "Free by Sixty-Three!"), it was a limited one. For one, the opinion did not extend beyond education; only separate *educational* facilities had been declared to be unequal. *Plessy* had not been directly overruled. But this limitation was only of a technical nature, for the psychosocial underpinnings of *Brown* were readily applicable to other areas, and inside the next two years the Supreme Court would apply the principle in *Brown* to state parks, public beaches and bathhouses, public golf courses, and public transportation. Marshall's prediction would prove to be vastly overoptimistic with respect to public education, but he was nonetheless right that *Brown* would prove the death knell for official state-sponsored segregation in all fields.

Brown also had a technical limitation. By its very language, the

Fourteenth Amendment only applied to the states ("No *state* shall . . . deny to any person within its jurisdiction the equal protection of the laws" (italics added), not the federal government. This limitation was addressed by *Brown*'s companion case, *Bolling v. Sharpe* (1954), which involved congressionally mandated school segregation in the District of Columbia. Under the Constitution, the District of Columbia is not a state and is subject to regulation by Congress. There is no express constitutional language requiring Congress to provide for equal protection of the laws. Nonetheless, the Court had previously found that the due process clause of the Fifth Amendment, which guarantees that the federal government cannot take life, liberty, or property without due process of law, required that the federal government treat individuals of different races equally. This became the basis for the decision in *Bolling*. In that case the Court noted that due process and equal protection were identical, but that they both stemmed from "our American ideal of fairness." The Court also noted that equal protection is a more explicit and a more narrow guarantee of fairness than due process. The Court had begun to develop a doctrine of equal protection from the due process clause in the Japanese internment cases *Korematsu* and *Hirabayashi*. In *Bolling*, the Court noted that racial discrimination "may be so unjustifiable as to be violative of due process."

Was a child's interest in pursuing an education a "liberty" protected from unfair restraint by the government? The answer was yes, for liberty under law "extends to the full range of conduct which the individual is free to pursue." If the case law had recognized that such liberties cannot be restricted "except for a proper governmental objective," *Bolling* established that segregated public education "is not reasonably related to any proper governmental objective." Thus the Court held that school segregation was an arbitrary deprivation of the liberty of black children in violation of the due process clause. Federally mandated segregated education was as unconstitutional as segregated schools maintained by state governments.

Brown, as well as *Bolling*, was limited in yet another and indeed most significant way. Both cases declared segregated education unconstitutional. Neither case specified a remedy. We now know, of course, why the opinion was silent on the subject. But at the time the Court simply offered reasoning that discussed "the considerable complexity" associated with formulating decrees in class action cases of such "wide applicability" and with such "great variety of local conditions." There would be yet another reargument, this one focused on the question of what remedy would be imposed. The Court would, of course, have available to it the views of the parties to the cases, but it invited the participation as amicus curiae not only of the Justice Department but also of the states requiring or permitting segregated public education.

Perhaps it was only fair to invite southern and other states allowing segregation to participate in the reargument out of which would emerge one year later, as *Brown II*, the opinion that would set forth the manner in which desegregation would take place. Yet it was ominous as well. Southern and border states had used every ounce of cleverness and determination at their disposal to maintain segregation in the years after *Gaines*. The failure of the Court to order immediate desegregation and the invitation to segregating states to help devise a desegregation formula promised more than wiggle room. It encouraged resistance, and it was clear from newspaper reports the day after *Brown* that resistance was promised by many of the southern states. Some states already had contingency plans in place to support segregated private schools or to end compulsory education altogether. Other states were merely studying such measures. There were also rumblings of resistance from southern members of Congress. The battle for a legal principle had been won. The war over remedy and effective implementation had scarcely begun.

CHAPTER 8

Brown II
"All Deliberate Speed"

Six months of conferences, cajoling, memos, drafting, and re-drafting had finally produced the Court's unanimous opinion declaring state-mandated segregation in public schools to be unconstitutional. It was a triumph for the decades of planning and preparation that had begun with early visionaries like Margold and Houston and that had been carried forward by able legal strategists and tacticians like Marshall, Motley, Greenberg, Black, Carter, Robinson, Nabrit, Redding, and the others. The decision also stood as a testament to the courage of parents like Oliver Brown, Harry and Liza Briggs, Sarah Bulah, and the other parents who dared, often at great personal risk, to challenge the prevailing racial order. The desegregation decision also represented a triumph for the new chief justice, Earl Warren. It put Warren's stamp on the Court with a decision of monumental significance at the beginning of his tenure. With *Brown* the stage would be set for the most active and controversial phase in the Supreme Court's history.

The *Brown* decision was momentous, but with respect to the issues of race and racial discrimination, even with respect to the issue of school segregation, the decision was hardly definitive. In many ways it fit Winston Churchill's observation during the Second World War immediately after the allied victory in North Africa. The British prime minister observed: "This is not the end, no it is not even the beginning of the end, but it is perhaps the end of the beginning." In a sense, *Brown* was the end of the beginning, the end of the idea as old as the Republic itself, that the law could formally discriminate—indeed totally exclude—on the basis of race and that the Constitution would support such discrimination. But if *Brown* proclaimed that that idea was unconstitutional, the decision hardly ended racial discrimination, even state-sponsored discrimination. What *Brown* did do was to act as a catalyst for a whole new phase of the civil rights movement. It would be a phase in which the champions of civil rights would continue the struggle for equal rights in the courts and in other venues. Members of the civil rights movement would find themselves confronting recalcitrant clerks at voter registration offices and gun-toting drivers enforcing segregation on municipal buses. They would challenge segregation at small-town lunch counters and risk their lives on the often dangerous back roads of the rural South. They would bring the movement to Washington D.C.'s Lincoln Memorial and ultimately the halls of Congress. Along the way the civil rights movement would encounter every conceivable kind of resistance from unofficial and official quarters.

The first part of that new phase would bring the civil rights movement back before the Supreme Court. The 1954 Warren opinion had simply pronounced school segregation unlawful. It did not address the question of how to dismantle the system of school segregation. That would be decided in another decision, generally known as *Brown II*, a necessary by-product of the Court's decision to separate right and remedy in the 1954 decision. The school desegregation cases were set over for another term for consideration of the appropriate remedy. The arguments in *Brown II* addressed the question of the specific nature of the remedy and the timetable for desegregation. The lawyers and consultants at the NAACP's headquarters debated among themselves. Kenneth Clark and Spottswood Robinson urged Marshall to insist on immediate implementation of the 1954 decision. A number of other advisers recommended a more gradual approach. Ultimately, Marshall and the other NAACP lawyers decided to argue that desegregation should commence promptly and be completed by 1956. The final round of the arguments in the school desegregation cases commenced on April 11, 1955, lasting for more than thirteen hours over four days. Just over a month later, on May 31, 1955, the final *Brown* decision, *Brown II*, was issued. In a compromise position, one that would allow decades to pass before full implementation of the original decree, the Supreme Court remanded the cases to the district courts with directions to implement desegregation with "all deliberate speed." The justices hoped that the ambiguous timetable would give white southerners an opportunity to adjust to what would be a drastic change in their customs, under the guidance of federal judges in local communities.

The *Brown* decision was greeted with elation in African American communities. The *Chicago Defender*, a nationally circulated Negro newspaper, published an editorial stating, "Neither the atom bomb nor the hydrogen bomb will ever be as meaningful to our democracy as the unanimous declaration of the Supreme Court that racial segregation violates the spirit and letter of our Constitution. This means the beginning of the end of the dual society in American life and the . . . segregation which supported it." In another black newspaper, the *Atlanta Daily World*, an editorial stated that "this case has attracted world attention; its import will be of great significance in these trying times when democracy itself is struggling to envision a free world. It will strengthen the position of our nation in carrying out imposed duties of world leadership."

The *Pittsburgh Courier*, a popular black weekly, addressed the case in cold war terms, declaring, "The conscience of America has spoken through its constitutional voice. . . . This clarion announcement will also stun and silence America's communist traducers behind the Iron Curtain. It will effectively impress upon millions of colored people in Asia and Africa the fact that idealism and social morality can and do prevail in the United States regardless of race, creed, or color." These editorials reflected the mood of hope and optimism that then prevailed among African Americans. *Brown* was seen as the dawn of a new era in race relations. The elimination of segregation in schools was merely the beginning. Afro-Americans were confident that *Brown*'s equality principle would be extended to remove racial barriers in other areas.

When Charles Houston and his colleagues were developing the "equalization" strategy in the mid-1930s, they had hoped that victories in court cases would inspire local communities to carry on the fight for civil rights after the lawyers moved on to other cities. This would happen not long after the *Brown* decision. In Montgomery, Alabama, in December of 1955, Rosa Parks, a seamstress and volunteer secretary for the local NAACP, refused a bus driver's demand that she yield her seat to a white passenger. A local ordinance required black passengers to sit in the rear of buses. Whites sat in front. If buses became full, black passengers were expected to stand and yield their seats to whites. Parks's arrest for violating the segregation ordinances led to the Montgomery bus boycott. Negroes refused to patronize public transportation until the local authorities accepted their demands for better treatment. During the boycott, Martin Luther King Jr., then twenty-six years old, emerged as the leader of that effort. After enduring more than a year of mostly empty buses, city officials finally acceded to the demands of the protesters. A lawsuit filed by Fred Gray, a black attorney in Montgomery, resulted in the Supreme Court's decision in *Browder v. Gayle* (1956), which struck down the ordinance requiring segregated public transportation. The Montgomery bus boycott was the first event in a new phase of the civil rights movement. The focus moved from the courts to the streets. *Brown* had helped to spark a flame that would quickly engulf the entire South.

On February 1, 1960, a group of freshmen at North Carolina Agricultural and Technical State College, an Afro-American institution in Greensboro, staged the first sit-in at a local lunch counter to protest segregation in public accommodations. Acting on a carefully rehearsed plan, the well-dressed students took seats in the white section of a lunch counter and refused to move when ordered to do so by managers of the facility. They were eventually arrested and taken to jail. The demonstration was carried out peacefully. The protesters did not respond to the jeers of white bystanders, nor did they resist when they were taken away by police officers. News of the event was carried in newspaper and television reports across the nation. Within two weeks of the Greensboro incident, fifty-four separate sit-ins were staged in fifteen cities. They employed the nonviolent tactics used by the

North Carolina students. These activities led to the organization of the Student Nonviolent Coordinating Committee led by, among others, John Lewis and Julian Bond.

In 1961 another group, the Congress of Racial Equality (CORE), organized "freedom rides." Led by CORE chief James Farmer, these activities consisted of interracial groups of protesters traveling on Greyhound and other interstate buses from cities in the North to southern destinations. The purpose of the freedom rides was to test an Interstate Commerce Commission ruling and a Supreme Court decision, both of which prohibited segregation on interstate carriers. When the demonstrators arrived at bus terminals in various locations in the South, they frequently encountered angry mobs of whites who beat them mercilessly while law enforcement officials stood by idly and watched. The demonstrators were then arrested and charged with disorderly conduct.

One thing that made this phase of the civil rights movement different from previous efforts was the presence of television camera crews. Unlike the litigation campaign, which unfolded in courtrooms outside of the public's view, the sit-ins and freedom rides were captured by film crews and shown on nightly news broadcasts that reached an international audience. The other new development was the increasing involvement of college students and other ordinary citizens who decided that the time had come to demand that they be treated with dignity and respect. Once the fire was lit, the flames could not be doused. Boycotts, mass marches, voter registration drives, and similar activities were conducted across the South by a growing number of grassroots civil rights organizations.

If Negroes saw *Brown* as just, long overdue, and a call to question other racial restrictions, many southern whites reacted to the decision with surprise and indignation. Their world had been turned upside down. Astonishment quickly turned to anger. On March 12, 1956, the Southern Manifesto was read into the *Congressional Record*. This document contained ninety-six signatures, nineteen from members of the Senate and seventy-seven from members of the House of Representatives. The Manifesto proclaimed, "The Supreme Court of the United States, with no legal basis for such action, undertook to exercise their naked judicial power and substituted their personal political and social ideas for the established law of the land." It also alleged that "outside agitators are threatening immediate and revolutionary changes in our public school systems. If done, this is certain to destroy the system of public education in some of the states." The Manifesto concluded with a pledge to "use all lawful means to bring about a reversal of the [*Brown*] decision which is contrary to the Constitution and to prevent the use of force in its implementation."

While southern politicians publicly proclaimed their dissatisfaction in the Southern Manifesto, other southern whites were privately seething at what they saw as an affront to the natural order of things. One letter from a Florida man to Chief Justice Earl Warren indicates both the strident objections to desegregation and the degree of racial hatred held by many:

Justice Earl Warren
Supreme Court U.S.A.

Sir: and the eight other Black Robed Death's Heads. I refrain from Calling you men. you have outraged the people of America. and her Constitution. you have obeyed the Counsel of the Negro's. the NAACP Why? The Communists are Behind it and you know it. Do you think the American people will allow you to take away Their Rights. No we are a white Nation we will never lower our selves To the level of the Black Race. They are not made in the Image and Likeness of god. They are Descendants of Cain. Cain murdred his brother Abel god put a mark on Him and His Seed. for the end of all Time. Nothing Can erace it: they Have Souls That will Become as white as Snow if they live according to gods law: the mark is Black and Smell is Reppelant. Do not Think you Can Defy or Change gods Decree [*sic*].

Some expressed racial animosities in letters. Others found deadlier means to show their hatred. One incident that provided

sumed inferiority of Negro students and its belief that segregated schools were necessary to address the differing mental capacities of black and white students. This decision, in which a lower court presumed it had the authority to reverse the Supreme Court's decision, was overruled by the Court of Appeals for the Fifth Circuit. Many judges across the South were reluctant to enforce *Brown*. In meetings, NAACP lawyers often joked about which of them had the worst judge.

Resistance went beyond the actions of lower court judges. Some politicians even attempted to develop a constitutional theory in an effort to fight the desegregation decision. Many state officials argued a right to resist or even ignore *Brown*. Their argument was often rooted in a nineteenth-century constitutional or quasi-constitutional theory known as the doctrine of "interposition and nullification." The theory held that state officials could shield a state's citizens from unconstitutional actions of the federal government. The doctrine had been asserted by various states in the nineteenth century. South Carolina had attempted to prevent the enforcement of federal tariffs in the 1830s, and some northern officials had urged noncompliance with the Fugitive Slave Act of 1850, among a number of examples. The theory was largely discredited, but a number of southern officials after *Brown* were taking the theory out of constitutional mothballs, dusting it off, and seeing if it might be put to service in resistance to the Supreme Court's desegregation requirement.

There would be an often fateful synergy between public officials asserting their powers of interposition and violent mobs determined to stop desegregation. One of the most dramatic confrontations involving school desegregation took place in Little Rock, Arkansas. On May 20, 1954, the Little Rock school board issued a policy statement indicating its intention to comply with *Brown*. On May 24, 1955, a federal court in Little Rock approved a plan that anticipated desegregation in stages, to be completed by 1963. In September of 1957, nine black students were slated to enroll in Little Rock's Central High School. On September 2, Arkansas governor Orval Faubus, perhaps acting on the doctrine of interposition and nullification, sent units of the Arkansas National Guard to Central High to prevent the students from enrolling. On September 3, the school board petitioned the federal district court for a two and one-half year delay in the implementation of the plan. The court refused the board's request and ordered it to proceed with desegregation. On September 4, Arkansas National Guard troops, acting on the governor's order, blocked the Negro students at the door of Central High School. Thurgood Marshall and Wiley Branton, a local NAACP lawyer, sought relief in the federal court. On September 20, the court granted the NAACP's request for an injunction to prevent Governor Faubus and the National Guard from interfering with the black students' efforts to enroll in Central High.

On September 23, the students entered the school through a side door to avoid a mob of angry whites that had gathered in front of the building chanting racist epithets and threatening violence. The students were unable to complete the day because rioting broke out on the school grounds. Reports of the confrontation at Little Rock generated international newspaper headlines. Dramatic images of white mobs and armed National Guard troops dominated nightly news reports. Television crews filmed scenes showing dozens of angry white adults crowding around young black students, uttering threats, and waving signs protesting the integration. Events rapidly escalated to a breaking point. On September 25, President Dwight D. Eisenhower dispatched federal troops to Little Rock. Eisenhower was a complex figure with respect to *Brown*. He privately expressed his disagreement with the school desegregation decision, yet he had allowed Herbert Brownell, his attorney general, to file amicus briefs in support of school desegregation. Although not a particularly strong supporter of integration, Eisenhower had been a relative moderate on the race issue as the commanding general of U.S. forces in Europe during the Second World War. He would also, in 1957, become the first president since Reconstruction to sign federal civil rights legislation. Regardless of his personal views on race and desegregation, he viewed the actions of the Arkansas officials as a challenge to his authority and to law and order more generally. He sent the 101st Airborne Division to Little Rock to quell the disturbances. When heavily armed federal troops arrived in Little Rock, the black students were finally allowed to attend classes. On November 27, 1957, army troops were withdrawn, but federalized National Guardsmen remained on duty at Central High School throughout the school year.

The federal district court's denial of the request to suspend, for two and one-half years, the operation of the school board's desegregation plan was appealed and affirmed by the Court of Appeals for the Eighth Circuit. That decision was appealed to the United States Supreme Court. In an opinion issued on September 29, 1958, the Supreme Court in *Cooper v. Aaron* reversed the lower court and reaffirmed *Brown* and strongly condemned the actions of the Arkansas officials. The court emphasized that Article 6 of the Constitution made the United States Constitution "the supreme law of the land." The opinion explained further that the 1804 decision *Marbury v. Madison* established the doctrine of judicial review. Under this principle, the courts rather than the executive or legislative branches of government have the final word regarding the interpretation of the Constitution and laws of the United States.

The Court found in *Cooper v. Aaron* that the actions of the Arkansas governor and state legislature, which claimed that they were not bound by the *Brown* decision, were in direct conflict with the supremacy clause of the Constitution. It held that "no state legislature or executive judicial officer can war against the Constitution without violating his undertaking to support it. . . . A governor who asserts a power to nullify a federal court order is similarly constrained." The court concluded, stating the "principles announced in [*Brown*] and the obedience of the states to them, according to the command of the Constitution, are indispensable for the protection of the freedoms guaranteed by our fundamental charter for all of us."

The Supreme Court's decision in *Cooper v. Aaron* and the president's deployment of heavily armed federal troops to Arkansas did not end the South's resistance to desegregation. School boards engaged in delaying tactics, forcing the NAACP to file separate cases in virtually every school district. Lawyers for the school boards tied up cases for years with legal maneuvers. School boards delayed for months in the development and submission of desegregation plans. When the plans were finally presented for court approval, they often proposed desegregation by one grade each year, which would prolong the process for at least twelve more years. In other instances, elected officials engaged in outright defiance, in part, to secure the votes of a white electorate that was adamantly opposed to integration.

By 1956 the Legal Defense Fund (LDF) had moved further away from the NAACP, the result of the need to become even more separate for tax purposes and because of personality conflicts and policy disagreements between the two organizations. In that year, the Legal Defense Fund filed suit in *Bush v. Orleans Parish School Board* in the U.S. District Court for the Eastern District of Louisiana. The case involving segregation in New Orleans public schools was assigned to James Skelly Wright, a southern judge sympathetic to school desegregation. The state filed a number of defenses, but Wright issued an order finding that segregation had to end "with all deliberate speed." *Bush* began what would be years of desegregation litigation in Louisiana. On November 4, 1960, just four days before the federal district court had scheduled the partial desegregation of New Orleans schools, the Louisiana state legislature went into extraordinary session in an effort to forestall court-ordered school integration. The legislature passed some twenty-five statutes designed to prevent the scheduled admission of five Negro girls to the New Orleans public schools. The girls were 5 out of 137 black students who had applied for admission to white schools. The Orleans Parish school board had made the decision to admit the five girls in response to court orders. The acts of the Louisiana legislature included an "interposition statute" in which the legislature declared that it did not recognize the Supreme Court decision in *Brown*.

Another statute passed during this session abolished the Orleans Parish school board and transferred administration of New Orleans public schools to the state legislature. The theory behind this measure was that it would be a violation of the doctrine of separation of powers for the courts to dictate to the legislature which measures they could or could not undertake. The legislative measures also included a provision prohibiting federal officers from enforcing *Brown* or lower court decisions designed to implement *Brown* in Louisiana. After the extraordinary legislative session, on November 13, 1960, as a last-ditch effort, this state superintendent declared a school holiday. The next day the LDF lawyers obtained an injunction preventing observation of the holiday.

In a scene that was depicted on a Norman Rockwell cover of the *Saturday Evening Post*, federal marshals escorted four black girls into two white elementary schools. Crowds of white adults gathered at the schools, jeering, insulting, and threatening the little girls. White parents withdrew their children from the schools. The police were able to restrain the crowds on the first day. Two days later, however, white mobs poured into the streets of New Orleans and a riot ensued. African Americans retaliated, throwing rocks and bottles at whites. On November 30, 1960, the U.S. District Court for the Eastern District of Louisiana held that the twenty-five emergency statutes enacted by the state legislature to prevent desegregation were unconstitutional. A three-judge panel headed by J. Skelly Wright especially attacked the Louisiana legislature's invocation of interposition:

> Interposition is an amorphous concept based on the proposition that the United States is a compact of states, any one of which may interpose its sovereignty against the enforcement within its borders of any decision of the Supreme Court or act of Congress. . . . In essence, the doctrine denies the constitutional obligation of the states to respect those decisions of the Supreme Court with which they do not agree. The doctrine may have had some validity under the Articles of Confederation. . . . Thus the Keystone of the interposition thesis, that the United States is a compact of states, was disavowed in the Preamble to the Constitution.

In early 1961, the trial court declared other parts of the specially enacted anti-desegregation legislation unconstitutional. Desegregation of the New Orleans public schools finally went forward.

The depths of the southern intransigence were further revealed when an African American attempted to enroll in the University of Mississippi. In 1961, James Meredith, a native Mississippian and Korean War veteran, attempted to enroll in the University of Mississippi. When his application was rejected, Meredith wrote a letter to the NAACP's Legal Defense Fund asking them to file a suit seeking to compel his admission to the university. The Legal Defense Fund agreed and sent staff attorney Constance Baker Motley to lead the effort. As Motley explained years later, Marshall's "joking theory was that black women were less subject to attack in the South than black men, since 'all white men had had black mammies.'" Motley was, in reality, the in-house expert in college and university cases. A trial was held, but the NAACP lost at the lower court level. The university claimed disingenuously that Meredith's application had been denied not because of his race but because he had failed to submit the required "alumni certificates," endorsements from university graduates. This, of course, would have been a virtually impossible task for an Afro-American in Mississippi in 1960. Nonetheless, the trial judge accepted this subterfuge. The ruling was appealed to the United States Court of Appeals for the Fifth Circuit. The appellate panel issued a decision reversing the trial court and ordered Meredith's admission.

Not long after the Fifth Circuit issued its decision, Mississippi governor Ross Barnett announced his intention to defy the federal court order, invoking state sovereignty and "interposition." On September 22, 1962, Meredith attempted to register for classes at Ole Miss. Governor Barnett refused to allow him to enroll. On September 12, the NAACP and the U.S. Department of Justice (which had intervened as a party to the case) filed an application for contempt in the federal proceeding seeking an order to require school officials to obey the ruling requiring Meredith's admission. During the hearing, school officials agreed to allow Meredith to matriculate. Unwilling to relent, Governor Barnett subsequently filed a civil action in state court seeking to enjoin Meredith's admission. The state court, ignoring the Constitution's supremacy clause, granted Barnett's request for an injunction.

On September 23, Meredith, accompanied by federal marshals, attempted to enter the university. State police and Mississippi's lieutenant governor prevented Meredith from registering. On September 28, the federal court issued an order holding Governor Barnett in contempt of court. United States marshals and the officials from the Department of the Army were dispatched to Oxford to assist Meredith in his efforts to register. Attorney General Robert Kennedy engaged in behind-the-scenes negotiations with Governor Barnett and other Mississippi officials in an effort to head off a violent confrontation. After negotiations failed, on September 29, President John F. Kennedy signed a proclamation ordering federal troops to Oxford. On September 30, 1,400 federal troops arrived in Oxford. Meredith was taken, under guard, to a dormitory on the campus. Hundreds of whites, who had gathered on the campus, rioted. Gunshots were exchanged. A French reporter was shot and killed in the fighting. Shotgun pellets injured some of the U.S. marshals. By 3:00 A.M., more federal troops arrived. Within a few hours, 2,500 armed federal soldiers occupied the Ole Miss campus with tanks and other military vehicles.

For several days the events at Oxford dominated national news reports. Television crews captured images of the violence, which were broadcast to an international audience. At times, it seemed that the Civil War was being refought in Oxford. Two weeks after the first riot, however, Meredith was finally able to register for classes. Federal troops, numbering at times as many as twenty-three thousand, occupied the town of Oxford. As time went by, the federal troops were gradually withdrawn. The last five hundred soldiers finally departed when Meredith graduated in 1963.

Alabama was another state that went to great lengths to avoid integration. A case seeking to desegregate the University of Alabama, *Lucy et al. v. University of Alabama*, was filed in 1953 and still pending when the Supreme Court issued the *Brown* decision in 1954. The NAACP lawyers subsequently decided to reactivate *Lucy*. The trial court ruled in the NAACP's favor, and on December 30, 1955, the lower court's decision was affirmed by the

Court of Appeals for the Fifth Circuit. When the plaintiff, Autherine Lucy, registered for classes in 1956, a riot broke out on the campus. The university's trustees later removed Lucy from the campus. The NAACP subsequently sued to compel the trustees to allow Lucy to attend classes. The court ruled that the university had not disobeyed the court's order to allow Lucy to attend the University. The NAACP's efforts were frustrated when that ruling was affirmed by the Court of Appeals for the Fifth Circuit.

In 1963 another suit was brought against the University of Alabama on behalf of two African American students. This case was filed after the confrontation in Mississippi over Meredith. As a consequence, Alabama officials knew that resistance would be futile. In order to make points with his segregationist constituency, Alabama governor George Wallace decided that the desegregation of the University of Alabama would not take place without a bit of political theater. He reached an understanding with the U.S. Justice Department. Having pledged to take a stand "at the schoolhouse door" to block the students' admission, Governor Wallace was allowed to proceed with a pretense of blocking the door and then stepping aside when the students and federal marshals accompanying them arrived. Wallace's dramatic staged resistance made national news and propelled the Alabama governor into the national political arena as an outspoken foe of integration.

Following the lead of other states, Georgia engaged in its own version of massive resistance. Efforts to desegregate Georgia's colleges and universities began in 1950 when a suit was filed against the University of Georgia on behalf of Horace Ward, a native of LaGrange, Georgia. While the case was pending, Ward was drafted. The case remained inactive while he was in the service, but it was reactivated after his discharge. LDF attorney Constance Baker Motley and Atlanta lawyer Donald Hollowell handled Ward's case. The judge ruled that Ward would first have to exhaust state administrative remedies prior to filing a claim in federal court. This meant that he would be required to appeal to the state board of education prior to suing in federal court. By this time six years had elapsed. Ward decided to move on and enrolled in Northwestern University Law School in Chicago. He later returned to Atlanta and eventually became the first black federal judge in Georgia.

In 1956 the LDF filed a desegregation suit against Georgia State College in Atlanta. Two African American women who were students at a local black college volunteered to be plaintiffs in the case. After suit was filed, state investigators researched the young women's backgrounds and found something in each woman's past that would prove to be embarrassing. The case went forward, however. Motley argued that the refusal to admit the students was not based on the women's backgrounds but in accordance with the state's policy and custom of excluding Negroes from colleges and universities in Georgia. To the surprise of the LDF lawyers, the judge issued a declaratory judgment holding the state's policy unconstitutional. Because of the embarrassing disclosures, however, the young women decided not to pursue their applications.

In 1959 the LDF filed a suit against the University of Georgia in Athens. The plaintiffs, Charlayne Hunter and Hamilton Holmes, were both from Atlanta, Georgia. They were outstanding students in high school, and there was nothing in their backgrounds that could cause any embarrassment. During the trial, the university's registrar testified that there was no official segregation in the university system and the segregation that existed was entirely voluntary. The judge rejected the university's argument and ordered that the plaintiffs be admitted in February of 1961. After an appeal to the United States Court of Appeals for the Fifth Circuit, which affirmed the lower court's decision, Hunter and Holmes enrolled in the university. Some rioting ensued when they attempted to register. The scenes were broadcast on national television reports. The disorder did not persist. White students occasionally harassed Hunter and Holmes, but they graduated on schedule.

The Alabama and Georgia cases were adjudicated at a time when the civil rights movement was in high gear. Martin Luther King Jr. was leading almost daily marches in Birmingham, Alabama. Police used high-pressure fire hoses and attack dogs to break up demonstrations. Several bombings occurred including one at a black church where children attending Sunday school were killed. In the summer of 1963, A. Philip Randolph, Martin Luther King Jr., and others organized the largest civil rights demonstration in the history of the United States. The March on Washington consisted of three hundred thousand demonstrators gathering on the Mall in Washington to protest segregation and discrimination. This was the site of King's "I Have a Dream" speech.

In November of 1963, President John F. Kennedy was assassinated. When Lyndon Johnson assumed the presidency, one of his priorities was the passage of civil rights legislation originally proposed by Kennedy. Congress subsequently enacted the Civil Rights Act of 1964, which outlawed discrimination in employment, in public accommodations, and by educational institutions receiving federal financial assistance. The next year Congress passed the Voting Rights Act of 1965, which helped curtail many of the practices that had effectively made the Fifteenth Amendment a dead letter in many states for much of the twentieth century. In urging passage of the measure, President Lyndon Johnson adopted the motto of the civil rights movement, stating, "and we shall overcome." *Brown* was now being buttressed by Congress and a sympathetic administration.

But the road to that acceptance had been a difficult one. The successes of the NAACP and the Legal Defense Fund had made the organizations targets for segregation's supporters. Some states decided on a frontal attack on the NAACP and its often vulnerable members in southern localities. Several state officials claimed that the NAACP was a foreign corporation doing business within their jurisdictions and as such were required to register with state officials. Local authorities demanded that NAACP officials submit financial and other information to them. The officials were most interested in obtaining membership lists. Although southern politicians consistently claimed that desegregation efforts were the work of a few "outside agitators," they knew that many local residents were either members of the NAACP or sympathetic to its program. If the identity of local

NAACP members could be obtained, punitive actions could be taken. Employers could be persuaded to fire workers. Loan applications could be denied. The White Citizens' Councils formed in the 1950s to fight integration were particularly active in using economic intimidation of NAACP members. Or matters could be dealt with the old-fashioned way. Crosses could be burned on lawns. Individuals could be subjected to threats of violence, bodily injury, and death. In some instances, the NAACP was accused of engaging in barratry, stirring up litigation, which violated the ethical rules of the legal profession and could be possible grounds for disbarment. Actions were also brought against individual lawyers. Some were threatened with disbarment proceedings. In Delaware, Louis Redding was charged with income tax evasion but was acquitted by a jury after a trial.

A number of cases were filed, many of which reached the Supreme Court. The NAACP almost always prevailed, but it had to devote a substantial portion of its time and scarce resources to defending the suits. The organization was unable to operate in Alabama for ten years. One unanticipated outcome of the southern challenges to the NAACP's activities was the development of new decisions by the Supreme Court expanding expressive and associational rights under the First Amendment. In *NAACP v. Alabama ex rel. Patterson* (1958), the Alabama legislature attempted to prevent the NAACP from operating in the state. The organization was held in contempt and fined $100,000 for failing to disclose its membership to state authorities. When the case reached the Supreme Court, the Court held that Alabama's actions violated NAACP members' First Amendment rights to freedom of association. In another case, *Louisiana ex rel. Gremillion v. NAACP* (1961), Louisiana attempted to prevent the organization from doing business in that state based on its failure to register with local authorities. The Supreme Court ruled, in 1960, that Louisiana statutes were unconstitutional because they had the purpose and effect of penalizing the legitimate exercise of First Amendment rights.

In another case, *Gibson v. Florida Legislative Investigation Committee* (1963), the president of the Miami, Florida, NAACP branch was held in contempt, fined, and imprisoned for refusing to divulge the organization's membership records. The Supreme Court reversed the contempt citation after finding that groups that are neither subversive nor engaged in illegal activities must have the right to associate, without state interference, under the First and Fourteenth Amendments. In *NAACP v. Alabama ex rel. Flowers* (1964), an Alabama state court enjoined the NAACP's operations in Alabama for failing to comply with corporate registration requirements. The Supreme Court reversed the Alabama court's decision in 1964, on the grounds that it interfered with NAACP members' First Amendment rights to freedom of association. In *Bates v. City of Little Rock*, the Supreme Court, in 1960, reversed, on First Amendment grounds, the convictions of local NAACP leaders who refused to turn over membership lists to local officials seeking to enforce a tax ordinance. Finally, in *NAACP v. Button*, the organization challenged Virginia laws that regulated the solicitation of cases. In a decision that allows public interest organizations to sponsor lawsuits, the Supreme Court found, in 1963, that the NAACP's activities were expressions protected by the First and Fourteenth Amendments.

Legal intimidation was one way to try and blunt NAACP efforts. Others preferred a more direct method: murder. Medgar Evers was the NAACP's field secretary in Mississippi. A veteran of the Normandy landings in June 1944, Evers was active in voter registration and in efforts to get greater cooperation among the civil rights organization in his native Mississippi. He was assassinated outside his home in Jackson in June of 1963. President Kennedy ordered his body to be buried at Arlington Cemetery. In 1964 the Student Nonviolent Coordinating Committee and other groups organized "Freedom Summer" during which hundreds of mostly white, middle-class college students traveled to Mississippi to register black voters. During that summer, local police and Ku Klux Klan members murdered three civil rights workers—Andrew Goodman, twenty-five years old, Michael Schwerner, twenty-one years old, both Jews from New York, and James Chaney, twenty-one years old, a Negro from Mississippi. The extreme Klan violence visited on Afro-American communities and civil rights workers caused some black men in the South to organize self-defense societies. The most successful of these was a group called Deacons for Defense and Justice, which operated in Louisiana and Mississippi. The organization, composed largely of veterans from World War II and the Korean conflict, armed themselves and patrolled Negro communities deterring Klan attacks.

The organizers of Freedom Summer elected a delegation, which was sent to the Democratic National Convention in Atlantic City, New Jersey, to challenge Mississippi's all-white delegation. More demonstrations were organized in the South, including one in Selma, Alabama, in which protesters were met with extreme violence. John Lewis, a leader of the Student Nonviolent Coordinating Committee, suffered a concussion that required a portion of his skull to be replaced with a steel plate. Television crews captured the horrifying brutality with which the police beat the peaceful protesters. In response, another, much larger, demonstration was held. Representatives of several civil rights organizations joined together in a march from Selma to Montgomery, Alabama, to protest black disenfranchisement. When the march ended, Ku Klux Klansmen murdered Viola Luizzo, an Italian American woman from Michigan, as she drove a group of black marchers back to Selma. These efforts played a pivotal part in convincing Congress to approve the 1965 Voting Rights Act.

In the mid-1960s, the civil rights movement entered a militant phase. A faction of the Student Nonviolent Coordinating Committee took a more defiant stance, disavowing the nonviolent approach. The organization also espoused a more separatist doctrine, rejecting the assistance of white supporters—even though many of those supporters had played a key and courageous role in Freedom Summer. The phrase "black power" became their rallying cry. Separatist leaders such as Malcolm X, of the Nation of Islam, and groups including the Black Panthers, a West Coast organization with a Marxist-Leninist ideology, never adhered to the nonviolent approach endorsed by King and the others. In several northern cities, urban riots broke out during the long, hot summers of the last half of the decade. In 1968, Martin Luther King Jr. was assassinated in Memphis, Tennessee. This event set off days of rioting in cities across the nation. The rioters' burning and looting left many central business districts in smoldering ruins. In the wake of King's death, Congress passed the Fair Housing Act of 1968, which prohibited discrimination in the sale or rental of housing on the basis of race, religion, gender, or national origin.

Despite the high level of protest activity, very little progress had been made toward school desegregation. In 1960, forty-six school desegregation cases were pending in southern states. Ten years after the *Brown* decision, only 1.2 percent of black students in the South attended schools with whites. In five states—Alabama, Mississippi, South Carolina, Florida, and Georgia—there were no black students attending white schools. By the late 1960s, however, the Supreme Court finally decided to put an end to the South's procrastination. In *Griffin v. County School Board of Prince Edward County* (1964), a case in which a school board involved in the original *Brown* cases had closed all of its schools to avoid desegregation, Justice Hugo Black stated, "There has been entirely too much deliberation and not enough speed in enforcing the constitutional rights which we held in *Brown*." The county was ordered to reopen its schools.

In *Alexander v. Holmes County Board of Education* (1969), the court ruled that the "continued operation of segregated schools under a standard allowing 'all deliberate speed' for desegregation is no longer constitutionally permissible. . . . The obligation of every school district is to terminate dual school systems at once and operate now and hereafter only unitary schools." In another case, *Green v. School Board of New Kent County*, the court held in 1968 that school officials "are clearly charged with the affirmative duty to take whatever steps might be necessary to convert to a unitary system in which racial discrimination would be eliminated root and branch." In a 1971 decision, *Swann v. Charlotte-Mecklenburg Board of Education*, the Supreme Court went a step further. It held that race-neutral student assignments would not satisfy a school board's desegregation obligation. The existence of racially identifiable schools would constitute a prima facie showing of discrimination. This meant that the courts would presume that if schools could be identified as black schools or white schools, the separate schools were the result of official discrimination. Public officials would have the burden of proving that the separate schools came about without deliberate discrimination. If school officials could not prove that separate schools were not the result of official discrimination, they would be responsible for taking affirmative steps to dismantle the dual system. School officials would be required to use all tools necessary to dismantle segregated school systems including the use of busing, where necessary, to achieve racial balance.

By making it clear that merely going through the motions without substantive change would not be acceptable, the Supreme Court finally took a position that would result in serious efforts to desegregate schools. Moreover, by shifting the burden of proof from the students and parents seeking desegregation to the school boards to demonstrate that they had eliminated all vestiges of the segregated system "root and branch," school officials could not persist in the dilatory tactics that prevented any meaningful integration during the fifteen years that elapsed since *Brown* was decided. Genuine progress toward desegregation finally commenced.

In the South, particularly in rural areas, school desegregation proceeded. In districts where there were only one or two high schools, the white and black high schools simply merged with students attending a single, racially integrated school. In urban areas, however, demographic patterns made school desegregation far more difficult. Beginning in the years during and after World War I, Negroes migrated, in large numbers, from rural areas in the South to urban areas in the North and Midwest. They were lured by the availability of employment opportunities in factories that paid far more than they could earn performing farm labor in the South. African Americans were also seeking to avoid the oppressive conditions that existed in the South where violence, lynching, and other forms of intimidation were commonplace. There were, moreover, greater educational opportunities for their children in northern schools.

The migration from field to factory continued through World War II and beyond. During the years that Afro-American families were moving north, whites were relocating from central city neighborhoods to the surrounding suburbs. Suburbanization increased exponentially during the post–World War II era, when the federal government heavily subsidized home ownership with Federal Housing Administration and Veterans' Administration mortgage programs. African Americans were frequently locked out of suburban areas as a result of racially restrictive covenants and other discriminatory practices. By the late 1960s, cities in northern industrial centers were becoming increasingly black, while surrounding suburbs were often virtually all white.

With the advent of busing to achieve racial balance, white flight to the suburbs accelerated. The NAACP attempted to address this problem in *Milliken v. Bradley* (1974), *Milliken I*, which involved efforts to integrate schools in Detroit, Michigan. In an earlier case, *Keyes v. School District No. 1, Denver, Colorado* (1973), the Supreme Court recognized that segregation was not limited to the South where laws required separate schools. Many northern cities pursued customs and policies that resulted in segregated schools. These policies included locating schools in all-white or all-black neighborhoods, deliberately assigning black students to racially identifiable schools, and otherwise engaging in practices that fostered segregation. In *Keyes* the Supreme Court held that localities that maintained segregated schools as a result of customs and official practice, rather than formal law, also had an affirmative duty to take action to desegregate schools.

In *Milliken I*, the NAACP claimed that state and local officials pursued policies that resulted in racially segregated schools in Detroit. The NAACP's argument persuaded the federal district court, which entered a metropolitan desegregation order that would have required that black students in Detroit schools be bused to schools in the surrounding suburbs. When the case reached the Supreme Court, the high tribunal reversed the lower court's decision to the extent that it included the suburban districts. The Supreme Court held that there could be no requirement to desegregate across municipal district lines without proof that the district lines had been deliberately designed to foster segregation. This, for all practical purposes, meant that suburban school districts would not be included in metropolitan desegregation plans.

This ruling would have a profound effect on desegregation efforts. It is difficult to demonstrate that suburban school districts were specifically designed to foster school segregation. It is perhaps even more difficult for courts to fashion remedies that take into account general and long-standing patterns of societal discrimination that produced patterns of residential segregation. *Milliken I*, in effect, meant that suburban districts were effectively insulated from desegregation plans, even though the absence of minorities in these areas was the product of years of discriminatory practices. The persistence of racially segregated housing patterns in most urban areas has resulted in school districts that are almost all black while the surrounding suburbs are largely white. As a result of persistent residential segregation and extreme isolation in many urban areas, a phenomenon that social scientists describe as "hypersegregation," African American students in many inner-city school districts are more segregated today than their grandparents were in the pre-*Brown* era.

CHAPTER 9

From Target to Icon
Brown and the Role of Courts in American Life

On Tuesday, September 15, 1987, Robert Bork, at the time a judge on the United States Circuit Court of Appeals for the D.C. Circuit, was testifying before the Senate Judiciary Committee. His testimony was part of what would prove to be an unsuccessful effort to have the Senate confirm him for an appointment as an associate justice of the United States Supreme Court. Bork, who had had a long and distinguished career as a jurist and legal scholar, had been nominated by President Ronald Reagan to fulfill the vacancy left by Justice Lewis Powell. Early on, Judge Bork used his testimony to praise the decision in *Brown*. He stated, "Reversing *Plessy* was clearly correct and represented perhaps the greatest moral achievement of our constitutional law." By 1987 Judge Bork's remarks were neither remarkable nor controversial. Few people in public life by that date were willing to criticize the 1954 decision. A person who did so ran a strong risk of being branded as an extremist, a part of a lunatic fringe, unfit for public office, certainly one who was clearly too dangerous for the nation's highest court.

Judge Bork had had a long record of supporting the 1954 school desegregation decision. As far back as 1968 in an article in *Fortune* magazine, Bork, then a professor at the Yale Law School, had expressed the view that *Brown* was correctly decided. Still there was a certain irony at Bork's confirmation hearing. Bork was known as a strong supporter of the view that judges should interpret the Constitution according to the original intentions of the framers of the different constitutional provisions. Prior to his Supreme Court nomination, Bork had argued vigorously from the bench and in his academic writings against expansive interpretations of constitutional provisions, against the notion of a judiciary empowered to help develop a living Constitution, flexible and responsive to modern needs and demands. Bork's conservative posture with respect to the role of the judiciary in American constitutionalism had played a major role in getting him a nomination to the nation's highest court from Ronald Reagan, postwar America's most conservative president.

During the confirmation hearing, Bork the staunch conservative felt obliged to defend *Brown* as consistent with the original understanding of the Fourteenth Amendment. Ironically, many of his liberal critics who opposed his nomination argued that *Brown* was a departure from the original understanding of the amendment. This curious debate can provide us with an interesting window on the afterlife of *Brown*. If the decision in *Brown v. Board of Education* had important, indeed far-reaching, things to say about America's enduring agony over race, it also caused several generations of jurists and scholars, lawyers and commentators, pundits and plain folk to ponder questions about the proper role of courts in American life. If Bork the conservative was willing to praise *Brown* in an effort to show that originalism was consistent with the Warren Court's reading of the Constitution on that occasion, more than a few of his liberal critics at the time of the confirmation hearings ironically argued exactly the opposite, that a faithful adherence to the intentions of the Thirty-ninth Congress would have prevented the school desegregation decision, forever enshrining separate but equal as the law of the land. *Brown* had become far more than a ruling on school segregation. It had become instead a Rorschach test on a wide array of issues in American life, race and the role of the judiciary most prominent among these. From 1954 on, the debate over *Brown* would become an arena for combat over the proper place of judges in policy making and the proper role of history in jurisprudence. By 1987 many conservatives were willing to agree that *Brown* was both legitimate and consistent with a proper reading of American history, while many of their liberal opponents saw the decision as calling into question the very legitimacy of looking to history as a guide to jurisprudence. Such had not always been the case.

It is no exaggeration to say that the Warren opinion in *Brown* precipitated a constitutional firestorm the likes of which the nation had not seen at least since the Taney opinion in *Dred Scott*, if then. To be sure, the Supreme Court had been involved in controversial opinions before, but *Brown* was different. The decision posed a direct challenge to the way millions of ordinary white Americans lived their lives. More significantly, *Brown* posed a challenge to the values of millions of ordinary white Americans, to their beliefs, their deeply rooted prejudices, their views concerning how proper lives should be lived, and of course the proper places of blacks and whites in America. It's hard to think of a parallel in the Supreme Court's history, at least in the Court's history prior to *Brown*. Certainly most of the Court's decision making prior to the Warren era involved topics that seemed remote to the average American. Institutionally the Court, despite the Fourteenth Amendment, had historically remained reluctant to interfere with the actions of state governments. A small break in that traditional reticence had begun in the 1930s when the Court began to look at state criminal procedures in the light of egregious violations of the rights of African American defendants in capital cases. The case of the Scottsboro Boys, a 1931 Alabama case in which eight black youths had been sentenced to death for the rape of two white women without legal representation, was probably the most famous of these. But these cases did not directly touch the lives of millions of white Americans, just those of a handful of Negro defendants lucky enough to get decent appellate review at a time when most Afro-American defendants in the South scarcely had decent trials to begin with. The Supreme Court's acquiescence in the Japanese American internment cases, *Hirabayashi* and *Korematsu*, affected the lives of over one hundred thousand people. But the Supreme Court there gave its imprimatur to a fait accompli, and the Court had had a long history of acquiescing when governments, state or federal, had felt the need to limit the rights of nonwhites. The Court perhaps came closest to touching the lives of millions of white Americans during the early stages of the New Deal when it set limits on the kinds of ameliorative legislation that the new Roosevelt administration and Congress could pass to fight the depression. But even those decisions simply prevented new measures. They did not interfere with existing practice and culture. And besides, the Supreme Court by the late 1930s was prepared to accept the expansion of congressional power that the New Deal required.

But *Brown* was different. Here the Supreme Court was directly challenging custom and culture. Segregation was a deeply ingrained part of the culture of the South and indeed other regions as well. If, as historian C. Vann Woodward has argued, the formal systematized and ritualized body of segregationist practices known as Jim Crow was only a little more than two generations old when Warren authored the Court's opinion in *Brown*, it was a twentieth-century manifestation of the durable desire to maintain white supremacy in the South. In a way not seen since Reconstruction, the core of white southern culture was being challenged by the federal government. This time the challenge came not by a Congress empowered by victory in Civil War, but by the Supreme Court, a body long known for its reluctance to interfere with state prerogative and its reticence concerning getting into the messy business of supervising the conduct of state officials, particularly when such power was to be exercised on behalf of blacks.

That the Court would make a pronouncement on an issue that would upset a deeply rooted cultural pattern, not to mention the strong prejudices of millions of white Americans, provoked a reaction that was immediate and intense, indeed at times ferocious. Despite the conservatism of *Brown II* with its refusal to press for immediate desegregation and its "all deliberate speed" language, language that insured that the process of dismantling the separate Jim Crow school system would be a painfully slow one, supporters of segregation were furious. That fury was, in part, responsible for the efforts of some southern politicians to resurrect the antebellum doctrine of interposition and nullification. It also caused most members of Congress from southern states to sign the Southern Manifesto denouncing *Brown* and declaring it to be constitutionally invalid. That fury and the politics of race baiting exacerbated by that fury were also responsible for Arkansas governor Orville Faubus's confrontational resistance to school integration in Little Rock.

Resistance to the 1954 decision also took other forms. The state of Virginia closed schools for all children rather than allow them to be integrated. Columnist James J. Kilpatrick, then a strong supporter of segregation, led the charge against school desegregation in that state, denouncing court-ordered desegregation as unconstitutional:

In May of 1954, that inept fraternity of politicians and professors known as the United States Supreme Court chose to throw away the established law. These nine men repudiated the constitution, spit upon the Tenth Amendment, and rewrote the fundamental law of this land to suit their own gauzy concepts of sociology. If it be said now that the South is flouting the law, let it be said to the higher court, You taught us how.

From the moment that abominable decision was handed down, two broad courses only were available to the South. One was to defy the Court openly and notoriously, the other was to accept the Court's decision and combat it by legal means. To defy the Court openly would be to enter upon anarchy, the logical end would be a second attempt at secession from the Union. And though the idea is not without merit, it is impossible of execution. We tried that once before.

The conservative magazine *National Review* attacked the decision as judicial usurpation:

National Review has contended, all along, that there are a number of issues involved in the segregation controversy which do not bear on the merits of the question whether Negroes and Whites should go to school together in the South. We have stated our views that the May 1954 decision by the Supreme Court was an act of judicial usurpation:; that it ran "patently counter to the intent of the Constitution."; that it was "shoddy and illegal in analysis, and invalid as sociology." And we have implied that it is not altogether clear whether a moral issue is at stake. If there is one at stake, it was there before the Supreme Court thought about it; and hence the moral fervor that has been attached to the Court decision itself is unconvincing, and, at worst, hypocritical.

Nor was the attack against *Brown* confined to champions of segregation or even to conservatives. Columbia University law professor Herbert Wechsler, who had served as an American prosecutor at the Nuremberg war crimes trials in 1946, authored a widely read article in the *Harvard Law Review* in 1959. It was titled "Toward Neutral Principles of Constitutional Law." In that influential article, Wechsler, a New Deal liberal, criticized the Warren opinion as being a violation of the right of free association of southern whites. The Wechsler article argued that it would be impossible to extract from the text or history of the Fourteenth Amendment a set of neutral principles that would reasonably cause the Court to prefer the right of Afro-American children to enter previously all-white schools over the right of white parents to keep their children from associating with Negro children. One of the nation's most distinguished jurists, Learned Hand, would also criticize *Brown* and the Warren Court more generally for extending the reach of judicial power in American life. The criticisms of *Brown* in the early stages tended to fall into three categories. First came critiques from many who could simply and accurately be characterized as racist. The Warren decision was disturbing precisely because it struck at the southern racial order. Segregationists were strong and virulent. They dominated the politics of the South, and they had more than a little support in other regions of the nation as well. This group usually couched its constitutional objections in the language of state's rights, the notion that despite the Fourteenth Amendment, the federal government and particularly the Supreme Court's ability to interfere with state activities—particularly where race was concerned—was severely limited.

There were other criticisms. Many felt uneasy about the Warren opinion's willingness to give the history of the Fourteenth Amendment rather short shrift. That the Court was willing to treat the intent of the framers with respect to school desegregation as a somewhat secondary issue, to put that issue in a relatively narrow corner of the decision and to state, "We cannot turn the clock back to 1868 when the Amendment was adopted, or even to 1896 when *Plessy v. Ferguson* was written," troubled a number of observers who felt that such reasoning smacked of a dangerous kind of judicial policy making. Not all of these critics were segregationists or even opponents of the *Brown* decision.

That the unanimous opinion also made extensive use of social science evidence further troubled many. What did Kenneth Clark's experiments with dolls or Gunnar Myrdal's documentations of prejudice and discrimination have to do with the Fourteenth Amendment? Was the Constitution to be held hostage to the changing fads and fancies of sociologists? Even many supporters of the *Brown* decision feared that Warren's reliance on social science evidence left the school desegregation decision on shaky constitutional grounds, changeable with new social science data or methodologies. Few of the critics stopped to consider or note that the controversial social science evidence located in what would become the famous and controversial footnote 11 was used to help the court resolve an issue older than *Plessy*, indeed older than the Fourteenth Amendment itself, the extent to which segregation, regardless of the equality of the tangible facilities provided, degraded and stigmatized, buttressing a caste system inconsistent with the principle of equality before the law. It was the issue that Charles Sumner and Robert Morris had raised before the Massachusetts Supreme Judicial Court in 1846 on behalf of Sarah Roberts and that Albion Tourgée had raised on behalf of Adolphus Plessy in 1896. Was the social science evidence critical in finally getting the anti-segregation principle recognized in American constitutionalism? It is hard to say. Research by legal historian Dennis Hutchinson indicates that the social science evidence was not as important to the outcome of the case as it has appeared to many observers. Still the use of the social science evidence was heavily criticized. Some of that criticism was made by people who appeared to show little appreciation for the long history of the issues, particularly the stigma issue, presented in the *Brown* decision.

Brown provoked an intense popular reaction. Impeach Earl

Warren signs appeared on billboards dotting the landscape in a good many states. But the *Brown* decision would only be the opening salvo in postwar America's debate over the proper role of the courts in America's governance. The Warren Court was about the business of doing something that had not been done since Reconstruction, and even then not by the Supreme Court. More than any other Court, the Warren Court brought the Fourteenth Amendment to life. The Court began this process with *Brown*. But the process did not end there. The Warren Court, headed by the former California attorney general and governor, who ironically enough had been a vigorous supporter of the wartime internment of Japanese Americans, would move into other areas, continually striking sensitive nerves in the national body politic. By the 1960s, the Court, perhaps spurred on by the moral capital it had gained with the *Brown* decision, produced decisions that touched on virtually every conceivable sensitivity in American life. In a nation with a strong tradition of public invocations of religiosity, the Warren Court proclaimed that official prayers in public schools violated the Constitution in *Engel v. Vitale* (1962). The Court, the nation's history of sexual prudery notwithstanding, found that a Connecticut statute prohibiting the distribution of birth control devices was unconstitutional in *Griswold v. Connecticut* (1965). American writings, at least since the days of Thomas Jefferson, had long celebrated the superiority of the yeoman farmer and small-town and rural America over the dangerous and alien cities. Despite that history, the Court proclaimed in *Baker v. Carr* (1962) that rural and urban Americans were entitled to equal representation before state legislatures. And perhaps most of all, the tradition in many states of harsh treatment of those accused of crimes did not stop the Warren Court from deciding that the accused had rights that local authorities could not ignore. In 1963, in the opinion in *Gideon v. Wainwright* authored by Justice Black, the Court held that criminal suspects had to be given attorneys at trial. Decisions in *Miranda v. Arizona* (1966) and *Escobedo v. State of Illinois* (1964) limited police interrogations and required police officials to inform suspects of their rights not to cooperate during interrogations. By 1967 the Court was even bold enough to take on the long-taboo subject of interracial marriage. In that year the Court struck down Virginia's ban on interracial marriage in the case of *Loving v. Virginia*.

One can debate and indeed many have debated these decisions both as to their wisdom as matters of policy and as to whether or not they were really correct applications of constitutional principles. We will not enter that debate or set of debates here, but two things are clear from the history of the Warren Court from *Brown* forward. First the Court repeatedly touched on sensitive areas of American culture. *Brown* was not an anomaly in this regard; it was instead the progenitor of a pattern in the Court's jurisprudence, a pattern of thought or jurisprudence that for better or worse was willing to take on the sensibilities of large portions of the American public when it believed that the Constitution dictated such.

Second, the Court was breathing a new life into the Fourteenth Amendment, a life that had been absent for much of the twentieth century. Again the Warren Court's decisions can and probably always will be debated, but it is clear that the Warren Court brought the two central concerns of the Fourteenth Amendment into the Court's jurisprudence. The first of these was the principle that the races should be treated equally before the law. The system of organized, systematic discrimination that had developed during the twentieth century was an ongoing violation of this principle both in terms of the quality of government service provided for Negroes and in terms of governmental support for a system of caste distinctions. The second Fourteenth Amendment principle that the Warren Court applied with unprecedented vigor was the application of rights deemed fundamental to the states. Indeed the Warren Court courted even greater controversy by declaring that there were fundamental rights not specifically mentioned in the Bill of Rights, the right to privacy being a major example. The Court's view was that these unenumerated rights were implied by the first ten amendments and were protected by the Constitution. These unenumerated rights also could not be violated by state governments.

It was this process of bringing the Fourteenth Amendment alive and making it central to the Court's constitutional jurisprudence that created the controversy that perennially surrounded the Warren Court. It also helped raise the deepest questions concerning the Court's role in a democratic society. State government traditionally has been and indeed still is the branch of government that most touches people in their daily lives. State governments have primary responsibility for criminal justice and law and order. People send their children to public schools run by state and local government. Americans traditionally have looked to state and local government to solve the problems of everyday life, whether those problems involve driver's licenses, high school basketball, obnoxious billboards, the prevention of crime, or the upholding of community mores. Classically, local and state governments have been the governments most responsive to local pressure, to the popular will. When the Warren Court challenged local practices—local practices that were more than custom but that also had the force of law—the Court was interfering with democratic governance in a way that had not previously occurred in American society. We should hasten to add that the Court was doing something else; it was making the Bill of Rights come alive in a way that had never before occurred in the nation's history. The Bill of Rights had been part of the nation's law almost from the beginning—1791 to be exact—but the Court for most of its history had relatively little to say concerning its provisions. The Court was almost totally silent on the subject in the nineteenth century. It only began seriously examining the Bill of Rights in the twentieth century. That process began with the Court's examination of the issue of freedom of speech and the First Amendment after the First World War. But overall the Supreme Court had little occasion to decide Bill of Rights issues. The Bill of Rights had originally been envisioned as only restraining the actions of the federal, not state, governments. While there is strong evidence that the framers of the Fourteenth Amendment, particularly Ohio congressman Jonathan Bingham and Michigan senator Jacob Howard, intended the amendment's privileges or immunities clause to make the Bill of Rights binding on the states, the Supreme Court had made that portion of the amendment a virtual dead letter in the 1873 *Slaughter House Cases.*

The Court would begin in the twentieth century a haphazard, somewhat intellectually incoherent process of applying the Bill of Rights to the states through the Fourteenth Amendment's due process clause. This jury-rigged approach to what has been termed incorporation, applying the Bill of Rights to the states, was helped along by a number of cases in the 1930s. These cases involved black suspects in criminal cases in southern states. They had been tortured into confessing to crimes they had not committed, as occurred in the case of *Brown v. State of Mississippi* (1936), or had been essentially denied attorneys in capital cases, as occurred in *Powell v. Alabama* (1932)—the so-called Scottsboro Boys case. The NAACP had played a prominent role in representing the defendants in that case. These cases, egregious violations of the very concept of due process, caused the Court to, in effect, start applying the Fifth Amendment's guarantee against self-incrimination and the Sixth Amendment's guarantee of a right to counsel against action by state governments.

Still, the process of applying the Bill of Rights to the states was still in its infancy when Earl Warren delivered the Court's opinion in *Brown.* Even by the 1960s when the Court began the process in earnest, applying the Bill of Rights to the states was still new, scarcely explored territory and quite controversial.

But applying the Bill of Rights to the states brought the provisions of the Constitution's earliest amendments alive in a way that had never before been seen in American life. Precisely because the federal government was remote and rarely touched the lives of most citizens, and also precisely because the many statutes and regulations of state governments had the greatest impact on the daily lives of most Americans, the Bill of Rights became more real with the Court's determination that the states could not violate guarantees provided by the federal Constitution. This incorporation of the Bill of Rights, when added to the *Brown* decision, further fueled charges by critics of the Court that the Warren Court was engaged in an unseemly activism, usurping the prerogatives of the democratically elected branches of government, particularly state governments.

The Court's critics charged that the high tribunal's decision making represented a real threat to democracy and self-governance. Many of these critics were simply racists and segregationists; others were people basically skeptical of parts of the Bill of Rights, particularly their modern applications to the states. It should nonetheless be added that there was, from an originalist's perspective, a certain unfortunate and at times necessary and at other times unnecessary sloppiness in the Warren Court's decision-making process that helped fuel many of the criticisms concerning its decisions. *Brown,* for example, was perfectly consistent with the central purposes of the Fourteenth Amendment—that the law should not be permitted to treat people of different races in radically different ways, one as inferior, the other as superior. It could be and has been argued that the *Brown* Court perhaps made a mistake by spending too much time focusing its historical energies on the narrow question of whether or not the Thirty-ninth Congress intended to outlaw school desegregation and not enough time on the broader central concern of the Fourteenth Amendment, insuring equal treatment under the law of people of different races.

Similarly the Warren Court's approach to the incorporation issue lacked a coherence that would satisfy those concerned with the problem of continuity between constitutional jurisprudence and the original intentions of the framers. The Warren Court worked on the development of a selective incorporation of the Bill of Rights—applying only those rights the Court deemed fundamental against the states. This was to be done through the Fourteenth Amendment's due process clause. This approach had at least two difficulties. First, selective incorporation appeared to be and undoubtedly was a simple exercise in judicial policy making, applying those provisions of the Bill of Rights justices believed to be important. Those believed to be unimportant or dangerous were simply ignored. Similarly, the due process clause of the Fourteenth Amendment seems like a dubious vehicle from which to apply the Bill of Rights to the states. It might make sense with respect to some of the provisions of the first ten amendments used to safeguard the rights of suspects in criminal proceedings (the Fifth Amendment's provision against self-incrimination and the Sixth Amendment's right to counsel for defendants in criminal cases are examples), but how could the First Amendment's guarantees protecting freedom of speech or the free exercise of religion, not to mention that amendment's establishment clause, be said to be derived from or applied through a clause guaranteeing due process? It was an incoherence that fortified the Court's critics. Again a better or seemingly better alternative, one more satisfying to originalists existed: the approach to incorporation urged by Justice Hugo Black. His was a view that supported total incorporation through the Fourteenth Amendment's privileges or immunities clause—the approach that had originally been intended by the clause's drafter, Jonathan Bingham.

We are spending a little time on this question of the Warren Court's jurisprudence and possible alternative reasonings in *Brown* and the incorporation cases because they present interesting examples of how the business of deciding judicial cases often differs from the reasoning, even the informed reasoning, of historians and historically informed laypeople. These differences contributed to the controversies over *Brown* and other major cases of the Warren era. They also contributed to the debate over the proper role of the judiciary in American life.

In both *Brown* and the incorporation cases, the Warren Court's reasoning was shaped, in part, by the Court's past and in part by the nation's sense of its past. Judges are creatures of precedent. They are more likely to be familiar with previous court rulings and the reasoning that produced those rulings than they are with the histories that produced specific constitutional provisions. And jurists tend to be reluctant to directly overrule previous opinions, proclaiming their fellow jurists wrong. Instead jurists have a tendency to try and develop new strains of judicial reasoning that don't fiercely clash with previous opinions but instead distinguish and evolve legal doctrine along new lines. Judges do this in part out of a concern that radical shifts from previous legal doctrine will cast some doubt on the whole judicial enterprise—how authoritative will the courts appear if they keep getting different results with their much-vaunted judicial reasoning? Judges also do this because their training is one that stresses distinguishing cases. Asking how a different set of facts, even a slightly different set of facts, or consideration of a different legal principle might change the outcome of a case is probably the first skill that fledgling attorneys learn. It is a skill learned in the initial weeks in law school. That skill is honed in legal practice, becoming yet sharper as the seasoned jurist exercises those skills on the bench. When the Warren Court began to look at the question of the extent to which the Bill of Rights applied to the states, it looked to the already existing body of law that had begun to restrict state action through the due process clause. The Court did not adopt the more radical, although historically more justifiable, alternative of proclaiming *Slaughter House* wrongly decided, grounding incorporation in the Fourteenth Amendment's privileges or immunities clause, as was suggested by Justice Black.

If the process of judicial decision making caused the Warren Court to overlook a strong, historically grounded rationale for its incorporation jurisprudence, the received wisdom concerning the history of the Reconstruction era that produced the Fourteenth Amendment probably played a role in causing the Warren Court to make a historical case for *Brown* that was significantly weaker than it had to be. The tragic-era legend of Reconstruction was so strong, both as a part of the popular culture and as the received wisdom from professional historians, that the members of the *Brown* Court might well be forgiven for assuming that the Thirty-ninth Congress might have meant very little indeed by the phrase "equal protection of the laws." In any event, the Warren Court's relative lack of historical grounding seemed to provide further ammunition for the Court's critics.

Bolling v. Sharpe, the companion case to *Brown*, also helped fuel critics' charges that the Warren Court's desegregation jurisprudence was not firmly rooted in the original understandings of the Constitution. You will recall that *Bolling* was based on the Fifth Amendment's due process clause and not on the Fourteenth

Amendment's equal protection clause. This was because *Bolling* dealt with the District of Columbia, federal territory governed by Congress, and not the actions of state government. Critics, prominent among them the late legal historian Raoul Berger, have noted that the Fifth Amendment was not originally intended to provide for equal protection of people of different races; indeed the Fifth Amendment became part of the Constitution at a time when slavery was legal and widely practiced.

In *Bolling* the Court had something of a dilemma. In light of the Civil War amendments, could it really be said that the equal protection or equal treatment principle did not apply to the federal government? It is true that the Fourteenth Amendment only mentions states, but could the great constitutional movement that eliminated slavery, established citizenship for all persons born in the United States, mandated equal protection, and eliminated racial restrictions on voting—the Thirteenth, Fourteenth, and Fifteenth Amendments—really have been meant to allow the federal government a right to discriminate that was denied the states? If so that would mean that not only the principle in *Brown* would have been suspect, as applied to the District of Columbia and other federal territories, but the principle in *Plessy* as well. Would the Court have been forced to acknowledge that there was no equal protection principle binding the federal government, that the federal government might, for example, have had schools for white children in the District of Columbia and provided no schools for black children? The Warren Court wisely rejected this reasoning in *Bolling*. Should the *Bolling* Court have tried a Fourteenth Amendment rationale rather than a Fifth Amendment one because it would have been more historically defensible? Perhaps. But the Court was faced with something of a logical dilemma in the case. The language of the Fourteenth Amendment referred to states, not the federal government. The history of the Fifth Amendment did not indicate that it was meant to insure equal treatment of the races. To allow the federal government a power to discriminate on the basis of race, when that power was denied to state governments, would have been absurd. The Court in *Bolling* had a ready body of precedent declaring that the Fifth Amendment's due process clause required equal treatment of people of different races. The Court's use of the Fifth Amendment when viewed in this context was not unreasonable.

We are focusing on the questions of historical reasoning and original intent not because there is an absence of persuasive arguments in favor of having jurists interpret the Constitution according to the needs or felt needs of the times. The debate over whether or not the Constitution should be interpreted largely in terms envisioned by the framers or whether Courts should view the Constitution as a "living document," as the proponents of that view would frame the issue, is a complex question that we cannot treat here. Strong arguments have been advanced for the competing propositions that departures from original intent simply become exercises in judicial policy making unconnected to the intended meanings of constitutional provisions and that slavish adherence to a doctrine of original intent produces a brittle constitutional jurisprudence incapable of meeting the real and evolving needs of our society. What is important for our purposes is that fidelity to history has long been something of a gold standard in American constitutional discourse. Like gold, history as currency tends to be strong and almost universally accepted. The party to a constitutional debate that can claim the support of history has a strong rhetorical and political advantage. There might be arguments, even persuasive ones, for taking a constitutional principle beyond what was intended by the framers, but that tends to be a harder case to make, particularly in the popular imagination. By not making the most compelling historical argument possible, the Warren Court helped insure that *Brown* would remain controversial.

If the Warren Court's often less than robust historical reasoning, not to mention the substance of its decisions, produced critics, the high court's decisions also produced supporters. Yale law professor Alexander Bickel, who as a law clerk to Justice Felix Frankfurter had drafted an important memo dealing with the issue of history and the school desegregation decision, authored a book in 1962 titled *The Least Dangerous Branch: The Supreme*

Court at the Bar of Politics. In it Bickel called for a Supreme Court that would interpret the Constitution according to enduring values embedded in the nation's fundamental charter, even if those values were not explicitly spelled out. Bickel expressed his support for the *Brown* decision by noting, "Government cannot take actions that have the consequence of placing one group in a position of permanent humiliation and inferiority." *Brown* caused other legal commentators to argue the value of the Court, the idea that it as a body not dependent on popular opinion and majority support could cut the Gordian knots of American politics that had stymied the elected branches of government. *Brown,* making the states respect the Bill of Rights, reapportionment— these were good things and unlikely to have occurred if the nation had waited for the elected branches of government to respond. Judicial activism, in this view, was a good thing, something to be encouraged, a way particularly of protecting relatively unpopular and powerless minorities. The Court would move the nation forward, solving the tough problems—making social progress. It is probably not coincidental that many of the most ardent champions of this point of view were law professors, particularly at elite law schools. They saw their writings and their former students, in the role of law clerks and ultimately judges, as playing pivotal roles in the shaping of this new era of social progress through judicial enlightenment.

The debate continued. Was *Brown* the beginning of a new wave of illegitimate usurpation of the democratic process by an unelected judiciary? Or were the courts, by virtue of their relative insulation from politics, able to tackle the entrenched inequities in American life? This debate was taking place against a background of often profound change, indeed upheaval in American race relations—a topic we will explore more fully in the next chapter. The ruling against school segregation was the beginning of a process that would get the government increasingly involved in dismantling the Jim Crow structures that had developed in the South since the beginning of the twentieth century. Two of the most important breakthroughs in this regard would come in the 1960s with the passage of the 1964 Civil Rights Act and the 1965

Voting Rights Act. The former prohibited racial discrimination in public accommodations and employment, while the latter provided for Justice Department supervision to protect the voting rights of minority voters in the South and other parts of the country. By the end of the 1960s or beginning of the 1970s, the kind of rigid, ritualistic, official public segregation that had existed for most of the twentieth century was slowly, and at times often painfully, coming to an end.

There was, of course, continued resistance to the dismantling of official segregation. Interestingly enough, that resistance would play an important part in *Brown*'s ongoing role as the centerpiece of the national debate over the role of the courts in American governance. The 1968 presidential election was, in part, a referendum on the changes that had occurred in American race relations during the 1960s. The candidate for the Democratic Party that year was Vice President Hubert H. Humphrey, a longtime supporter of desegregation and someone who had played a critical role in supporting the civil rights legislative program of President Lyndon Johnson. The Republican candidate, Richard Nixon, had been a supporter of the *Brown* decision and desegregation more generally in the 1950s. Soon after the 1954 desegregation decision, Nixon, then vice president, praised Warren remarking, "And, speaking for a unanimous Supreme Court, a great Republican Chief Justice, Earl Warren, has ordered an end to racial segregation in the nation's schools." But by 1968 Nixon was courting the white southern vote through a campaign emphasizing judicial restraint and an opposition to busing to achieve school integration. This was part of Nixon's "southern strategy" designed to capture the votes of white southerners, who had traditionally voted for Democrats, for the Republican Party. That year there was also a major third party campaign by Alabama governor George C. Wallace. Wallace had gained fame in the early 1960s as a supporter of segregation—particularly with his stand against the integration of the University of Alabama in 1962. The Wallace campaign had a barely disguised segregationist agenda.

Nixon's victory in 1968 had mixed implications for both *Brown* and the future of school desegregation. On the one hand, during the Nixon administration the federal courts actually became more effective in dismantling the dual school systems still existing in the South. Often over the objections of the Nixon Justice Department, the federal courts struck down locally developed "freedom of choice" plans that required black parents to assume the burden of integrating previously all-white schools—a move that often subjected the parents to local intimidation. The Supreme Court played a pivotal role by limiting the extent to which state and local officials could continue to delay school desegregation efforts. On the other hand, with the Nixon administration's efforts to get the votes of the white South, the courts in the early years of the administration increasingly had to exercise supervisory powers to insure compliance. The administration was reluctant to use the carrot and stick of federal spending, education funds from the Department of Health, Education, and Welfare to induce state officials to proceed with school integration.

The role of the federal courts in implementing school desegregation further fueled the controversy over judicial activism. Nixon helped make the role of the judiciary and the composition of the Supreme Court national political issues. Announcing that he wanted to place justices on the high court who would be "strict constructionists," by which Nixon meant supporters of a jurisprudence of strict adherence to original intent, Nixon sought through judicial nominations to rally the political support of those who opposed the activism of the Warren Court. Although Nixon expressed his support for *Brown*, his call for strict constructionists on the Court and particularly his announced intention to place southern conservatives on the Court was seen by many as an attack on *Brown* along with the rest of the legacy of the Warren era.

Brown became an especially high-profile issue for four of Nixon's nominations for the Supreme Court. The nominations of Clement Haynsworth, George Harold Carswell, William Rehnquist, and Lewis Powell all illustrate the changing role that *Brown* was playing in the late 1960s and early 1970s. The 1969 nomination of Clement Haynsworth, a judge then sitting on the United States Court of Appeals for the Fourth Circuit, was per-

{ *Brown v. Board of Education* }

ceived by many civil rights advocates as an effort to turn back the clock on civil rights and especially to weaken the *Brown* decision. While it is unlikely that anyone believed that the core principle pronounced in *Brown I*—that the maintenance of officially separate schools for black and white children was unconstitutional—would be overturned, many feared that justices hostile to *Brown* could thwart the work of *Brown II*—developing means of actually desegregating schools and forcing school districts to dismantle separate school systems. Haynsworth, who was from South Carolina, had had a conservative record on desegregation issues. While on the Fourth Circuit he had authored an opinion stating that the decision of officials in Prince Edward County to close public schools rather than desegregate did not violate the Supreme Court's decision in *Brown*. The Supreme Court reversed his opinion in *Griffin v. County School Board* (1964). While on the Fourth Circuit Haynsworth was particularly reluctant to enforce *Brown*. He authored decisions that supported delays in the implementation of school desegregation including a dissenting opinion that would have allowed black or white students to withdraw from schools where they were in a racial minority. During Senate confirmation hearings, Haynsworth never endorsed *Brown* nor conceded that it had been correctly decided.

With *Brown* dependent on the courts for effective enforcement, the prospect of a judge with a proven reluctance to enforce the decision excited great fears among civil rights champions. Civil rights groups mobilized to oppose the nomination. Haynsworth's nomination was also opposed by many labor unions. Combined pressure from both labor and civil rights organizations contributed to the Senate's rejection of the Haynsworth nomination.

Following the Haynsworth nomination, Nixon submitted the name of George Harold Carswell for a position on the high court. Carswell had taken positions even less supportive of desegregation than Haynsworth. At his confirmation hearing, it was brought out that Carswell had publicly supported white supremacy in 1948 and that he had generally been a supporter of segregation. As a United States district court judge, Carswell had been frequently reversed for issuing opinions supportive of segregation. Like Haynsworth, Carswell refused to endorse *Brown* during his confirmation hearing. Carswell also engendered strong opposition, and his nomination was defeated in the Senate.

Both the Haynsworth and the Carswell nominations were part of a time in which the *Brown* decision, or at least its effective implementation, was still very much contested territory. While Richard Nixon was a president who did not oppose the basic decision in *Brown*, he knew that there was political capital to be made in making an indirect attack on the desegregation decision. That attack would be made through the appointment of justices hostile to and perceived as hostile to the 1954 ruling. Such nominations would shore up Nixon's support in the South and make *Brown* a continuing issue—at times explicit, at times implicit—in American political life. Similarly, the successful efforts of the civil rights movement to block these nominations continued the debate over *Brown* and the proper function of the judiciary.

In many ways the debate over *Brown* and its implications for the wider debate over the role of the judiciary in America would be fundamentally altered with Nixon's nomination of William Rehnquist to the Supreme Court in 1971. Rehnquist, who had been a conservative political activist in his native Arizona, had had a long history with the *Brown* decision. As a law clerk to Justice Robert Jackson while the *Brown* case was being decided, Rehnquist authored a memo critical of the case for desegregation and supportive of the Court's earlier decision in *Plessy v. Ferguson*. Rehnquist also had a history of conflict with the NAACP in Arizona and opposition to anti-discrimination legislation in that state. He had also publicly and vigorously supported the Carswell nomination, arguing that the failed nominee's record was the result of a "constitutional conservatism," not racism. Rehnquist came to the Senate as a court nominee who was clearly a staunch conservative, one who indeed had a history of resistance to civil rights measures. How would he handle the issue of *Brown* during the confirmation process and what would that mean?

During his Senate confirmation hearings, Rehnquist, who would later become chief justice, repeatedly reaffirmed the correctness of the 1954 decision, indicating that the unanimous nature of the decision had made *Brown* the law of the land that should continue to be followed. He also stated his view that the Warren opinion was historically defensible. During the hearings Rehnquist took some pains to distinguish between *Brown*, which he indicated he would not challenge as a justice, and the Warren Court's decisions in criminal procedure, which he believed were still open to judicial reconsideration.

The nomination of Lewis Powell to the Supreme Court also helped reinforce *Brown's* position as a virtually untouchable icon of constitutional jurisprudence by the early 1970s. Nominated at the same time as Rehnquist, Powell had also had, to be charitable, a checkered history with respect to the 1954 desegregation decision. As chairman of the Richmond, Virginia, school board, Powell presided over a body that had resisted school desegregation. By 1961, some seven years after the *Brown* decision, the Richmond public schools were still rigidly segregated. Powell had also privately expressed opposition to *Brown* and as an attorney had represented Prince Edward County in its efforts to close public schools rather than desegregate. He also supported the state of Virginia's policy of giving tuition vouchers to students attending segregated schools as a means of avoiding integration. Powell would also proclaim his fidelity to *Brown* during the course of his confirmation hearing, indicating that the decision had set a precedent that must be respected.

One modern legal commentator, Brad Snyder, has gone so far as to say that the Rehnquist and Powell hearings helped place the 1954 decision in the upper, or perhaps more accurately the untouchable, canon of American constitutional law. The Rehnquist hearing was particularly telling in this regard. For the first time a conservative gave a detailed defense of the decision. In an important way, the battle over *Brown's* basic legitimacy had been settled. If there was still room for public debate over the question posed by *Brown II*, how to implement desegregation, the essence of *Brown I*, the principle that government could not mandate discrimination, now had widespread public acceptance, any silent, unexpressed, private doubts notwithstanding. The principle was one issue that serious contenders for public office or public influence were not willing to dispute, at least publicly.

In terms of public, political debate, the debate over the essential soundness of the *Brown* decision was over. There was still, to be sure, something of an academic debate to be had on the subject. In 1977, legal historian Raoul Berger authored the controversial book *Government by Judiciary: The Transformation of the Fourteenth Amendment*. In that study Berger, who acknowledged that the school desegregation mandated by *Brown* was just as a matter of policy, nonetheless argued that the decision was a stunning example of judicial overreach and a violation of the original understanding of the Fourteenth Amendment. The Berger study reiterated many of the views of the earlier critics of the Warren opinion and was based on the view that the Fourteenth Amendment took root in a northern political climate that was so racist as to preclude the kind of far-reaching, egalitarian interpretation essayed by Earl Warren in *Brown*. Berger's was a controversial and provocative thesis but ultimately one that primarily engaged the nation's historians and law professors, not its politicians and prospective jurists. While the book brought about lively debates in law reviews and historical journals, few in the business of fashioning law and public policy were prepared, by the late 1970s, to publicly agree with Berger that *Brown* had been incorrectly decided.

What had happened? How had *Brown* been transformed from its status as a matter of intense public controversy in the 1950s and 1960s into a decision that would rarely be critiqued and only then in somewhat rarefied academic circles by the 1970s? Certainly part of the answer lies in the transformation of racial attitudes that had begun to occur in the 1960s. The civil rights movement of the 1960s, the fight for desegregation and voting rights, helped to transform the attitudes of white Americans toward issues of race relations in ways that are still unfolding—a point we will explore in the next chapter in greater detail. The movement was in many ways a national morality play, played out for the first time in the living rooms of tens of millions of Americans through the medium of television. The drama of peaceful demonstrators set upon by public officials defending segregation and willing to uphold its virtues through the use of clubs, fire hoses, and attack dogs caused many, even many who had previously accepted traditional notions of Negro inferiority or who had not thought much about race at all, to reconsider previously held beliefs. If segregation meant setting attack dogs on peaceful demonstrators or killing little girls by bombing churches or murdering young men registering voters in the Mississippi Delta, then maybe segregation was an evil and a great evil that had to be eradicated. That rethinking didn't necessarily mean that all white Americans were willing to enlist en masse in the cause of breaking down all existing racial barriers and inequalities. It does mean that many were becoming less and less comfortable with the traditional, outwardly visible manifestations of the nation's historic caste system. In that atmosphere *Brown* would gain increased acceptance. By the 1970s, rejection of *Brown* put a person in the uncomfortable position of appearing to support the segregationists of the 1960s, a public posture that fewer and fewer people were willing to adopt.

The civil rights movement of the 1960s also brought about a political revolution in the South. The Voting Rights Act of 1965 changed the political landscape in the region. From the beginning of the twentieth century until the 1960s, black voters had been effectively disenfranchised in the South. Southern politicians in the first five decades of the twentieth century could not only ignore the wishes of their black constituents, they could and often did engage in a vicious politics of race baiting to gain and hold office. With the passage of the Voting Rights Act of 1965, that would change. With effective federal enforcement of the Fifteenth Amendment's guarantee of the right to vote, Afro-American voters became a major political force in southern politics. The old antiblack, race-baiting politics of the past became increasingly less tenable. Even those who had previously been opponents of desegregation had to trim their sails somewhat to survive in the new political atmosphere. This, too, contributed to a new mood in southern and national politics, a mood in which direct opposition to *Brown* was less and less viable in public life.

The *Brown* decision benefited from the change in racial attitudes that occurred in the country during the 1960s. But the

1954 case's role as constitutional touchstone would not end with its acceptance across the political spectrum in the 1970s. The debates over judicial power, individual rights, state prerogative, and the proper role of history and original intentions in constitutional jurisprudence—debates that had heightened public interest since the Warren opinion was handed down—would continue to intensify in the 1970s and beyond. *Brown* would continue to play a vital role in these debates even after the development of the widespread consensus that *Brown* was properly decided.

The new consensus on *Brown* helped transform the debate over constitutional methodology, particularly the question of the role of history and original intentions in constitutional jurisprudence. In the years immediately after *Brown*, many of the decision's supporters worked to establish *Brown's* legitimacy by trying to demonstrate that it was consistent with the intentions of those nineteenth-century men of the Thirty-ninth Congress who drafted the Fourteenth Amendment. By the 1970s, the debate over history was beginning to take a somewhat different shape. Many liberal legal commentators were beginning to ask, How legitimate could a jurisprudence rooted in originalism be if it called *Brown* into question, if it made the great desegregation case problematic? Many conservatives found themselves scrambling to reconcile their support for a jurisprudence rooted in original intent with the new, widespread consensus over *Brown*.

Of course other issues were at stake, issues that went beyond the issue of desegregation advanced in *Brown v. Board of Education*. The Supreme Court's decisions in the areas of criminal justice, religion in public life, and the right to privacy remained enduring areas of public controversy. These controversies would not end with the retirement of Chief Justice Earl Warren in 1969. Under the new chief justice, Warren Burger, the Court would continue examining sensitive areas of American life. The Court's 1973 decision in *Roe v. Wade*, severely restricting the ability of state governments to regulate abortions, was and indeed remains a decision every bit as controversial as *Brown* was when it was first decided. The 1973 decision was in some ways even more controversial because the opposition to *Brown* tended to be regionally centered, while the opposition to *Roe* (as well as support for the decision) was nationwide.

Roe would have an important bearing on the development of the debate over *Brown* and the proper role of history in constitutional jurisprudence. While we do not intend to discuss either the policy or constitutional arguments that might be made for or against *Roe*, it is safe to say that from the point of view of those who argue for constitutional interpretation based on the framers' intentions, support for the 1973 decision was weak. *Roe* has become perhaps the sharpest constitutional controversy of our time, generally, although not exclusively, pitting liberal and conservative constitutional commentators against each other. In part the continued battle over *Brown* and the proper role of history in constitutional jurisprudence has been a way for combatants to argue the merits of the abortion decision. One side, opponents of the decision, usually conservatives, make the case that *Roe v. Wade* was illegitimate in part because it had a weak historical foundation. Those arguing this point hasten to add that their use of history would not have precluded the Warren decision in *Brown*. Their opponents, usually liberal, argue that *Roe v. Wade* was an important and necessary decision and that an exclusive reliance on the intentions of the framers is not key to legitimate jurisprudence and that such would have precluded the desegregation decision in *Brown*.

It is perhaps within this context that Robert Bork's praise for *Brown* during his unsuccessful 1987 Senate confirmation hearing might best be understood. In a short thirty-three years, the 1954 school desegregation decision had undergone a curious odyssey. Highly controversial, indeed often reviled when it was first handed down, the case had undergone a transformation in the public mind. It had become an icon whose basic premise—that the state should not engage in official discrimination—few were willing to publicly question. Curiously enough *Brown* has, in recent years, taken on a new role. It has become a yardstick against which the legitimacy of other cases and indeed differing strategies of constitutional interpretation are measured.

Brown and Race

The Divided Legacy

It is relatively easy to assess *Brown*'s importance in American legal history. Historians and legal scholars as well as practicing attorneys and sitting jurists would readily agree as to its place as one of the handful of pivotal cases in the life of the nation and in the history of the Supreme Court. It easily takes its place among the milestones of American jurisprudence, ranking alongside the famous (*Marbury v. Madison*), the infamous (*Dred Scott v. Sanford*), and the still highly contested (*Roe v. Wade*) handiworks of the nation's highest tribunal. The case, as we have seen, has become something of a constitutional lodestar, a measuring stick for constitutional methodologies and ideologies for both the legal profession and the lay public.

And yet *Brown* was not a case about legal process nor about the Court's proper role in the American system of governance. The decision instead concerned the nation's most enduring and vexing problem: race. Did *Brown* make a difference? What difference did it make? A half century after the 1954 decision, it is not at all difficult to find those who would urge that the majority opinion authored by Chief Justice Earl Warren heralded a new era in American race relations, that it helped precipitate the downfall of Jim Crow. It is also easy to find those who argue that *Brown* was fatally flawed, a decision too weak to have effectively made a difference in the lives of Americans of African descent. Others will argue that the changes that have come about are due to causes other than *Brown*, the civil rights revolution and resulting legislation of the 1960s, and structural changes in American society and the economy. Still others will argue that there has really been relatively little in the way of change or progress, that the seeming progress that has occurred has been more illusory than real, that blacks remain entrenched at the bottom of the American social hierarchy despised and apart, perpetual outsiders, perennial victims of discrimination.

Before we can answer the question of what difference *Brown* made, we have to ask how American race relations and the circumstances of African Americans have changed in the last half century. That is a complex question. The Colored and White signs, once ubiquitous in many parts of the country, have come down from the bus stations and water fountains, the park benches and rest rooms. The last vestiges of Jim Crow law were eradicated by statute and court decision more than a generation ago.

Black men and women are found in places that would have been inconceivable on that Tuesday afternoon in December in 1953 when Thurgood Marshall asked the Supreme Court, "Why . . . you have to single out Negroes and give them this separate treatment?" Colin Powell, the son of black West Indian immigrants, now serves as secretary of state. A black woman, Condoleeza Rice—who as a child lost a friend to Klan terrorism, one of the little girls murdered in the bombing of a Negro church in Birmingham, Alabama, in 1962—now serves as head of the National Security Council. African American students are routinely enrolled in all-white, indeed even previously legally segregated, universities. The same may be said for black faculty members, even though their presence is still rare in most academic disciplines. Afro-American men and women are to be found in major law firms and the executive offices of major corporations—not in numbers that correspond to the black portion of the population at large to be sure—but present, and present in sufficient numbers so that the black man or woman in such a position cannot simply be dismissed as a token or as freakish or idiosyncratic. Black politicians are routinely found in state legislatures and the United States House of Representatives. The occasional black governor or senator even serves a term or two, every now and then. African American officers, even flag rank officers, have long since ceased to be a rarity in the racially integrated armed forces—a far cry from the experiences of Negro servicemen and women in the Jim Crow army and navy of the two world wars. Black cabinet members routinely advise presidents of both parties. Southern white politicians now turn their backs on the naked racism of their predecessors and regularly court the Afro-American vote. Indeed some, like the late South Carolina senator Strom Thurmond or West Virginia senator Robert Byrd, implicitly and at times explicitly repudiate their own pasts. Thurmond, the 1948 candidate of the segregationist Dixiecrat Party, vigorously courted the large black vote in his home state for the last three decades of his career, from the 1970s on. Robert Byrd, a former member of the Ku Klux Klan, denounces his former association.

These changes reflect deep, perhaps seismic changes in American racial attitudes over the past half century. The liberalization of racial attitudes that started becoming part of American culture before the Second World War, a liberalization that provided an important, perhaps critical backdrop to the *Brown* decision, has continued. Indeed that liberalization has spread and intensified. The raw racism that prevailed in daily life, popular culture, and academic treatise at the beginning of the last century has become an embarrassing relic, defended by only a marginalized few today in public life. Few in the modern behavioral or biological sciences support the kind of scientific racism that was heartily championed at the best universities a century ago. Affirmative action programs exist to try and increase the number of minority students admitted to universities or minority employees hired by firms. And even though those programs are under heavy criticism and face an uncertain future, even the critics of such programs couch their criticism in the rhetoric of the civil rights movement of the 1960s, claiming that they are seeking "color-blind" methods to increase the inclusion of those previously excluded.

The changes in racial attitudes among white Americans are perhaps even more profound than has generally been acknowledged. Social science surveys as well as day-to-day practice indicate an acceptance of interracial relations in family life, marriage, and adoption that clearly would have been unthinkable in 1954 when the *Brown* decision was handed down. Even if one suspects that a significant portion of the responses to social surveys should be discounted as people telling the pollsters the "right" or "socially acceptable" answer, the fact that tolerance for interracial marriage or transracial adoption has become the "right" answer in the last half century itself reflects a profound cultural change. This rejection of outright racial bigotry even occurs in some quite unexpected precincts in modern America. Private schools in southern communities that originally started out as "Seg Academies," institutions founded to allow white students to avoid integrated public schools, now routinely enroll black students. Southern white fundamentalist Protestant churches often have black parishioners. Rural white southern voters vote for African American representatives—former congressmen J. C. Watts of Oklahoma and Mike Espy of Mississippi are perhaps the most prominent examples of this. Surprisingly, even the occasional right-wing antigovernment militia will sometimes have a black member or two. Multiracialism and a rejection of the kind of racism that prevailed in the first half and indeed beyond the first half of the twentieth century has taken strong root in modern America. It has even done so in venues that would have been inconceivable just a few decades earlier.

But that is only part of the story. Racism still exists. It is not hard to find. But it lacks the kind of official support that it had in generations past. It is not as overwhelming a part of American culture as it was throughout most of the twentieth century, but still, reports of its total demise are woefully premature. Segregation continues. It has lessened to be sure, but African Americans remain the most segregated of the racial and ethnic groups in the United States, with the exception of Indians on reservations. At the dawn of the twenty-first century, nearly half of the black population still lives in communities that are 90 percent or more black. The poverty rate for black families is roughly three times that for whites. The percentage of African American children raised in female-headed, fatherless households has risen dramatically since the *Brown* decision. More than 50 percent of all African American children are raised in such families. The percentage of black children born out of wedlock approaches 70 percent. The unemployment rate for black men is double that for white men. The problem is even more acute when the unemployment rate for young black men is considered.

The list of social disadvantages for contemporary African Americans is long. Inner-city black communities have high, often staggering, crime rates. The homicide rate for young black men between the ages of fifteen and twenty-four is more than ten times the national average. A strong alienation often exists between black communities and the law enforcement officers whose task it is to protect those communities. This in turn, of course, only serves to exacerbate the problem of crime and violence in many black communities, especially poor ones.

And public education remains segregated. This segregation is not like the official school segregation that was at issue in *Brown*. There are, to be sure, still local school officials who attempt subterfuges designed to steer white students to some schools, black students to others. But today opponents of segregated education face a problem in many ways more intractable and certainly less amenable to judicial remedy than that faced by Thurgood Marshall and his associates five decades ago. Inner-city schools remain segregated because middle-class parents, white and increasingly black ones as well, have by and large withdrawn their children from those schools. The movement of the middle class to the suburbs out of the jurisdiction of urban public schools, coupled with the increased use of private schools for those middle-class children who remain in major cities, has led to a segregation in education for poor black children in many cities every bit as stark as, and in some cases starker than, it was at the time *Brown* was decided.

Indeed the social science evidence indicates that a resegregation of schools has occurred in recent decades. According to a recent report by the Civil Rights Project at Harvard University, titled "A Multiracial Society with Segregated Schools: Are We Losing the Dream?" (2003), school desegregation made steady progress through the 1980s, particularly in the South. Since that decade, school segregation or resegregation has increased due to suburbanization and the flight of middle-class students to private schools.

This continued segregation in education is accompanied by significant problems in inner-city education. Black educational achievement as measured by standardized test scores remains, on average, lower than that for white—significantly so. This in turn continues to fuel the national debate over affirmative action, particularly in university admissions. Should black students, as well as students from other disadvantaged minority groups, be given some sort of break in university admissions—"racial preferences" cry the concept's opponents; "affirmative action" reply its supporters—or should university admissions be color-blind, race neutral, despite the burden of race throughout American history?

To many African American children, education remains separate and unequal despite *Brown* and its successor cases. There are also distressing indications—more than indications really—that decades, if not centuries, of discrimination in education and employment have produced results that have taken on a cultural life of their own. Reliable observers tell us that many inner-city children have come to reject those attitudes and habits that are requisite for academic success. Excelling at school, doing well on standardized tests, studying hard, demonstrating an interest in class—these practices are seen as "acting white," a rejection of one's racial identity. To the extent that these observations are accurate, they bespeak a frightening internalization of older racist norms that put an exceedingly low ceiling on black intellectual capacity.

So which picture is more representative of the current reality of race relations and the status of Americans of African descent at the beginning of the twenty-first century? Is that reality better captured by the increasingly integrated world of the black middle class and more and more even that of the stable black working class? Or is it better represented by the continually depressed circumstances in the inner city? Should we judge race in modern America by looking at university-educated business managers, college professors, military officers, and presidential advisers? Or do we gain a more accurate picture by looking at junior high school students in ghetto neighborhoods who are functionally illiterate? Should we applaud the tremendous changes that have occurred, recognizing the very real progress that we often take for granted? Sixty years ago, the black man driving the municipal bus that takes us to work would have been barred from that job because of his race. Thirty years ago, the African American woman who advises us on how the new tax laws will affect our investments would have been kept out of that job because of her race and her sex. Or should we decry the fact that young black men, most of whom are innocent of any crime, are far more likely to be hassled by police because of their color and that they are hassled even by good cops because of the disproportionate involvement of young black men in street crime?

Is the glass half empty or half full? We won't stop debating the issue, nor should we. But even this debate can provide a key to understanding the impact of the *Brown* decision on race relations in America. For those Americans whose ancestors were brought from Africa in chains to what would become the United States, the question of race has always involved two distinguishable albeit interrelated questions. The first was the question of caste, the second the question of inequality. Caste, of course, helped produce and exacerbate inequality. This was done when the law commanded that black students had to attend the under-resourced schools for colored children. It also occurred when social, economic, and indeed legal barriers reserved the best jobs for white men and women. The American caste system did more than simply stigmatize and set the Negro apart; it did much to create and sustain profound tangible inequalities, inequalities that persist to this day in educational and occupational attainment, residential patterns, wealth accumulation, and other measurable indexes of success and failure in American society.

And yet caste involved something more. The system of caste helped create and sustain an immense psychological chasm between black and white Americans. Black and white Americans would inhabit different communities and have different identities in the nation they shared. This would ironically be most true in the South, despite often strong cultural affinities between black and white southerners. This sense of being apart would often make African Americans strangers in their own land. It was a sense of difference constantly reinforced by a rigorous system of exclusion, a system of exclusion backed, indeed made possible, by the law's mandate.

Brown's importance lay in its setting the nation's law on the path of rejecting the kind of racial exclusion that had made African Americans a people apart since before the nation's founding. The 1954 decision provided a foundation for later court decisions and legislative enactments that established a new set of norms concerning law and race. Before *Brown*, the Fourteenth Amendment notwithstanding, American law gave its sanction to a patent system of racial inequality. *Brown* began the process of withdrawing the law's sanction from the system of caste and castelike distinctions that had been a part of American life from the beginning. *Brown* did not do it alone. The decision would become a catalyst for profound changes in legal norms. It was able to do so in large part because of the remarkable courage of ordinary men and women. That courage started with parents like Harry Briggs of South Carolina, Sarah Bulah of Delaware, and Oliver Brown and the others who stood up for better lives for their children by challenging the entrenched system of school segregation in their communities. It also took great extraordinary courage for Negro parents after *Brown* to risk their children's lives by sending them to the white schools that the Supreme Court claimed could no longer be segregated. The 1954 decision was important. But without the willingness of parents to take their children to the theoretically newly desegregated schools of the South, the Warren opinion would have been a dead letter. Anyone who has seen the newsreels from that era with snarling and vicious mobs poised to attack children attempting to enter schools knows of the incredible bravery of the parents and students who helped turn the Warren opinion into living law.

Brown was not self-executing. It took courageous men and women and boys and girls to make it more than an empty judicial opinion. It also took courageous Americans of all races who struggled in the civil rights movement to make *Brown* the foundation of a modern body of civil rights law firmly rejecting the older system of caste. The civil rights struggles of the 1960s, which led to among other things the critical Civil Rights Act of 1964 and the Voting Rights Act of 1965, played a crucial role in dismantling legal support for the American system of race as caste. The argument made in Benjamin Roberts's lonely lawsuit on behalf of his daughter Sarah in the 1840s would finally become national law in America in the second half of the twentieth century.

In the second half of the twentieth century, the law came to accept, somewhat belatedly, the position argued by Charles Sumner in 1848 and later by Thurgood Marshall in 1953. The state and its laws cannot single out Americans of African descent, indeed any Americans, for separation and stigmatization because of race. The law's statement in this regard has had a powerful influence on American life. It doubtless helped accelerate the rejection of racism as an American cultural norm. As a nation Americans tend to view the Constitution with an importance, indeed perhaps reverence, that takes it beyond the status of simple positive law. The decision in *Brown v. Board of Education* that segregation was unconstitutional had a profound effect not only on American law but on American life as well. When that decision was combined with later reinforcing decisions and civil rights legislation, it gave a significant boost to those larger forces in the society and the culture that were saying that discrimination was wrong and indeed un-American. The synergy between the *Brown* decision and the cultural forces arguing that the day of raw racism was or should be over made the Warren opinion a powerful catalyst both for removing castelike barriers and for changing racial attitudes.

Brown's importance in the history of American race relations is assured. But if *Brown* should be seen as having a central importance in the fight against caste and racism, *Brown* also provides an important lesson in the law's limitations. *Brown* played an important role in challenging the system of caste and exclusion that had developed in American society. But the law has found the system of structural inequality a more vexing problem. The often profound socioeconomic inequalities between blacks and whites can be traced to slavery, segregation, and long-term patterns of exclusion. These were sanctioned, indeed often mandated, by law. Yet it is not clear the extent to which the law will or can provide remedies in the future for the legacy of exclusion in the past. What is clear is that the terrain would have been much bumpier and the playing field an awful lot less level without the efforts of those men and women who developed the strategy, argued the case, and changed history in *Brown v. Board of Education.*

1850   *Roberts v. City of Boston:* Massachusetts Supreme Judicial Court holds that segregation in public schools is consistent with Massachusetts Constitution, which states that "all men are free and equal."

1857   *Dred Scott v. Sandford:* U.S. Supreme Court decision states that Negroes cannot be citizens of the United States. The Court also holds that Congress has no power to end slavery in federal territories.

1860   Abraham Lincoln is elected president on a Republican Party platform that opposes the expansion of slavery to new states and territories.

1861   Eleven slave states secede from the United States, and the Civil War ensues.

1863   President Lincoln issues Emancipation Proclamation, freeing all slaves located in states or parts of states in rebellion.

1865   The Civil War ends. Thirteenth Amendment is ratified, outlawing slavery. Reconstruction begins.

1868   Fourteenth Amendment is ratified. Amendment makes citizens of all persons born in the United States. Amendment also contains equal protection clause and clauses protecting the rights of individuals from state action under the due process and privileges or immunities clauses.

1870   The Fifteenth Amendment is ratified. Amendment prohibits racial discrimination in voting.

1873   Supreme Court decides the *Slaughter House Cases.* Cases severely limit power of Fourteenth Amendment's privileges or immunities clause.

1875   U.S. Supreme Court decides *United States v. Cruikshank.* Case limits ability of Congress to protect citizens against private infringement of constitutional rights.

1877	Rutherford Hayes takes office as president, bringing end of Reconstruction.
1879	*Strauder v. West Virginia* is decided by the U.S. Supreme Court. Decision overturns statute limiting jury service to white men. Statute is found to be inconsistent with general tenor of the Civil War amendments.
1883	Supreme Court decides the *Civil Rights Cases*, holding that neither the Thirteenth nor the Fourteenth Amendment empowers Congress to prohibit racial discrimination in public accommodations.
1886	Supreme Court decides *Yick Wo v. Hopkins*. This case, involving discrimination against Chinese immigrants running laundries, is important because Court found discrimination in the acts of public officials even though the statutes did not mention race or racial discrimination.
1896	*Plessy v. Ferguson* is decided by the U.S. Supreme Court, pronouncing state-mandated segregation consistent with the equal protection clause, so long as the separate facilities are equal.
1908	Supreme Court decides *Berea College v. Commonwealth of Kentucky*. Court upholds state statute mandating segregation in private educational institutions.
1909	NAACP is founded.
1914	Supreme Court decides *McCabe v. Atchison, Topeka and Santa Fe Railway Company*. Court declares that the right to equal accommodations is a personal right that is due immediately on demand.
1917	Supreme Court decides *Buchanan v. Warley*, declaring a statute forbidding sales of property to Negroes violates the freedom of contract.
1929	Charles Hamilton Houston is appointed vice dean of the Howard University Law School.
1930	The Garland Fund agrees to fund an NAACP legal campaign to eradicate Jim Crow, and Nathan Margold

is hired as special counsel to the NAACP to coordinate this effort.

1930   Thurgood Marshall enters Howard University Law School.

1931   Nathan Margold issues a report on potential uses of Garland Fund monies. Report outlines attack on school segregation to force school authorities either to equalize black schools with white ones or to desegregate.

1933   Thurgood Marshall graduates from Howard University Law School and is admitted to the Maryland bar.

1934   Charles Hamilton Houston is appointed staff counsel to the NAACP. He changes Margold strategy with litigation emphasis on graduate and professional schools.

1936   *Pearson v. Murray* is decided by the Maryland Court of Appeals. Court holds that out-of-state scholarship for black law students does not satisfy equal protection clause.

1936   Thurgood Marshall is appointed as an assistant staff counsel to Charles Hamilton Houston at the NAACP.

1938   Charles Hamilton Houston resigns his position with the NAACP, and Thurgood Marshall is appointed chief counsel.

1938   Supreme Court decides *State ex rel. Gaines v. Canada*. Court holds state must provide in-state opportunity for legal education for blacks.

1941   President Franklin Roosevelt, under considerable prodding from black labor leader A. Philip Randolph, issues Executive Order 8802 prohibiting employment discrimination in federal government and defense industries.

1943   Supreme Court decides *United States v. Hirabayashi*. *Hirabayashi* and another Japanese internment case, *United States v. Korematsu* (1944), help establish doctrine that Fifth Amendment's due process clause makes equal protection principle binding on the federal government.

1948   President Harry S. Truman issues executive orders calling for policies of nondiscrimination in the federal civil service and the armed forces.

1948   *Sipuel v. Board of Regents of the University of Oklahoma* and *Fisher v. Hurst* are decided by the U.S. Supreme Court. The Supreme Court confirms that to provide equal educational opportunity, the state need not integrate a law school but need only establish a separate but equal one.

1950   *McLaurin v. Oklahoma State Regents for Higher Education* is decided by the U.S. Supreme Court. The Supreme Court rules that if a state decides to open an educational institution to black students, it would injure black students and the quality of the education they sought to segregate them within the institution.

1950   Supreme Court decides *Sweatt v. Painter.* Court orders Heman Sweatt admitted to the University of Texas Law School. Court finds, on basis of intangible differences, that the separate law school established at a black institution is not equal.

1950–   NAACP files school desegregation cases in federal
1952   district courts. These cases collectively come to be known as *Brown v. Board of Education.*

1952   The U.S. Supreme Court accepts and consolidates appeals in state school desegregation cases. Court also invites petition attorneys in District of Columbia case *Bolling v. Sharpe* to bypass appellate court for direct appeal to Supreme Court. *Bolling* is consolidated with others.

December First set of Supreme Court oral arguments in *Brown*
1952   *v. Board of Education.*

June 1953 *Brown* restored to docket for second set of oral arguments. The parties are ordered by the Court to address whether the legislative history of the Fourteenth Amendment supports segregation or desegregation in schools, whether the Congress or the judiciary is empowered to abolish school segregation, and whether immediate desegregation would be necessary or advisable if the Court were to rule against the school districts.

September 1953	Chief Justice Fred Vinson dies.
October 1953	Earl Warren takes office as chief justice.
December 1953	Rearguments take place.
May 1954	The Supreme Court issues a unanimous opinion in *Brown v. Board of Education*, declaring that "separate educational facilities are inherently unequal." Another hearing is scheduled to determine appropriate remedy.
April 1955	Oral arguments are held on the issue of appropriate remedy to be issued in *Brown v. Board of Education*.
May 1955	The Supreme Court issues a unanimous opinion on the issue of a remedy. Immediate desegregation not ordered. School boards ordered to proceed with "all deliberate speed."
1957	Little Rock crisis. In the face of mob opposition encouraged by Arkansas politicians, President Eisenhower orders federal troops to protect students and to enforce a federal court order to desegregate Central High School in Little Rock.
1964	The Civil Rights Act of 1964 is signed into law. Federal law makes racial discrimination illegal in public accommodations, in employment, and in federally funded higher education.
1965	The Voting Rights Act of 1965 is signed into law, enforcing the Fifteenth Amendment.
1968	The Open Housing Act of 1968 is passed, making discrimination in the sale and rental of housing illegal.

1968   The U.S. Supreme Court decides *Green v. School Board of New Kent County*, intending to end the delay entailed by the "all deliberate speed" formula. School officials are said to have an affirmative duty to eliminate the effects of segregation "root and branch."

BIBLIOGRAPHICAL ESSAY

Note from the Series Editors: The following bibliographical essay contains the major primary and secondary sources the author consulted for this volume. We have asked all authors in the series to omit formal citations in order to make our volumes more readable, inexpensive, and appealing for students and general readers. In adopting this format, Landmark Law Cases and American Society follows the precedent of a number of highly regarded and widely consulted series.

In one sense this bibliographical essay is a little harder than usual to write. From the beginning, we envisioned this book as one that would examine *Brown v. Board of Education* not only as a legal case but also as a study that would connect the desegregation case to broader themes in American culture. In a real sense, everything we had previously read or written as students of American law and history helped inform us and indeed helped serve as background and sources in the writing of this volume. Presumably we are not unique in making such a claim. Most historical writings rest on a considerably broader foundation than the relatively small number of sources actually cited. All that having been said, we shall try in this essay to cull out the most relevant sources, those that best informed us about the history of *Brown* and its antecedents, and the sources that we believe would provide a good background for further exploration on the part of the reader. The bibliography that follows this essay will provide a more extensive list of the sources consulted.

A few other general words about sources are in order before we discuss specific chapters. Our principal primary sources were the cases that we examined. Examinations of cases and the legal doctrines emerging from those cases is, of course, the very essence of what legal historians do. We would like to suggest that legal cases also provide a very important window into the cultural and social mores of different times. Certainly we found that our explorations of some of the major cases dealing with race and caste in American history not only told us about the evolution of legal doctrine but also provided us with an incomparable education in social history as well. We will not spend too much time discussing the cases in this bibliographic essay. They were discussed in the different chapters and are listed in the bibliography. Despite the relative lack of discussion of the cases in this essay, readers should realize that they were of critical importance in the writing of the book. Many secondary sources proved quite helpful in writing this volume. Four of these have a general importance. John Hope Franklin and Alfred A. Moss Jr. provide a superb overall introduction to the field of African American history in *From Slavery to Freedom: A History of African Americans* (2000). Anybody writing on *Brown v. Board of Education* quickly comes to appreciate and realize his indebtedness to the pioneering research of Richard Kluger in his insightful study, *Simple Justice: The History of Brown v. Board of Education and Black America's Struggle for Equality* (1975). Kluger's work would clarify and identify many of the major issues posed by *Brown* for future scholars who would work in the area. Another important general examination of *Brown* is provided in James T. Patterson's *Brown v. Board of Education: A Civil Rights Milestone and Its Troubled Legacy* (2001). Patterson's study is particularly valuable for its detailed discussion of the grassroots support behind the NAACP's desegregation effort and its discussion of the difficulties of implementing the *Brown* decision. A creative exploration of *Brown* and possible alternative ways to have framed the desegregation decision are provided by Jack Balkin and his associates in *What "Brown v. Board of Education" Should Have Said: The Nation's Top Legal Experts Rewrite America's Landmark Civil Rights Decision* (2001). Although some of the reasoning provided in the mock opinions in Balkin's volume are unlikely to have been expressed in 1954, the opinions do provide important and generally well-reasoned constitutional alternatives to the actual decision.

Roberts v. City of Boston (1850) played a critical role in the development of the separate but equal doctrine. Constitutional historian Leonard Levy was one of the first to explore *Roberts* and its critical legacy. A good summary of Levy's research in this area and the importance of *Roberts* in later state and federal jurisprudence on segregation can be found in Levy's *The Law of the Commonwealth and Chief Justice Shaw* (1957). Many historians have explored the history of the African American community in antebellum Boston. The best overall study of the subject is James Oliver Horton and Lois E. Horton, *Black Bostonians: Family Life and Community Struggle in the Antebel-*

lum North (1979). The Hortons' study provides an especially valuable treatment of the antebellum struggle against discrimination in Boston.

Thomas D. Morris's *Southern Slavery and the Law, 1619–1860* (1996) provides the most comprehensive treatment available of the law of slavery in the southern United States, both in terms of formal legal doctrine and in terms of the actual treatment of slaves before courts in particular cases. Those wishing to examine the legal and social status of free Negroes in the antebellum South should begin with Ira Berlin's *Slaves without Masters: The Free Negro in the Antebellum South* (1975). Reconstruction clearly brought pivotal legal, political, and social change for Americans of African descent. Those wishing to learn more about this critical period in American history would do well to consult Eric Foner's *Reconstruction: America's Unfinished Revolution, 1863–1877* (1989).

A valuable discussion of *Plessy v. Ferguson* can be found in Charles A. Lofgren, *The Plessy Case: A Legal-Historical Interpretation* (1987). For a broader examination of the origins and downfall of Jim Crow, consult C. Vann Woodward's classic *The Strange Career of Jim Crow* (2002). As we indicated, an important reason for the Supreme Court's willingness to ignore egregious violations of the Fourteenth and Fifteenth Amendments in the early twentieth century can be found in the historical writings of the era. The widespread agreement among educated Americans of the early twentieth century that Reconstruction was a tragic mistake contributed to the minimal enforcement of the egalitarian principles added to the Constitution during that era. For those wishing to understand the historical literature that shaped most Americans' views of Reconstruction in the early twentieth century, we would suggest examining William A. Dunning, *Reconstruction Political and Economic, 1865–1870* (1907); Claude G. Bowers, *The Tragic Era: The Revolution after Lincoln* (1929); and Paul Buck, *The Road to Reunion* (1937). Although these writings were originally intended as secondary sources on Reconstruction, today they have new lives as primary sources on early twentieth-century racial attitudes.

W. E. B. Du Bois was clearly the central figure in the organization's development before the First World War. Those wishing an introduction to the young Du Bois's views on race would do well to consult his classic 1903 book, *The Souls of Black Folk* (in *Three Negro Classics*, ed. John Hope Franklin, 1965). His rival Booker T. Washington's 1915 autobiography, *Up from Slavery* (also in *Three Negro Classics*), provides an important contrast with the Du Bois narrative. Helpful general histories of the NAACP are to be found in Charles Flint Kellogg, *NAACP: A History of the National Association for the Advancement of Colored People*, vol. 1, *1909–1920* (1967), and Kenneth W. Goings, *The NAACP Comes of Age: The Defeat of Judge John Parker* (1990). Students of the history of the NAACP would also be well served by reading the autobiography of NAACP general secretary Walter White in *A Man Called White: The Autobiography of Walter White* (1948). The development of the NAACP's litigation strategy is ably covered in Mark V. Tushnet, *The NAACP's Legal Strategy against Segregated Education, 1925–1950* (1987).

There is a useful body of literature on the architects of the NAACP's school desegregation strategy. For an examination of Charles Hamilton Houston's life, see Genna Rae McNeil, *Groundwork: Charles Hamilton Houston and the Struggle for Civil Rights* (1983). Houston's legal career and his contribution as vice dean of Howard Law School are also well covered in J. Clay Smith, *Emancipation: The Making of the Black Lawyer, 1844–1944* (1993). William H. Hastie, lawyer, jurist, and legal scholar, was also instrumental in developing the NAACP's legal campaign. Details of Hastie's career can be seen in Gilbert Ware, *William Hastie: Grace under Pressure* (1984). A veritable cottage industry has grown up around the life and work of Thurgood Marshall. The following are particularly helpful in improving our understanding of Marshall's contribution to the school desegregation struggle: Juan Williams, *Thurgood Marshall: American Revolutionary* (1998); Randall W. Bland, *Private Pressure on Public Law: The Legal Career of Justice Thurgood Marshall* (1993); and Mark V. Tushnet, *Making Civil Rights Law: Thurgood Marshall and the Supreme Court, 1936–1961* (1994).

State ex rel. Gaines v. Canada (1937) was an important milestone on the road to *Brown*. The Missouri case attracted a significant amount of attention at the time, generating a number of primary sources that were useful to this study. Conditions at the all-black Lincoln University Law School were described in "Jim Crow Law School" in *Newsweek* (October 1939). The *Gaines* case was also extensively commented on in the contemporary law review and educational literature. See, e.g., "Recent Decisions: Constitutional Law: Equal Protection: Exclusion of Negroes from State University Law School," *Cornell Law Review* (1939); and Charles H. Thompson, "The Missouri Decision and the Future of Negro Education," in *Journal of Negro Education* (1939). For valuable secondary discussions of *Gaines*, see Lucille H. Bluford, "The Lloyd Gaines Story," in *Journal of Educational Sociology* (1959); and Raymond T. Diamond, "Confrontation as Rejoinder to Compromise: Reflections on the Little Rock Desegregation Crisis," in *National Black Law Journal* (1989).

A number of works provided useful information about the evolution of American racial attitudes in the twentieth century. Thomas F. Gossett's *Race: The History of an Idea in America* (1997) and George Fredrickson's *The Black Image in the White Mind: The Debate on Afro-American Character and Destiny, 1817–1914* (1971) provide good overviews of the development of racial attitudes, including the development of scientific racism in the United States. Those wishing a more comprehensive history of scientific racism in American social science would do well to examine Elazar Barkan's *The Retreat of Scientific Racism: Changing Concepts of Race in Britain and the United States between the World Wars* (1992). Don Martindale's "American Sociology before World War II," in *Annual Review of Sociology* (1976), was particularly helpful in informing our understanding of the early development of that discipline. Students of the history of social science would also be well served by reading Gunnar Myrdal et al., *An American Dilemma: The Negro Problem and Modern Democracy* (1944), and T. W. Adorno et al., *The Authoritarian Personality* (1950). Both studies helped influence attitudes toward race and racial prejudice among both social scientists and the lay public and were written shortly before the *Brown* decision.

The two world wars of the twentieth century had profound effects on the lives and attitudes of Americans black and white. The best overall study of Negro participation in the military history of the United States is Bernard C. Nalty's *Strength for the Fight: A History of Black Americans in the Military* (1986). We have spent some time discussing the movies as barometers of popular racial attitudes. Two books by film historian Thomas Cripps are especially valuable for those researching the history of Afro-Americans in films: *Making*

Movies Black: The Hollywood Message Movie from World War II to the Civil Rights Era (1993), and *Slow Fade to Black: The Negro in American Film, 1900–1942* (1993).

A number of sources proved quite helpful in our examination of the actual litigation in *Brown*. The briefs filed in *Brown* and transcripts of the oral arguments in that landmark case are conveniently assembled in *Landmark Briefs and Arguments of the Supreme Court of the United States: Constitutional Law*, vols. 49 and 49A, edited by Philip B. Kurland and Gerhard Casper (Arlington, Va.: University Publications of America, 1975). The two volumes are an invaluable resource, conveniently putting the written records in *Brown I* and *Brown II* as they were presented to the Court in easily accessible form. The Papers of the NAACP (1982) are another important source for primary documents. This collection, which is organized and indexed, contains correspondence, reports, memoranda, and other documents from the official files of the NAACP. It is stored in the Library of Congress and available on microfilm.

A number of autobiographical accounts by counsel involved in *Brown* supply important perspectives on the litigation. Jack Greenberg's *Crusaders in the Courts* (1994) contains an in-depth history of the activities of the NAACP's Legal Defense Fund. Greenberg's memoir provides an insider's perspective on both *Brown* and the era of "massive resistance" that followed. Constance Baker Motley's autobiography, *Equal Justice under Law* (1998), also makes a valuable contribution to the historical record, particularly her portrait of Marshall's reactions to the pressures of the *Brown* litigation. NAACP executive director Roy Wilkins's autobiography, *Standing Fast* (1982), also provides an important perspective on the case. Two important works provide valuable information about the principal attorneys on the other side of the litigation. William H. Harbaugh's *Lawyer's Lawyer: The Life of John W. Davis* (1973) examines the life of the principal attorney representing the states arguing for segregation. Also valuable is Paul Wilson's autobiography, *A Time to Lose: Representing Kansas in Brown v. Board of Education* (1995).

Our knowledge of the Supreme Court's deliberations on *Brown* and the role of the different judicial personalities in the crafting of that decision was greatly enhanced through our examinations of the papers of Justice Harold Burton and Justice Felix Frankfurter, both found in the Library of Congress. The Frankfurter Papers also gave an important indication of the critical role of then law clerk Alexander Bickel in the proceedings. Bickel's memo on the Fourteenth Amendment, "Segregation Cases: Legislative History of the Fourteenth Amendment," can be found in the Frankfurter Papers. Bickel revised that memo and published it as a law review article, "The Original Understanding and the Segregation Decision," in *Harvard Law Review* (1955). We also examined Horace Edgar Flack, *The Adoption of the Fourteenth Amendment* (1908), as an example of the conventional wisdom on the Fourteenth Amendment against which Frankfurter and Bickel were struggling. Students of the subject interested in the controversial role of Philip Elman in *Brown* would do well to examine his interview with legal historian Norman Silber: "The Solicitor General's Office, Justice Frankfurter, and Civil Rights Litigation, 1946–1960: An Oral History," in *Harvard Law Review* (1987). There are problematic aspects to the Elman interview, as indeed there are with all sources. It is quite likely that Elman overstated his role. Nonetheless the interview provides a good examination of some of the activities occurring behind the scenes in *Brown* and a good glimpse into the role of the Justice Department in the litigation.

Judicial biographies were also key to our understanding of the Supreme Court, its key personalities, and the deliberative process that went into the *Brown* decision. A number of biographies were particularly helpful in informing us about the personalities of the jurists who participated in *Brown* and the role that their life experiences and outlooks may have played in the crafting of the decision. Felix Frankfurter's life and career have been covered in a number of works. Three studies, Liva Baker's *Felix Frankfurter* (1969); H. N. Hirsch's *The Enigma of Felix Frankfurter* (1981); and Philip Kurland's *Mr. Justice Frankfurter and the Constitution* (1971), proved to be particularly helpful for our purposes. A particularly important account of Frankfurter's view of judicial restraint and its implementation in the tragic case of Willie Francis can be found in William Wiecek's "Felix Frankfurter, Incorporation, and the Willie Francis Case," in *Journal of Supreme Court History* (2001). Earl Warren's career has also been the subject of considerable biographical examination. We found Bernard Schwartz's *Super Chief: Earl Warren and His Supreme*

Court: A Judicial Biography (1983) particularly valuable. William O. Douglas's autobiography, *The Court Years, 1937–1975* (1980), provides an important insider's account of *Brown* and other issues that came before the Court during Douglas's tenure. Gerald T. Dunne's *Hugo Black and the Judicial Revolution* (1977) and Roger K. Newman's *Hugo Black: A Biography* (1994) both provide well-researched, detailed accounts of the life and career of a pivotal justice in the *Brown* litigation. Mary Frances Berry's biography of Justice Stanley Burton, *Stability, Security, and Continuity: Mr. Justice Burton and Decision-Making in the Supreme Court, 1945–1958* (1978), and John D. Fassett's *New Deal Justice: The Life of Stanley Reed of Kentucky* (1994) both provided useful information on justices who have not been the subjects of much historical study.

A variety of sources proved helpful in our examinations of the implementation of *Brown*, the struggle for desegregation post-*Brown*, and the controversy more generally over race and civil rights in the 1950s and 1960s. Jack Bass's *Unlikely Heroes: The Dramatic Story of the Southern Judges of the Fifth Circuit Who Translated the Supreme Court's Brown Decision into a Revolution for Equality* (1981) focuses on the federal appellate judges who presided over the former Fifth Circuit, which covered the southern states where most of the desegregation battles were fought. His study provides a particularly illuminating examination of the role of the appellate court judges in supervising often reluctant trial judges and recalcitrant elected officials. Another valuable examination of this period is J. Harvie Wilkinson III's *From Brown to Bakke: The Supreme Court and School Desegregation, 1954–1978* (1979). We also found the popular press of the era to be a particularly helpful source of information on the desegregation struggle and racial attitudes. We consulted *Crisis*, *Time*, *Ebony*, *National Review*, *The Nation*, and other periodicals that covered the desegregation struggle from different perspectives. Individual articles can be found in the bibliography.

Brown, of course, had an important afterlife both in terms of the question of the proper role of courts in American governance and in terms of the enduring issue of race in American society. One very perceptive essay on *Brown* and its role in current judicial politics is Brad Snyder's "How the Conservatives Canonized *Brown v. Board of Education*," in *Rutgers Law Review* (2000). No discussion of *Brown* and the modern debate over the role of the judiciary in American life would be complete without mention of Raoul Berger's *Government by Judiciary: The Transformation of the Fourteenth Amendment* (1977). Although many have rightly criticized both Berger's history and his legal conclusions, his work represents a major point of view in the debate.

The question of where we are in terms of race some fifty years after *Brown* is both important and complex. Many scholars have emphasized the progress that has occurred in the ensuing five decades. See, e.g., Stephan and Abigail Thernstrom, *America in Black and White: One Nation, Indivisible* (1997). Others have emphasized the continuing burden of race and racism on Americans of African descent. See, e.g., Derrick Bell, *Faces at the Bottom of the Well* (1992). A valuable source for examining the phenomenon of resegregation of public schools since the 1990s is the January 2003 report by the Civil Rights Project at Harvard University: "A Multiracial Society with Segregated Schools: Are We Losing the Dream?"

BIBLIOGRAPHY

ARTICLES

"The Admission of Negroes to the University of Maryland." *School and Society* 46 (September 11, 1937): 335.

Barksdale, Norval P. "The Gaines Case and Its Effect on Negro Education in Missouri." *School and Society* 51 (March 9, 1940): 308–9.

Bickel, Alexander M. Memo, "Segregation Cases: Legislative History of the Fourteenth Amendment," in *Papers of Justice Felix Frankfurter.* Revised version later published as "The Original Understanding and the Segregation Decision." *Harvard Law Review* 69 (1955): 1–65.

Bluford, Lucille H. "The Lloyd Gaines Story." *Journal of Educational Sociology* 32 (1959): 242–46.

Chin, Gabriel J. "The Plessy Myth: Justice Harlan and the Chinese Cases." *Iowa Law Review* 82 (1996): 151–82.

Clark, Kenneth. "Segregation as a Factor on the Racial Identification of Negro Pre-School Children: A Preliminary Report." *Journal of Experimental Education* 8, no. 2 (1939).

Clement, Rufus E. "The Impact of War upon Negro Graduate and Professional Schools." *Journal of Negro Education* 11 (1942): 365–74.

———. "Legal Provisions for Graduate and Professional Instruction for Negroes in States Operating Separate School Systems." *Journal of Negro Education* 8 (1939): 142–49.

Clift, Virgil A. "Pattern of Discrimination in Public Higher Education." *School and Society* 72 (October 7, 1950): 225–28.

"Controversy Follows Psychological Testing." *American Psychological Association Monitor Online* 30, no. 11 (December 1999). www.apa.org/monitor/Dec99/SS4.html. Accessed May 1, 2003.

Cottrol, Robert J. "The Long Lingering Shadow: Law, Liberalism, and Cultures of Racial Hierarchy and Identity in the Americas." *Tulane Law Review* 76 (2001): 11–79.

———. "Static History and Brittle Jurisprudence: Raoul Berger and the Problem of Constitutional Methodology." *Boston College Law Review* 11 (1985): 353–87.

Cottrol, Robert J., and Raymond T. Diamond. "The Second Amendment: Toward an Afro-Americanist Reconsideration." *Georgetown Law Journal* 80 (1991): 309–61.

"Decision of the Missouri Supreme Court on the Admission of Negroes to State Universities." *School and Society* 48 (December 3, 1938): 726–27.

Diamond, Raymond T. "Confrontation as Rejoinder to Compromise: Reflections on the Little Rock Desegregation Crisis." *National Black Law Journal* 11 (1989): 151.

Dudziak, Mary. "Oliver Wendell Holmes as a Eugenics Reformer: Rhetoric in the Writing of Constitutional Law." *Iowa Law Review* 71 (1986): 833–67.

Fairfax, Roger A. "Wielding the Double-Edged Sword: Charles Hamilton Houston and Judicial Activism in the Age of Legal Realism." *Harvard Black Letter Law Journal* 14 (1998): 17–44.

Frankenberg, Erica, Chungmei Lee, and Gary Orfield. "A Multiracial Society with Segregated Schools: Are We Losing the Dream?" *The Civil Rights Project: Harvard University*. www. civilrightsproject. harvard.edu. Accessed May 1, 2003.

Goza, Claude. "Note: Constitutional Law—Equal Protection of the Laws—Admission of Negro to Law School of the State University." *Georgia Bar Journal* 1 (May 1939): 54–55.

Harris, Nelson H. "Negro Higher and Professional Education in North Carolina." *Journal of Negro Education* 17 (1948): 335–40.

Hogan, Percy A. "History of the University of Missouri Law School." *Missouri Law Review* 5 (1940): 269–92.

Hunter, John M. "Evaluation of Graduate Work Offered by Negro Colleges." *Quarterly Review of Higher Education among Negroes* 15 (1947): 338–47.

Jackson, Reid E. "Financial Aid Given by Southern States to Negroes for Out-of-State Study." *Journal of Negro Education* 13 (1944): 30–39.

Jenkins, Martin D. "Enrollment in Institutions of Higher Education of Negroes, 1947–48." *Journal of Negro Education* 17 (1948): 206–15.

"Jim Crow Expelled." *New Republic* 123 (October 16, 1950): 9.

"Jim Crow Law School." *Newsweek* 14 (October 1939): 32.

Johnson, George M., and Jane M. Lucas. "The Present Legal Status of the Negro Separate School." *Journal of Negro Education* 16 (1947): 280–89.

"Less Sound and Fury." *National Review* (March 28, 1956): 5.

Marshall, Thurgood. "An Evaluation of Recent Efforts to Achieve Racial Integration in Education through Resort to the Courts." *Journal of Negro Education* 21 (1952): 316–27.

Martindale, Don. "American Sociology before World War II." *Annual Review of Sociology* 2 (1976): 121–43.

Myers, Alonzo E. "The Colleges for Negroes." *Survey* 86 (1950): 233–39.

"Negro Students in Texas." *New Republic* 122 (June 26, 1950): 7–8.

"Not Equal." *New Republic* 123 (August 21, 1950): 9.

"Recent Decisions: Constitutional Law—Equal Protection of the Laws—Refusing Negro Admission to State-Maintained Law School as Denial of Equal Protection." *Brooklyn Law Review* 8 (1939): 442–44.

"Recent Decisions: Constitutional Law: Equal Protection: Exclusion of Negro from State University Law School." *Cornell Law Review* 24 (1939): 419–22.

Redd, George N. "Present Status of Negro Higher and Professional Education: Critical Summary." *Journal of Negro Education* 17 (1948): 400–409.

Rochelle, Charles E. "Graduate and Professional Education for Negroes." *American Association of Collegiate Registrars Journal* 19 (1944): 191–205.

Savage, William S. "The Influence of the Gaines Case on Negro Education in the Post War Period." *Quarterly Review of Higher Education among Negroes* 11 (1943): 1–5.

Saveth, Edward N. "Jim Crow and the Regional Plan." *Survey* 85 (1949): 476–80.

Silber, Norman. "The Solicitor General's Office, Justice Frankfurter, and Civil Rights Litigation, 1946–1960: An Oral History." *Harvard Law Review* 100 (1987): 817–52.

Snyder, Brad. "How the Conservatives Canonized *Brown v. Board of Education.*" *Rutgers Law Review* 52 (2000): 383–494.

Stoney, George C. "In Defense of the Regional Plan." *Survey* 86 (1950): 300–302.

Thompson, Charles H. "The Missouri Decision and the Future of Negro Education." *Journal of Negro Education* 8 (1939): 131–41.

———. "The Prospect of Negro Higher Education." *Journal of Educational Sociology* 32 (1959): 309–16.

Villard, Oswald Garrison. "Issues and Men." *Nation* 147 (December 24, 1938): 693.

Ware, Leland B. "Setting the Stage for Brown: The Development and Implementation of the NAACP's School Desegregation Campaign, 1930–1950." *Mercer Law Review* 52 (2001): 631–73.

Washington, Harold R. "History and the Role of Black Law Schools." *Howard Law Journal* 18 (1974): 385–422.

The Week. *National Review* (March 7, 1956): 3.

Wesley, Charles H. "The Outlook for the Graduate and Professional Education of Negroes." *Journal of Negro Education* 11 (1942): 423–34.

Wiecek, William. "Felix Frankfurter, Incorporation, and the Willie Francis Case." *Journal of Supreme Court History* 26 (2001): 53–66.

BOOKS (FICTION)

Dixon, Thomas Jr. *Clansman: An Historical Romance of the Ku Klux Klan.* New York: Gordon Press, 1975.

Johnson, James Weldon. *Autobiography of an Ex-Colored Man.* In *Three Negro Classics*, ed. John Hope Franklin. New York: Avon Books, 1965.

Mitchell, Margaret. *Gone with the Wind.* New York: Macmillan, 1936.

BOOKS (NONFICTION)

Adorno, T. W., et al. *The Authoritarian Personality.* New York: W. W. Norton, 1950.

Baker, Liva. *Felix Frankfurter.* New York: Coward-McCann, 1969.

Balkin, Jack, ed. *What "Brown v. Board of Education" Should Have Said: The Nation's Top Legal Experts Rewrite America's Landmark Civil Rights Decision.* New York: New York University Press, 2001.

Ball, Howard. *A Defiant Life: Thurgood Marshall and the Persistence of Racism in America.* New York: Crown Publishers, 1998.

Barkan, Elazar. *The Retreat of Scientific Racism: Changing Concepts of*

Race in Britain and the United States between the World Wars. New York: Cambridge University Press, 1992.

Bass, Jack. *Unlikely Heroes: The Dramatic Story of the Southern Judges of the Fifth Circuit Who Translated the Supreme Court's Brown Decision into a Revolution for Equality.* New York: Simon and Schuster, 1981.

Bell, Derrick. *Faces at the Bottom of the Well.* New York: Basic Books, 1992.

Berger, Raoul. *Government by Judiciary: The Transformation of the Fourteenth Amendment.* Cambridge, Mass.: Harvard University Press, 1977.

Berlin, Ira. *Slaves without Masters: The Free Negro in the Antebellum South.* New York: Pantheon Books, 1975.

Berry, Mary Frances. *Stability, Security, and Continuity: Mr. Justice Burton and Decision-Making in the Supreme Court, 1945–1958.* Westport, Conn.: Greenwood Press, 1978.

Bickel, Alexander M. *The Least Dangerous Branch: The Supreme Court at the Bar of Politics.* New Haven, Conn.: Yale University Press, 1962.

Bland, Randall W. *Justice Thurgood Marshall, Crusader for Liberalism: His Judicial Biography.* Bethesda, Md.: Academia Press, 2001.

Bowers, Claude G. *The Tragic Era: The Revolution after Lincoln.* Cambridge: Houghton Mifflin, 1929.

Buck, Paul H. *The Road to Reunion.* Boston: Little, Brown, 1937.

Cottrol, Robert J. *The Afro-Yankees: Providence's Black Community in the Antebellum Era.* Westport, Conn.: Greenwood Press, 1982.

Cripps, Thomas. *Making Movies Black: The Hollywood Message Movie from World War II to the Civil Rights Era.* New York: Oxford University Press, 1993.

———. *Slow Fade to Black: The Negro in American Film, 1900–1942.* New York: Oxford University Press, 1993.

Douglas, William O. *The Court Years, 1939–1975: The Autobiography of William O. Douglas.* New York: Random House, 1980.

Du Bois, W. E. B. *Black Reconstruction: An Essay Toward a History of the Part Which Black Folk Played in the Attempt to Reconstruct Democracy in America, 1860–1880.* New York: Russell and Russell, 1935.

———. *The Souls of Black Folk.* In *Three Negro Classics,* ed. John Hope Franklin. New York: Avon Books, 1965.

Dudziak, Mary. *Cold War Civil Rights: Race and the Image of American Democracy.* Princeton: Princeton University Press, 2000.

Dunne, Gerald T. *Hugo Black and the Judicial Revolution.* New York: Simon and Schuster, 1977.

Dunning, William A. *Reconstruction Political and Economic, 1865–1870.* New York: Harper and Brothers, 1907.

Eastland, Terry. *Counting by Race: Equality from the Founding Fathers to Bakke.* New York: Basic Books, 1979.

Fassett, John D. *New Deal Justice: The Life of Stanley Reed of Kentucky.* New York: Vantage Press, 1994.

Flack, Horace Edgar. *The Adoption of the Fourteenth Amendment.* Baltimore: Johns Hopkins University Press, 1908.

Foner, Eric. *Reconstruction: America's Unfinished Revolution, 1863–1877.* New York: Harper and Row, 1989.

Franklin, John Hope, and Alfred A. Moss Jr. *From Slavery to Freedom: A History of African Americans.* Boston: McGraw-Hill, 2000.

Fredrickson, George M. *The Black Image in the White Mind: The Debate on Afro-American Character and Destiny, 1817–1914.* New York: Harper and Row, 1971.

Goings, Kenneth W. *The NAACP Comes of Age: The Defeat of Judge John Parker.* Bloomington: Indiana University Press, 1990.

Gossett, Thomas F. *Race: The History of an Idea in America.* New York: Oxford University Press, 1997.

Greenberg, Jack. *Crusaders in the Courts: How a Dedicated Band of Lawyers Fought for the Civil Rights Revolution.* New York: Basic Books, 1994.

———. *Race, Relations, and American Law.* New York: Columbia University Press, 1959.

Harbaugh, William H. *Lawyer's Lawyer: The Life of John W. Davis.* New York: Oxford University Press, 1973.

Herskovits, Melville J. *The Myth of the Negro Past.* New York: Harper and Brothers, 1941.

Hirsch, H. N. *The Enigma of Felix Frankfurter.* New York: Basic Books, 1981.

Horton, James Oliver, and Lois E. Horton. *Black Bostonians: Family Life and Community Struggle in the Antebellum North.* New York: Holmes and Meier, 1979.

Kellogg, Charles Flint. *NAACP: A History of the National Association for the Advancement of Colored People*. Vol. 1, *1909–1920*. Baltimore: Johns Hopkins University Press, 1967.

Kluger, Richard. *Simple Justice: The History of Brown v. Board of Education and Black America's Struggle for Equality*. New York: Alfred A. Knopf, 1975.

Kurland, Philip B. *Mr. Justice Frankfurter and the Constitution*. Chicago: University of Chicago Press, 1971.

Lemann, Nicholas. *The Big Test: The Secret History of the American Meritocracy*. New York: Farrar, Straus, and Giroux, 2000.

Levy, Leonard W. *The Law of the Commonwealth and Chief Justice Shaw*. New York: Harper and Row, 1957.

Lofgren, Charles A. *The Plessy Case: A Legal-Historical Interpretation*. New York: Oxford University Press, 1987.

McNeil, Genna Rae. *Groundwork: Charles Hamilton Houston and the Struggle for Civil Rights*. Philadelphia: University of Pennsylvania Press, 1983.

Morris, Thomas D. *Southern Slavery and the Law, 1619–1860*. Chapel Hill: University of North Carolina Press, 1996.

Motley, Constance Baker. *Equal Justice under Law*. New York: Farrar, Straus, and Giroux, 1998.

Myrdal, Gunnar, et al. *An American Dilemma: The Negro Problem and Modern Democracy*. New York: Harper and Brothers, 1944.

Nalty, Bernard C. *Strength for the Fight: A History of Black Americans in the Military*. New York: Free Press, 1986.

Newman, Roger K. *Hugo Black: A Biography*. New York: Pantheon Books, 1994.

Patterson, James T. *Brown v. Board of Education: A Civil Rights Milestone and Its Troubled Legacy*. New York: Oxford University Press, 2001.

Pollack, Jack Harrison. *Earl Warren: The Judge Who Changed America*. Englewood Cliffs, N.J.: Prentice-Hall, 1979.

Schwartz, Bernard. *Super Chief: Earl Warren and His Supreme Court: A Judicial Biography*. New York: New York University Press, 1983.

Simon, James F. *The Antagonists: Hugo Black, Felix Frankfurter, and Civil Liberties in Modern America*. New York: Simon and Schuster, 1989.

Smith, J. Clay. *Emancipation: The Making of the Black Lawyer, 1844–1944*. Philadelphia: University of Pennsylvania Press, 1993.

Thernstrom, Stephan and Abigail. *America in Black and White: One Nation, Indivisible*. New York: Touchstone, 1997.

Tushnet, Mark V. *Making Civil Rights Law: Thurgood Marshall and the Supreme Court, 1936–1961*. New York: Oxford University Press, 1994.

———. *The NAACP's Legal Strategy against Segregated Education, 1925–1950*. Chapel Hill: University of North Carolina Press, 1987.

Urofsky, Melvin I. *A Mind of One Piece: Brandeis and American Reform*. New York: Charles Scribner's and Sons, 1971.

Washington, Booker T. *Up from Slavery*. In *Three Negro Classics*, ed. John Hope Franklin. New York: Avon Books, 1965.

White, G. Edward. *Earl Warren: A Public Life*. New York: Oxford University Press, 1982.

White, Walter Francis. *A Man Called White: The Autobiography of Walter White*. New York: Viking Press, 1948.

Wilkins, Roy. *Standing Fast*. New York: Viking Press, 1982.

Wilkinson, J. Harvie III. *From Brown to Bakke: The Supreme Court and School Desegregation, 1954–1978*. New York: Oxford University Press, 1979.

Williams, Juan. *Thurgood Marshall: American Revolutionary*. New York: Times Books of Random House, 1998.

Wilson, Paul. *A Time to Lose: Representing Kansas in Brown v. Board of Education*. Lawrence: University Press of Kansas, 1995.

Woodward, C. Vann. *The Strange Career of Jim Crow*. Oxford: Oxford University Press, 2002.

———. *Tom Watson: Agrarian Rebel*. Savannah, Ga.: Beehive Press, 1973.

BRIEFS

The following briefs are all from *Landmark Briefs and Arguments of the Supreme Court of the United States*, vol. 49, ed. Philip B. Kurland and Gerhard Casper. Arlington, Va.: University Publications of America, 1975.

Brief for Appellants in Brown v. Board of Education, filed in U.S. Supreme Court, October Term 1952, 23–39.

Appendix to Appellants' Briefs: "The Effects of Segregation and the Consequences of Desegregation: A Social Science Statement," 43–66.

Brief for Appellants in Nos. 1, 2, and 4 and for Respondents in No. 10 on Reargument, October 1953, 481–748.

Brief for Appellees in Brown v. Board of Education, October 1952, 67–111.

Brief for the United States as Amicus Curiae in Brown v. Board of Education, October 1952, 113–47.

Brief of American Federation of Teachers as Amicus Curiae in Brown v. Board of Education, October 1952, 195–213.

Brief of American Jewish Congress as Amicus Curiae in Brown v. Board of Education, October 1952, 215–39.

Brief of American Veterans Committee, Inc. as Amicus Curiae in Brown v. Board of Education, October 1952, 241–59.

Brief of Congress of Industrial Organizations as Amicus Curiae in Brown v. Board of Education, October 1952, 261–75.

Brief on Behalf of American Civil Liberties Union, American Ethical Union, American Jewish Committee, Anti-Defamation League of B'Nai B'rith, Japanese American Citizens League, and Unitarian Fellowship for Social Justice, as Amicus Curiae in Brown v. Board of Education, October 1952, 149–93.

Brief for Board of Education on Reargument, October 1953, 749–57.

Brief for State of Kansas on Reargument, October 1953, 759–852.

Oral Argument in Bolling v. Sharpe, December 10, 1952, 395–411.

Oral Argument in Bolling v. Sharpe, December 11, 1952, 413–40.

Oral Argument in Briggs v. Elliott, December 9, 1952, 307–28.

Oral Argument in Briggs v. Elliott, December 10, 1952, 329–46.

Oral Argument in Brown v. Board of Education, December 9, 1952, 277–305.

Oral Argument in Davis v. Prince Edward County School Board, December 10, 1952, 347–93.

Oral Argument in Gebhart v. Belton, December 11, 1952, 441–79.

Supplemental Brief for the United States as Amicus Curiae on Reargument, November 1953, 853–1054.

The following briefs are all from *Landmark Briefs and Arguments of the Supreme Court of the United States: Constitutional Law,* vol. 49A, ed. Philip B. Kurland and Gerhard Casper. Arlington, Va.: University Press of America, 1975.

Brief of the Attorney General of the State of Oklahoma as Amicus Curiae, November 1954, 1021–1138.

Brief of the Attorney General of the State of Texas as Amicus Curiae, November 1954, 1039–1170.

Oral Argument in Brown v. Board of Education, Gebhart v. Belton, Bolling v. Sharpe, Briggs v. Elliott, and Davis v. Prince Edward County School Board, April 11, 1955, 1071–1139.

Oral Argument in Brown v. Board of Education, Gebhart v. Belton, Bolling v. Sharpe, Briggs v. Elliott, and Davis v. Prince Edward County School Board, April 12, 1955, 1141–1211.

Oral Argument in Brown v. Board of Education, Gebhart v. Belton, Bolling v. Sharpe, Briggs v. Elliott, and Davis v. Prince Edward County School Board, April 13, 1955, 1213–1289.

Oral Argument in Brown v. Board of Education, Gebhart v. Belton, Bolling v. Sharpe, Briggs v. Elliott, and Davis v. Prince Edward County School Board, April 14, 1955, 1291–1317.

CASES

Adams v. U.S., 319 U.S. 312 (1943).

Alexander v. Holmes County Board of Education, 396 U.S. 19 (1969).

Alston v. School Board of City of Norfolk, 112 F.2d 992 (4th Cir., 1940).

Baker v. Carr, 369 U.S. 186 (1962).

Barrows v. Jackson, 346 U.S. 249 (1953).

Bates v. City of Little Rock, 361 U.S. 516 (1960).

Berea College v. Commonwealth of Kentucky, 211 U.S. 45 (1908).

Bluford v. Canada, 32 F. Supp. 707 (W.D. Mo., 1940).

Bob-Lo Excursion Co. v. People of State of Michigan, 333 U.S. 28 (1948).

Bolling v. Sharpe, 347 U.S. 497 (1954).

Briggs et al. v. Elliott et al., 98 F. Supp. 529 (U.S.D.C. East. Div. of S.C., Charleston Div., 1951).

Brotherhood of Railroad Trainmen v. Howard, 343 U.S. 768 (1952).

Browder v. Gayle, 352 U.S. 903 (1956).

Brown v. Board of Education of Topeka, Shawnee County, Kansas (Brown I), 347 U.S. 483 (1954).

Brown v. Board of Education of Topeka, Kansas (Brown II), 349 U.S. 294 (1955).

Brown v. State of Mississippi, 297 U.S. 278 (1936).

Buchanan v. Warley, 245 U.S. 60 (1917).

Bush v. Orleans Parish School Board, 364 U.S. 500 (1960).

Canty v. Alabama, 309 U.S. 629 (1940).

Chambers v. State of Florida, 309 U.S. 227 (1940).

Civil Rights Cases, 109 U.S. 3 (1883).

Clyatt v. United States, 197 U.S. 207 (1905).

Commonwealth v. Aves, 35 Mass. (18 Pick.) 193 (1836).

Commonwealth v. Jennison, Proc. Mass. Historical Society, 1873–1875 (April 1783).

Cooper v. Aaron, 358 U.S. 1 (1958).

Cumming v. Board of Education of Richmond County, 175 U.S. 528 (1899).

Davis v. County School Board of Prince Edward County, 103 F. Supp. 337 (U.S. D. C. E. D. Va., Richmond Div., 1952).

District of Columbia v. John R. Thompson Co., Inc., 346 U.S. 100 (1953).

Dred Scott v. Sanford, 60 U.S. (19 How.) 393 (1857).

Engel v. Vitale, 370 U.S. 421 (1962).

Epps v. Carmichel, 93 F. Supp. 327 (M.D.N.C. 1950).

Escobedo v. State of Illinois, 378 U.S. 478 (1964).

Fisher v. Hurst, 333 U.S. 147 (1948).

Gebhart et al. v. Belton et al. (includes Gebhart v. Bulah), 91 A. 2d 137 (S. C. of Del., 1952).

Gibson v. Florida Legislative Investigation Committee, 372 U.S. 539 (1963).

Gideon v. Wainwright, 372 U.S. 335 (1963).

Giles v. Harris, 189 U.S. 475 (1903).

Giles v. Teasley, 193 U.S. 146 (1904).

Gong Lum v. Rice, 275 U.S. 78 (1927).

Green v. School Board of New Kent County, VA, 391 U.S. 430 (1968).

Griffin v. County School Board of Prince Edward County, 377 U.S. 218 (1964).

Griswold v. Connecticut, 381 U.S. 479 (1965).

Guinn and Beals v. United States, 238 U.S. 347 (1915).

Hall v. De Cuir, 95 U.S. 485 (1877).

Henderson v. United States, 339 U.S. 816 (1950).

Hirabayashi v. United States, 320 U.S. 81 (1943).

James M. Hurd and Mary I. Hurd v. Frederic E. Hodge, 68 S.Ct. 162 (1948).

Keyes v. School District No. 1, Denver, Colorado, 413 U.S. 189 (1973).

Korematsu v. United States, 323 U.S. 214 (1944).

Lane v. Wilson, 307 U.S. 268 (1939).

Lochner v. New York, 198 U.S. 45 (1905).

Louisiana ex rel. Francis v. Resweber, Sheriff, et al., 329 U.S. 459 (1947).

Louisiana ex rel. Gremillion v. NAACP, 366 U.S. 293 (1961).

Loving v. Virginia, 388 U.S. 1 (1967).

Lucy et al. v. Adams, Dean of Admissions, University of Alabama, 350 U.S. 1 (1955).

Marbury v. Madison, 5 U.S. (1 Cranch) 137 (1803).

McCabe v. Atchison, Topeka and Santa Fe Railway Company, 235 U.S. 151 (1915).

McLaurin v. Oklahoma State Regents for Higher Education, 87 F. Supp. 526 (D.C.Okl. 1950).

McLaurin v. Oklahoma State Regents for Higher Education, 87 F. Supp. 528 (D.C.Okl. 1950).

McLaurin v. Oklahoma State Regents for Higher Education, 339 U.S. 637 (1950).

Milliken v. Bradley (Milliken I), 418 U.S. 717 (1974).

Milliken v. Bradley (Milliken II), 433 U.S. 267 (1977).

Miranda v. Arizona, 384 U.S. 436 (1966).

Moore v. Dempsey, 261 U.S. 86 (1926).

Morgan v. Commonwealth of Virginia, 328 U.S. 373 (1946).

Muller v. State of Oregon, 208 U.S. 412 (1908).

NAACP v. Alabama ex rel. Flowers, 377 U.S. 288 (1964).

NAACP v. Alabama ex rel. Patterson, 357 U.S. 449 (1958).

NAACP v. Button, 371 U.S. 415 (1963).

Nixon v. Condon, 286 U.S. 73 (1932).

Nixon v. Herndon, 273 U.S. 536 (1927).

Patton v. State of Mississippi, 331 U.S. 804 (1947).

Pearson v. Murray, 182 A. 590 (Md., 1936).

Plessy v. Ferguson, 163 U.S. 537 (1896).

Powell v. Alabama, 287 U.S. 45 (1932).

Roberts v. City of Boston, 59 Mass. (5 Cush.) 198 (1850).

Roe v. Wade, 410 U.S. 113 (1973).

Shelly v. Kraemer, 334 U.S. 1 (1948).

Sipuel v. Board of Regents of the University of Oklahoma, 332 U.S. 631 (1948).

Slaughter House Cases, 89 U.S. (16 Wall) (1873).

Smith v. Allwright, 321 U.S. 649 (1944), overruling *Grovey v. Townsend*, 295 U.S. 45 (1935).

State ex rel. Bluford v. Canada, 153 S.W. 2d 12 (Mo., 1941).

State ex rel. Gaines v. Canada (Gaines I), 113 S.W. 2d 783 (Mo., 1937).

State ex rel. Gaines v. Canada (Gaines II), 305 U.S. 337 (1938).

State ex rel. Gaines v. Canada (Gaines III), 131 S.W. 2d 217 (Mo., 1939).

State ex rel. Hawkins v. Board of Control, 47 So.2d 608 (Fla., 1950).

State ex rel. Michael v. Witham, 165 S.W. 2d 378 (Tenn., 1942).

Steele v. Louisville and Nashville Railroad, 323 U.S. 192 (1944).

Stell et al. v. Savannah-Chatham Board of Education, 387 F. 2d. 406, 220 F. Supp. 667 (USDC, So. Dist. of Ga., 1963).

Strauder v. West Virginia, 100 U.S. (10 Otto) 303 (1879).

Swann v. Charlotte-Mecklenburg Board of Education, 402 U.S. 1 (1971).

Sweatt v. Painter, 210 S.W. 2d 442 (Tex. App. 1948).

Sweatt v. Painter, 339 U.S. 629 (1950).

Terry et al. v. Adams et al., 345 U.S. 461 (1953).

United States v. Cruikshank, 92 U.S. (2 Otto) 542 (1876).

Watts v. State of Indiana, 338 U.S. 49 (1948).

Westminster School District of Orange County v. Mendez, 161 F.2d 774 (9th Cir., 1947).

Wrighten v. Board of Trustees of University of South Carolina, 72 F. Supp. 948 (E.D.S.C. 1947).

Yick Wo v. Hopkins, 118 U.S. 356 (1886).

FILMS

Bataan. Metro Goldwyn Mayer, 1943.

Birth of a Nation. David W. Griffith Corp., 1915.

Crash Dive. Twentieth Century Fox, 1943.

Gone with the Wind. Selznick International Pictures, 1939.

Home of the Brave. Screen Plays Corp., 1949.

Internet Movie Database. http://US.IMDB.com/search.html. Accessed May 1, 2003.

The Jackie Robinson Story. Eagle-Lion Films, Inc.

The Negro Soldier. War Department, 1944.
Wings for this Man. War Department, 1945.

PAPERS

Justice Harold Burton Papers. Library of Congress.
Justice Felix Frankfurter Papers. Library of Congress.
NAACP Papers. Library of Congress.

SONGS

"The Darktown Strutters' Ball" (1917). Words and music by Shelton Brooks.
"They're Either Too Young or Too Old" (1943). Lyrics by Frank Loesser, music by Arthur Schwartz. Version quoted as sung by Helen O'Connell with the Jimmy Dorsey Orchestra.

INDEX

Due process, 218, 245
    fairness and, 181
    guaranteeing, 220
    violation of, 106, 131
Due process clause, 106, 219, 221, 223, 248
    violation of, 181–82
Dunning, William A., 36
Dunning School, 83

Eastland, Terry, 111
Economic liberalism, racial liberalism and, 153
Economic participation, 179
Economic rights, 50
Education
    alternative facilities for, 101
    black/white children and, 178
    compulsory, 182
    desegregation and, 117, 174
    discrimination in, 58, 77, 106, 152, 200, 239
    inner-city, 239
    Jim Crow, 109
    legal, 112, 113, 247
    as liberty, 181
    opportunities for, 86, 205
    public, 84, 179
    secondary, 59
    segregated, 58, 62, 66, 105, 106, 117, 119, 123, 126, 127, 131–32, 134, 178, 182, 238, 239
    state-supported, 13
    universal, 178
    See also Schools
Edwards, James, 98
Eighth Amendment, cruel and unusual punishment and, 156
Eisenhower, Dwight D.
    Brown and, 170, 192
    civil rights legislation and, 192
    concentration camps and, 97
    Frankfurter and, 162
    Little Rock and, 192, 249
    Warren and, 159, 160
Elman, Philip, 165
    Brown and, 161–62, 169, 170, 171
    clerkship of, 162
    Frankfurter and, 170–71, 174
    right and remedy and, 169, 170
Emancipation, 12–13
Emancipation Proclamation (1863), 23, 245
Emergency statutes, nullification of, 195
Employment
    discrimination in, 99, 155, 200, 225, 249
    opportunities for, 205
Enforcement Act (1870), 27
Engel v. Vitale (1962), school prayer and, 215
English, Horace B.,130
Epps v. Carmichael (1950), 114

Equality, 7, 51, 132, 135, 148, 185
    concept of, 35, 48, 123
    de jure, 4, 12–13
    forcing, 36
    instructional, 131, 140
    Negro, 18
    physical, 140
    separation and, 8, 246
    social, 32
Equality before the law, 7, 12, 33
Equalization, 125, 126, 127, 185–86
    desegregation and, 135
    in South Carolina, 141
Equal opportunity, 62, 72, 115, 137, 179
    providing, 64–65
Equal Opportunity League, 49
Equal protection, 5, 6, 25, 43, 64, 102, 221, 222
    expanding, 163–64
    Fourteenth Amendment and, 177
    litigating, 118
    segregation and, 111
Equal protection clause, 17, 24, 42, 75, 100, 138, 245, 246, 247
    Brown and, 181
    interpreting, 177, 178, 180
    McLaurin and, 109
    separate but equal and, 7
    violation of, 76, 133
Equal rights, 2, 160
    in antebellum Boston, 12–13
    immigrants and, 82
    securing, 31, 37
Equal treatment, 5, 35, 45, 60, 62, 64, 168
Equity, 43, 44, 45, 143–44
Escobedo v. State of Illinois (1964), interrogations and, 215–16
Espy, Mike, 237
Eugenics movement, 38
Evers, Medgar, 202
Executive Order 8802 (1941), 247

Fair employment practices, 91, 155
Fair Employment Practices Commission, 155
Fair Housing Act (1968), 204
Fairness, due process and, 181
Farmer, James, 187
Faubus, Orval, 191–92, 211
Federal Housing Administration, 206
Fifteenth Amendment, 24, 39, 222, 249
    Brown and, 200
    criticism of, 37
    demands of, 36, 40, 46
    enforcement of, 47, 48, 231
    Giles and, 47
    racial discrimination and, 25
    ratification of, 245
    repudiation of, 35
    vote and, 5